Visual Basic 2005
for
Psychologists

Visual Basic 2005
for
Psychologists

by

Otto H. MacLin
University of Northern Iowa

Mark R. Dixon
Southern Illinois University

James W. Jackson
Southern Illinois University

Foreword by

Steven C. Hayes
University of Nevada, Reno

CONTEXT PRESS

Reno, NV

Visual Basic 2005 for Psychologists
Paperback pp. 323

Distributed by New Harbinger Publications, Inc.

Library of Congress Cataloging-in-Publication Data

MacLin, Otto H., 1958-
Visual basic 2005 for psychologists / by Otto H. MacLin, Mark R. Dixon, James W. Jackson ; foreword by Steven C. Hayes.
p. cm.
Includes bibliiographical references and index.
ISBN-13: 978-1-878978-59-2 (pbk.)
ISBN-10: 1-878978-59-4 (pbk.)
1. Psychology--Data processing. 2. Microsoft Visual BASIC. I. Dixon, Mark R., 1970- II. Jackson, James W., 1977- III. Title.

BF39.5.M28 2007
150.285'5362--dc22

2007039506

© 2007 CONTEXT PRESS
933 Gear Street, Reno, NV 89503-2729

Printed in the United States of America

Table of Contents

Foreword

Nothing delays research progress quite so much as the delay between an idea and its implementation. I have see over and over again that those who are able to program their own research projects finish more quickly and do so in a higher quality way than those who are entirely dependent on the expertise of others.

Programming has become a key ally to the intellectual development of the field. I am sometimes told by psychology students or faculty that they do not have time to learn how to program. In fact, taking the long view, they do not have time to waste *not* knowing how to program. The hours put into learning pay off very quickly, usually within a matter or weeks. It does not make sense to delay the process, especially when learning tools are available that shorten the learning curve so dramatically.

This book is such a tool.

Of the many modern programming languages available, none is more popular than Visual Basic. Flexible and powerful, Visual Basic allows for control of virtually every parameter related to the conduct of experimental research. Flexible control over the presentation of stimulus materials, and careful measurement of the dimensions of responding are essential to successful research programs in psychology and all of the behavioral sciences. Visual Basic gives the researcher the tools needed to accomplish those ends.

In the present volume, Mark Dixon, Otto MacLin, and James Jackson take readers from the earliest stages of Visual Basic programming to the use of this language to program complex human studies. It has the considerable advantage of being written by young professionals who just a few years ago helped many of their fellow graduate students learn to program, and since have helped many of their own students learn how to take advantage of this powerful technology. The authors are driven by the sense of satisfaction that comes from empowering others. The examples and sample programs are precisely relevant to the preparations psychologists and psychology students will want to be able to program. Now in its second edition, it is more refined and helpful than ever.

This book will empower psychology. It will empower you.

Steven C. Hayes
University of Nevada

Preface

Looking Ahead

We can not stress enough the importance of learning how to program your own experiments. The time you spend learning Visual Basic 2005 will be nothing compared to the time you will spend attempting to explain to a computer programmer what you want your experiment to look like and what it needs to do. These folks don't come cheap, they don't work on your schedule, and they don't really care about your deadlines. Take the time now to learn how to program, and it will pay for itself soon enough. Learning how to program is a liberating endeavor, much like knowing how to speak the foreign language of a distant country that you will be visiting. There is so much you can do with the repertoire, and so little you can do without it.

There are so many ways to use the power of Visual Basic 2005 in your professional research career. They include conducing basic operant research in the laboratory, collecting observational data in an applied setting, computerizing traditional paper survey instruments, and computing data transformations. Every project you conduct as a behavioral psychologist could probably be enhanced in some way with a form of computerization. Teaching students and other professionals how to do the same will benefit our entire science, in addition to your own career.

By teaching you Visual Basic, we are giving you the tools to create many things. Many people might think we are crazy for doing so. Instead we should have opened a software company and designed custom programs for top dollars. Others have done so. Our reinforcers are simply different.

This book is dedicated to the many people we have met during the past four years following the publication of the original text *Visual Basic for Behavioral Psychologists*. We have been fascinated hearing about their new programming endeavors and how these individuals were able to master the art of programming – something once thought of as impossible. We hope that this new text will again spark such a movement within the field and that the resulting research advances our field in basic laboratory investigations as well as through the real-world applications that follow. We would also like to thank Steven C. Hayes and Emily Neilan Rodrigues of Context Press who gave us the opportunity to make this book and challenged us to improve upon our former work.

Otto H. Maclin, Mark R. Dixon, and James W. Jackson
Makanda, IL
July 2007

Chapter 1: Introduction

Overview

Technology and Research

As we venture into the 21st century, computerized technology is accelerating at exponential rates. Computerized equipment that was state of the art five years ago is now obsolete. Such rapid changes in technology may have a considerable impact on the research agenda of the behavioral psychologist. Equipment and software purchased with start-up or grant funds are often outdated before the end of the project. Furthermore, additional monies are regularly needed to hire computer programmers to reprogram software to handle changes in experimental parameters or new hardware. This often leaves the behavioral psychologist at the mercy of technical staff that have varying degrees of knowledge about the purpose of the experiment.

Furthermore, behavioral psychologists interested in the study of human operant behavior are under increasing demands to automate their experimental procedures. Tabletop procedures where stimuli are presented to the subject by a human experimenter are often criticized for potentially containing methodological flaws. While these flaws can be reduced through careful training of experimenters, they can never be completely eliminated. Using a computer to present stimuli eliminates many uncontrolled variations in stimuli positioning, orientation, and inter-trial intervals. Computerization also eliminates experimenter demand characteristics and any across-experimenter variability.

This text is designed to provide the behavioral psychologist with the necessary skills to adapt their human operant research agenda to the changing face of science in the 21st century. We will show you how to atomize your experimental apparatus, stimulus presentations, and data collection procedures. We will also provide you with specific programming routines (code) that you can customize and incorporate into your own experiments. But most importantly, we will provide you with the skills to program your own research, whatever that research may be.

In this book we have attempted to illustrate the creation of some popular types of experiments a researcher of human operant behavior may wish to conduct. The list is far from exhaustive. Yet we believe we will present the skills necessary for you to program any other type of experiment you can conceptualize albeit similar or totally different from the ones found in this text. We will walk you through the experiment programming experience step-by-step. In doing so, we believe that two goals will be accomplished upon successful completion of each chapter. First, you will learn more specific techniques about Visual Basic 2005 and observe their application in an actual computer program. Second, you will craft an actual working program that may be useful in the classroom, the laboratory, or the applied setting.

If nothing else, each chapter's program can serve as a backbone for your own experimental creations.

If you have ever purchased or browsed through commercially available textbooks on programming in Visual Basic 2005, you may have discovered that most of the information found in them is irrelevant to psychological research. They are written for computer programmers more generally. In this book we have attempted to greatly accelerate the learning curve for crafting your own computer programs for your own research agenda by only including those programming routines that are necessary for research purposes. The programming repertoire we present in this book has evolved over many years of hunting, searching, and foraging for the correct answers to many programming questions in vast sources of texts, list-serves, chartrooms, emails, and personal connections. Our programming abilities are a repertoire that has been considerably shaped by the contingencies of reinforcement for programming (or the punishers for failure to correctly program) that will be delivered to you the reader in somewhat of a "rule-governed" fashion.

To reduce and hopefully eliminate the deduction that programming will become easy after reading this book, or that a program can be created in a liner fashion from start to finish, we have programmed each experiment found in this text in a rather roundabout manner. That is, we will have you take steps backwards and often times run you into a dead end before finishing the program that is created in each of the chapters. We feel this approach more accurately approximates the real programming experience. Our non-liner method may frustrate you as you work through the chapters, but we believe it will prepare you in the long run for your own programming adventures that lay ahead.

Utility of Programming in Visual Basic 2005

Visual Basic 2005 is an "object orientated" programming language that is relatively easy to use. What is meant by "object orientated" is that the programming language is based on the placement of objects on the screen that perform some type of action when they are clicked on or triggered by keystrokes or timers. By being an "object orientated" language, Visual Basic 2005 takes the labor out of many once time consuming tasks. In previous versions of the "BASIC" programming language, programmers needed to write pages and pages of "code" in order to get an object to increase or decrease in size. In comparison, Visual Basic 2005 allows this type of operation in less than two sentences or even with the simple click of the mouse. If you are familiar with programs such as Microsoft Word, PowerPoint or Excel, you already possess some of the necessary skills to program in Visual Basic 2005. For example, Visual Basic 2005 uses the same procedures to cut, paste, and copy images or text within the program as well as utilizes the mouse pointer to drag, drop and resize objects on the computer screen.

Another useful feature of Visual Basic 2005 is that it is seamlessly connected to other common desktop software programs developed by Microsoft. We are not attempting to develop a loyalty to a particular brand of software for all your computing application needs, but this feature is quite valuable to expanding Visual Basic's capabilities. For example, you might wish to design a variety of experimental conditions using different stimuli and reinforcers. Using the streamlining capabilities of Visual Basic, you as the researcher could enter these values beforehand in an Excel spreadsheet, and have Visual Basic 2005 "read" them into your program during the running of the experiment. All your condition changes now are just made in Excel, not the actual computer program. Plus, your data output file can be written directly into Word or Excel formats for easy data analysis.

The ease of creating a computerized experiment in Visual Basic 2005 will also allow the behavioral psychologist to reduce the time necessary to run a given experiment. The researcher will not need to train graduate students or research assistants in the meticulous methodological procedures of a given study. Once the experiment is programmed, they will only need to show the assistant which button to click on the mouse to start the procedure. Additionally, by using a computerized procedure it may allow for the simultaneous running of multiple subjects given the appropriate research facilities. By placing the experiment on a server or the web, the behavioral psychologist could increase his/her sample sizes or experimental conditions significantly without adding any additional time for data collection.

System Requirements and Installation Procedures

Hardware and Software

Before we get started working with Visual Basic, you will need to make sure that your computer contains the appropriate hardware and software to run the program. Our experiences with Visual Basic 2005 and above will require you to have:

IBM-compatible computer equipped with CD-ROM drive, monitor and mouse
Pentium-based microprocessor (Pentium 4 or above)
Audio card and speakers (for multimedia purposes)
Microsoft Windows XP Professional or above operating system
1 Gigabite of RAM (or more)

While these are the recommended minimum requirements for running Visual Basic 2005, newer equipment and software along with faster processors will improve performance.

Editions of Visual Basic 2005

While Visual Basic 2005 comes in different varieties or editions (Express Edition, Academic Edition, Professional Edition, and Enterprise Edition) we recommend that you purchase either the Professional or Enterprise Edition. All of the mobile programming discussed in this text may not function properly with only the Express or Academic Edition. We have developed and tested all our programs found in this text using both the Professional Edition of Visual Basic 2005 and the free downloadable Express Edition available on the Microsoft website.

Installation

To begin the installation process, place the Visual Basic 2005 CD into your CD-ROM drive. The installation process will begin automatically. If, for some reason it does not, click on the start button in the bottom left corner of your screen. Next, click on *Run*, click on *Browse*, change directories to your CD-ROM drive, and then double-click on *setup.exe*. Now click on *OK*. Visual Basic 2005 should begin installing. If installation is still not accomplished, please see the owner's manual that accompanies your software.

One option that will appear during installation is the type of install you want to undertake. A "minimum install" will only place the essential files for most components of Visual Basic 2005 to operate correctly. While this will save hard drive disc space, it is not recommended for programming the types of programs we will present in this text. The "standard install" is also not recommended. Most of the programs found in the following chapters will work correctly with this option, but not all of them. Therefore, we strongly recommend that you conduct a "full install" of Visual Basic 2005 / Visual Studio to minimize any programming incompatibilities between information found in this text and your attempts to reproduce the programs on your own computer.

Programming Interface

The Project

Open the Visual Basic 2005 program by first clicking on the *Start* button in the bottom left corner of your computer screen, then on *Programs*, and finally on *Microsoft Visual Basic*. Depending on your installed version, your third option may say something like "Visual Studio 2005" or "Visual Basic 2005." Once the program opens you will see a small window entitled "Start Page" prompting you to make a selection between *Create Projects* or to open an existing project. Select *Create*, and then *Windows Application*, and then click *OK*. This option is probably already highlighted as the default option when the program loaded. In the future you can use the *Existing* tab to quickly access projects that you previously worked on.

It should be noted at this time that throughout the course of this book some buttons or names will appear using *italics*. This has been done by the publisher to assist with reading ease and clarity, but these items are not written in *italics* in Visual Basic 2005. When VB 2005 code is written, it is set apart in a different font. When these lines of code are too long to fit on a single line, the subsequent lines are indented to indicate that the previous line of code is continuing.

Project Explorer

Programming in Visual Basic 2005 takes place in, what is called, a "Solution." This "solution" can be conceptualized as the environment that houses your program. As a default, Visual Basic 2005 has named this solution for you as "WindowsApplication1." As you examine your computer screen, along with Figure 1.1, you will see a novel looking tool bar down the left side of the screen along with four smaller windows containing a variety of information within the larger main window of Visual Basic.

Take note of the smaller window in the upper right hand side of the screen. This window is called the "Solution Explorer." The "Solution Explorer" is your outline of the various components that currently exist in your program. Currently your program, entitled "WindowsApplication1" contains a file folder consisting of a form called "Form1.vb". Right now if you were to run your program, a blank window with

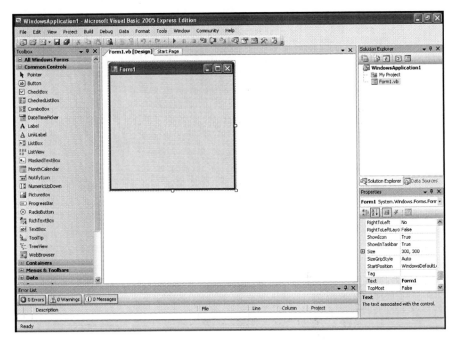

Figure 1.1 displays an overview of the Visual Basic 2005 programming environment.

a name of "Form1" would appear on the computer screen. Try this by clicking on the *Debug* option in your main toolbar at the top of the screen followed by the *Start Debugging* sub-option. To terminate the program, again click on "Debug" but now select the sub-option *Stop Debugging*.

As you add more materials into your computer program besides a blank window called Form1.vb, the detail of the Solution Explorer will grow. Clicking on the Solution Explorer files and directories is quite useful when your program becomes larger and you need to locate specific portions of the program quickly. If for some reason you accidentally close the Solution Explorer window, and it will happen, simply click on *View* and then *Solution Explorer* from the main toolbar. folders) is unnecessary to create the programs you will probably make for research purposes.

Forms

To the left of the "Solution Explorer" window is a larger window called "Form1" containing a window "Form1" inside of it. This layout mimics what you also see in the "Solution Explorer", yet in graphical form. Again, we currently have a solution called "WindowsApplication1" and a form called "Form1" within it. You already saw Form1 in action. So far, it doesn't do much. Yet this little form can quickly become quite powerful.

Properties Window

Directly below the "Solution Explorer" window is a slightly larger window entitled the "Properties Window." In our current project, the name in the Properties Window reads "Properties-Form1." This window displays a variety of modifiable properties of the form. Some of these properties are more important for psychological research than others, with the most commonly used options described here. Other form properties will be detailed in later chapters as their use becomes more context relevant.

For now, take a look at your first form property, the name. You can change the name of your form to something more descriptive than "Form1." To do this simply double-click on the "(name)" option. It should be the first available option. The text "Form1" will become highlighted. Change this text to your new form name. For illustration purposes, lets call the form "frmGreetings." This name might be relevant if our form served to greet users or subjects when they begin to interact with our program. The name of your Properties Window should now have changed to "frmGreetings". Figure 1.2 displays this change.

A few sections below the "(name)" option is the "Backcolor" option. Click on this option, select *custom* and change the color to a shade of yellow. Note the changes in frmGreetings in Figure 1.3.

Below *BackColor* is the *FormBorderStyle* property. This property of the form determines if a user will be able to resize the form during run time (i.e. minimize or maximize the window). It is likely to be the case that you will not want your subject to alter the size of the screen's form during run time of the experiment. Doing so may disrupt subject attention to the stimuli conditions programmed into the experiment. Alter the BorderStyle property in different ways, and run the program each time, trying to change the size of the form. Note the differences with each property option. You may have had a problem trying to run your program at this time depending on your version of Visual Basic 2005. A new error window may have popped up saying there were build errors. Click on the *NO* Button when asked if you want to continue. To fix this error, click on *WindowsApplication1* in the *Solution Explorer* (to highlight this selection), then click *Project* on the main menu, then on the *Properties* option. Now change the *Startup option* from *Form1* to *frmGreetings*, and click *OK*. Try running the program, it should now work.

Scrolling down the Properties Window you will find an option entitled *WindowState*. The default option for WindowState is *Normal*. This means that during

error

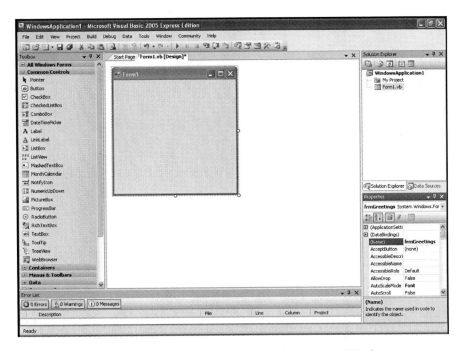

Figure 1.2 shows the alterations made in the Properties Window following the renaming of Form1.

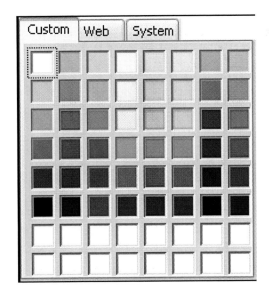

Figure 1.3 displays the BackColor property color customization window.

run time your form will appear with the same size dimensions that existed by default when you began your program. Yet, if you want the form to become larger, say the entire size of the computer screen, all you need to do is change this property to *Maximized*. Run the program. Your yellow frmGreetings form should encompass the entire computer screen. Note though, that it will no longer be possible to stop the program using the *Run* and *Stop* sequence as before – frmGreetings covered it up. Stop the program using the X in the top right hand corner of frmGreetings. If you selected a BorderStyle of *None* and wish to stop the program you will need to actually use a CTRL-ALT-DELETE command sequence. Varying levels of program termination and form size can work to your advantage when attempting to reduce subject distraction during your experiment.

Form Layout

The Start Position property provides you with a way of altering your form's look during run time on your computer screen. You can shift your form's position by changing this property. Try moving your form here, and then try running the program. Note how your form is positioned in different sections of the monitor screen based on the selection you made. The Start Position property only works to aid you when your form is in the WindowState *Normal* mode. Most programs you will create will contain forms that are Maximized.

Toolbox

The most dynamic window that resides on your Visual Basic 2005 desktop is the Toolbox. This window contains all the necessary devices for you to create your own experiments. These "tools" which are contained within the toolbox can be incorporated into your program by using your mouse button to select, drag, and drop them onto your existing form. Because we are creating Windows-based programs (as opposed to web-based or other types) the Windows Forms tools are displayed by default. If not, click on this option.

The first tool is the default mouse pointer. You can click here if you accidentally selected a tool you don't want and need to obtain a different one, or if you clicked on a tool by mistake and simply want to return to other activities within your form and program. Another important tool is a Label, and is depicted with a large capital letter *A*. Placing this tool on your form will result in a rectangular box with the text "Label1" located within it. Note that the default property highlighted in the Properties Window is "Text" - "Label1." Double-click on the section and type in a different caption, like *Hello* and press Return. Notice how your Label on your form now has changed its text from *Label1* to *Hello*.

Figure 1.4

*Figure 1.4 and 1.5 display the effects of altering your form's position
with the Start Position Property.*

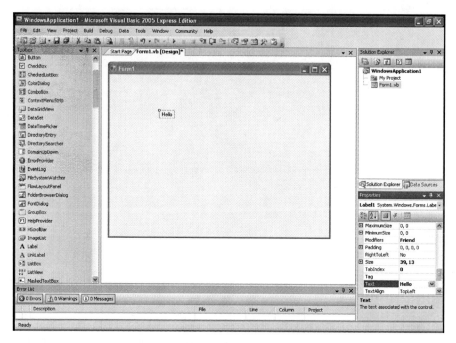

Figure 1.6 displays the form and Label.

Another tool is the PictureBox. Adding a PictureBox to your form will give you the ability to place graphics into your computer program. Add a PictureBox to your form and note the default property highlighted in the Properties Window is "Image (none)." Double-click on the "(none)" section and notice that you are presented with an explorer window to select a picture from your computer's files. Click on *"Local Resources."* Browse for a picture, select it, and click *OK*. Your picture should now reside in your PictureBox. The PictureBox contains a property called *SizeMode* located a few options below the Image property. Altering this property to *StretchImage* will allow your graphic to be resized to fix exactly within the display box. This is a very valuable property which will save you considerable time if you are left having to resize all your graphical images to fix exactly within your Picture objects. This tool also contains the ability for participants to respond, or click, directly on it during an experiment. This is of considerable value if you are presenting stimuli directly within a PictureBox and wish for the participant to make a response to that stimulus rather than an adjacent Button or CheckBox.

Another tool is the TextBox and is depicted with a small case "a b |" display. Placing this tool on your form will result in a rectangular box with no text located within it. This TextBox looks very similar to your Label box, yet the important difference is that a TextBox allows a user to enter information during run time by typing in the box, while a Label will not. A Label is used to display information, while a TextBox is often used to acquire information from the participant. There are

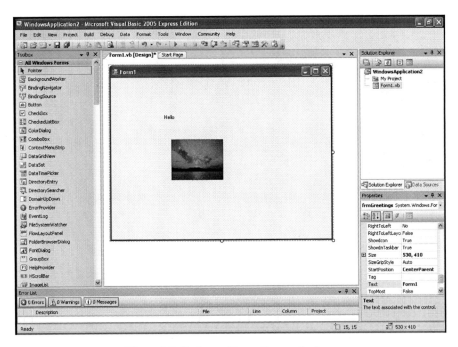

Figure 1.7 displays a PictureBox on the form.

exceptions to this case, but in general this rule does hold true. Notice that the default property highlighted in the Properties Window is "Text" followed by a blank space. Double-click on the blank section and type in a line of text, like *Welcome to my form* and press Return. Notice how your TextBox on your form has now placed in *Welcome to my form* on the TextBox. Now locate the Font property for your TextBox and double-click on it. Notice that you are now presented with more property options like Name, Size, Unit, Bold, etc., that allow you to make a variety of changes to the characteristics of your font for the text in your TextBox. Play around with some changes, and note the changes on your form. Run your program and notice how you can edit the text of your TextBox and how you cannot edit the text of your Label.

A GroupBox is a rectangular object on the form that can hold other tools within it. It is essentially a type of "mini form" within your existing form. Add a GroupBox to your form and note that the text displayed above it is *GroupBox1* and that the default property highlighted in the Properties Window is "text" – "GroupBox1." Double-click on the "text" property and change the text to *How are you?* and press Return. Notice how your text has changed. Within your new Frame you can place specific tools to enhance the design style of your form's layout. There are other and more pragmatic properties to the GroupBox tool that will be covered in later chapters.

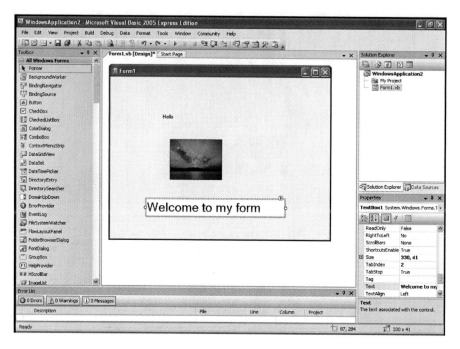

Figure 1.8 displays the form, PictureBox, Label, and TextBox.

Another important tool is the Button. A Button is a tool that a user or participant clicks the mouse pointer on during an experiment. It can be thought of as a computerized version of a lever in a traditional operant chamber. The Button can be used as the primary response operanda in many experiments. Two or more Buttons can also function as response options in choice situations. Add two Buttons to your form, within your GroupBox. You can stretch or shrink them by manipulating the sides of the Button. Make them about the same size, and locate the "text" property of Button1. Change that property to *Great*. Note the change on the form. Now select Button2 and change the "text" property to *Bad*. Note the change on your form.

The CheckBox and RadioButton tools allow you to create a means for participants to select from an array of options presented to them. You might use these tools to create a means of assessing participant age, sex, race, and other demographics. They might also be used in survey research to measure self-reports to different psychological questions.

The ComboBox and ListBox tools provide you with yet another way in which a participant can select from a list of options presented to them. These tools work best on forms containing many objects and materials because they only require minimum space and can store a large number of response options.

Figure 1.9 displays the form, PictureBox, Label, TextBox, and GroupBox.

Figure 1.10 displays the form with the newly added two Buttons.

The *Timer* tool has considerable utility for programmers of behavioral research. It is sometimes called the *Timer Object*. The Timer is depicted by a little stopwatch in the toolbox. Add a Timer tool to your form. Notice how it immediately was removed from your form and placed in the empty space below it. this is done because the Timer Object is never visible during runtime. Look in the Properties Window and notice that this little tool has only a few properties compared to other tools like the TextBox, Label, GroupBox, etc. Altering the *Interval* property of the Timer from "0" milliseconds to some value can control the duration stimuli are displayed on the form, specify the length of an experimental phase, or delay the onset of a reinforcer.

There are other tools within the toolbox that we have not mentioned here, but will be highlighted in subsequent chapters as their utility becomes more apparent. However, most programming can be completed with the simple tools we have outlined above.

Error List Window

The Error List Window found on the bottom of your screen is a new feature in VB 2005. Its purpose is to provide you with a listing of problems that occur during the test running of your program. Hopefully this window will remain relatively

Figure 1.11 displays the form with the added Timer.

empty as you learn to program, but if not, it does highlight where your errors are, and provides you with "hints" about how to fix the error(s).

Beyond the Visual Interface

Menu Bar

The Menu Bar in Visual Basic 2005 is quite similar to the Menu Bar found on your other popular Microsoft Office products. Some of the response options are in fact identical. You have the *Cut, Copy, Paste* features, the *Open* and *Save* features, and the *Undo* and *Redo* features. Other response options are more idiosyncratic to Visual Basic. Here you can *Add a project, add a windows form,* or *add a new component.* Like the other Microsoft products, these options are simple shortcuts to perform actions that are also found in the dropdown menus located at the top of the screen under headings such as *File, Edit, Properties,* etc. We will highlight the most commonly used response options of this Menu Bar as we construct the programs found in the following chapters. Explore them a little now to become familiar with their location. Often sought after options are the "Properties Window" and "Toolbox". There have been many times that we have accidentally closed one of these windows, and need to pop them back open quickly. It can become rather frustrating when you can't remember how to do so.

Code

By now you probably double-clicked on your form somehow and accidentally opened a window containing a white background and the title text of "Public Class frmGreetings." If not, do so now. Simply place your mouse pointer anywhere on your form and double-click. This underworld of your form is actually called the *Edit Level, Code Level,* or *Programming Level* where you write syntax to make your form do the things you want it to do during the running of the experiment. It is here where you make stimuli in PictureBoxes appear and disappear, Timers turn on or off, sounds play, screens change colors, etc. Believe it or not, you will be able to do so by the end of the next chapter. With the right direction, the programming all of these fascinating events is relatively quite easy to do.

An Unfortunate Flaw

There will be times when you attempt to run your program, and your form just does not show up. Your mouse can still move on the screen, but the form seems to be missing. This is a flaw in the VB 2005 program that will hopefully be solved in future editions. To minimize the probability of this happening, make your WindowState property *Maximized.* If all else fails, stop the program, and just try running it again. This flaw is annoying, yet it will not affect the running of the final program once it is totally built.

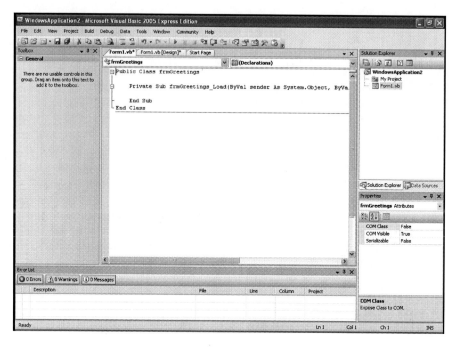

Figure 1.12 displays the "Code" or "Edit" level of the form.

Chapter 2:
Simple Routines in Visual Basic

Windows States, Screen Colors, and Key Previews

Window States

Open a new "Windows Application" project and change the name of the Project and solution to *Forms*. It is a good practice to start off by saving your form and project immediately before you begin working on it. This helps avoid any loss of information from computer crashes or unexpected power outages. To save all your related forms and information found in your Forms Solution, click on *File* in the main menu, then click on *Save All*.

Select the form by clicking on it, change the name of the form to *frmForm* in the Solution Explorer, and change the text to *This is a form* in the Properties window. Now run the program using the menu. You can use the controls box in the upper right corner to minimize and maximize the form during run time. Close the form.

Allowing the subject to be able to change the size of the form is sometimes undesirable when running experiments. Also, it may be more useful for subjects to see the experiment encompass the entire computer screen to reduce distractions. It is easy to configure these options prior to running the program. To do so, change the *WindowState* property to *Maximize*. Now run the program using the menu. Close the program using the control box in the upper left corner.

Screen Colors

You can change the background color of the form by altering the BackColor property in the property toolbox. Simply click on *BackColor* and choose your preferred color. There are a wide variety of colors you can choose from. These colors can add contextual cues to specific programming procedures, or just a flash of color to a rather boring preparation. You may wish for the screen color to change when the subject clicks a specific object, or after a given amount of time has elapsed. Both of these options are easily constructed, as you will see below.

Key Preview

The key preview information is useful for creating programs that would require a subject to press a specific key in order for a specific event to happen. For example, you might have a subject press the *X* key to turn off a loud aversive noise, but only after he/she has pressed the *G* key twice. Or, you might have the space bar advance images in a signal detection task. The key preview function allows you to figure out which keycode is associated with each key, and with that information you can compose code for the computer do something if the keycode = 34 (or whatever the number of your desired key might be).

Double-click the form to go to the edit level. There are two drop down boxes at the top of the editor. The left drop down lists the objects residing on the form. Currently there are no objects other than the form, and two items called *(General)* and *(frmForm Events)*. Select *(frmForm Events)*. The *(General)* option found here will be discussed later.

The right drop down box will now list all of the events or *(frmForm Events)* associated with the form (or whatever other object is highlighted in the left drop down box). With the *(frmForm Events)* listed in the left box, select *KeyUp* in the right box. A new subroutine will appear called Form_KeyUp (ByVal sender as Object, ByVal e as System.Windows.Forms.KeyEventArgs) handles Mybase.KeyUp. Directly below this line and above the line *End Sub* type:

```
me.Text = e.KeyCode
```

Now return to the properties toolbox of frmForm and change the form property of *KeyPreview* to *True*. Run the program using the menu and try typing in numbers or letters. Notice that the text displays different numbers each time you press a key. This is because each key has a unique number associated with it. Each time you press a key and then let it up, the associated number is displayed in frmForm's text. Close frmForm using the upper right control box.

Under your last line of code type:

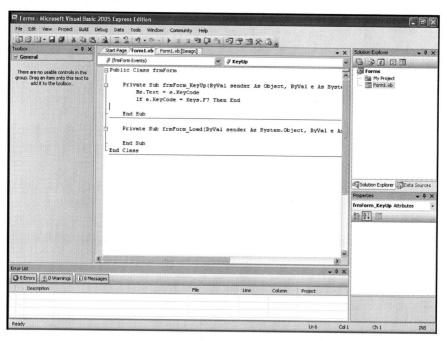

Figure 2.1 displays an example of the keypreview function.

```
If e.KeyCode = Keys.F7 then End
```

Now run the program and press the F7 key. Your program should automatically end.

Altering Form Properties

Form Resizing and Buttons

Double-click on the form to go to edit level. Using the left event drop down box, select *(frmForm Events)* and using the right drop down box, select *SizeChanged*. A new subroutine called *frmForm_SizeChanged...* will appear. Below this line type:

```
me.Text = me.Height & "," & me.Width
```

Run the program using the menu. Use the control box to restore the form. Move the mouse cursor to the edge of the form. The cursor will turn into a double headed arrow, then press down on the left mouse key and resize the form. Notice how the form properties *Height* and *Width* are displayed in the text and change each time you resize the form. This information may be useful if you are designing a program with multiple forms where each will occupy only a portion of the computer screen.

Return to your project and click on the Button object in the toolbox. Place the Button on your form and change the name of the Button in the properties box to *cmdButton*. Resize the Button by clicking on it, and then move your mouse cursor to the edge of the Button. When the mouse cursor changes to a double arrow, hold down the left mouse button and resize the Button by moving the mouse in any desired direction. You can also resize the Button by changing the *Size* properties in the properties box.

You can also move the entire Button by pressing down on the left mouse key when it is over the Button. Then simply drag cmdButton to any desired location on the form. Another way to move cmdButton to the left or right is by changing the *Location* property in the property box. If cmdButton disappears don't worry, you have probably entered a value that is larger or smaller than the visible area of frmForm. Now try moving cmdButton by changing the *Location* property in the properties box. While this appears rather trivial right now, keep in mind that you can change object properties while the program is running. This can be very useful in a variety of experiments. We will illustrate such usage in later chapters.

Now, change the text property of cmdButton to *Color Switch*. Double-click on cmdButton and insert the code directly below the subroutine cmdButton_Click...:

```
me.Backcolor = Color.Bisque
```

Run the program, and click on the Button. You will see that your screen changes from whatever color you chose earlier to a light tan color. You could add other Buttons for other colors too.

Utilizing a Button with code to terminate the program is also very useful. For example, if you are attempting to assess a subject's persistence on a given task like a slot machine and you allow them to quit when they "feel" they can't win any more. Some human subjects' committees may even require a program termination option to be in your experiment. Such an option allows the subject to terminate the program at anytime they feel uncomfortable.

Change the text property of cmdButton to *Close*. Double-click on cmdButton and insert the code directly below the subroutine cmdButton_Click:

```
End
```

While you have previously been starting your program using the icon on the menu, you can also run it by pressing the *F5* key. Give this a try and click on the *Close* button. The program should end.

You might be wondering right now what this "code" you are typing in actually means. Especially that "me" word. Well "me" is shorthand for the active form in the program. When you have more than one form in your program "me" becomes quite important.

Events

An event is something that happens, most often due to the user clicking on the mouse or pressing a key on the keyboard. When the user clicks on the cmdButton, as described above, this is called an event. The same is true with the KeyUp procedure that you created earlier. Visual Basic 2005 programs are most often run via a series of events that occur right after each other. Your experiments will undoubtedly be event driven by the subject. Let's begin an example of an event that links multiple forms together.

Linking Multiple Forms

Open the Forms Solution if it is not already open, and add a new form using the menu. Click on *Project*, then *Add WindowsForm*, then click on the *WindowsForm* Icon. Rename the form *frmForm2*. Change the text of frmForm2 to *Form 2*. Change the WindowState to Maximized. Now add a Button and rename it *cmdPreviousForm*, and change the text of cmdPreviousForm to *Previous*. Next, double-click on cmdPreviousForm to enter edit mode and under cmdPreviousForm_Click type:

```
me.Visible = False
```

Now press the enter key. On the next line type:

```
Dim x as New frmForm()
x.Show()
```

Return to frmForm by double-clicking on its name in the Solution Window. Add a Button and rename it *cmdNext* and change the text property of cmdNext to *Next*. Move cmdNext to any new location on the form. Double-click on cmdNext to enter edit mode, type the following code below cmdNext_Click:

```
me.Visible = False
```

Press the enter key and then type:

```
Dim x as New frmForm2()
x.Show()
```

Press the F5 key to run the program: Click on the *Next* Button: Click on the *Previous* Button. Notice how the Buttons take you from one form to another.

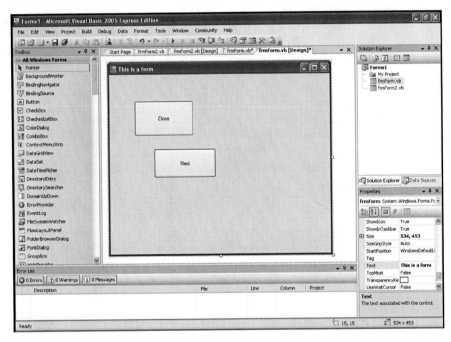

Figure 2.2 displays an example of the incorporation of Buttons with multiple forms.

Notice how the screen flickers when you change from one form to another. This is because you are hiding one form before showing the next. If you reverse the order of the code under cmdNext so that the show property of *X* is *True* before you change the visible property of frmForm to *False* then the flicker will not occur. Change the order of the code under frmForm2 as well, and run the program using the F5 key.

While the *me. Visible=False* code explains itself the *DimX...* code probably does not. What happens here is that we need to take the frmForm2 Object (i.e. Windows Form) and make it equal an arbitrary entity (i.e., *X*). Then we simply tell *X* to show itself. Variables such as *X* will be explained in more detail as we progress.

Labels

Open the VB 2005 Solution *Forms* if it is not already open and go to frmForm by double-clicking on its name in the Solution Explorer. Add a Label to the form by clicking on the Label icon in the toolbox. Change the name property of the Label to *lblInstructions* and change the text property of lblInstructions to *Click on the NEXT button to go to the next form*. Move the Label to the upper left corner of frmForm and run the program.

Changing the Font properties in lblInstructions can be done rather easily. Click on lblInstructions to select the object, and then locate the font property in the property box. Double-click on the font property so that more font options appear. This is very much like font options that are used in Word and Excel. This is because VB 2005 uses existing Windows libraries to make VB 2005 a more powerful program, as well as one that you should be somewhat familiar with if you use other Microsoft products. Using the font dialog box, change the font size and any other properties you might desire. Finally, close the font options by double-clicking on font property again and change *AutoSize* property to False. Run the program.

In addition to changing font properties, you can also change the TextAlign property of lblInstructions. The default alignment of the text for lblInstructions is set to the left. Yet, if you wish to center the text, select lblInstructions by clicking on it, locate the TextAlign property in the toolbox, and change the alignment property to center. Run the program.

Another possibility you may wish to consider when using Labels for providing instructions to your subject is changing some of the Label properties while the program is running. This might be done to ensure orientation to a specific Label at a specific time. To do this, add another Button to frmForm, change the name to *cmdLeft*, and change the text of cmdLeft to *Left*. Double-click on cmdLeft to enter edit mode and type the following code under cmdLeft_click:

```
lblInstructions.TextAlign = ContentAlignment.MiddleLeft
```

Now, add another Button and position it to the right of cmdLeft. Change the name of this new Button to cmdRight, and change the text property to *Right*. Double-click on cmdRight to enter edit mode and type the following code under cmdRight_click:

```
lblInstructions.TextAlign = ContentAlignment.BottomRight
```

Run the program. Try clicking on the Left and Right Buttons.

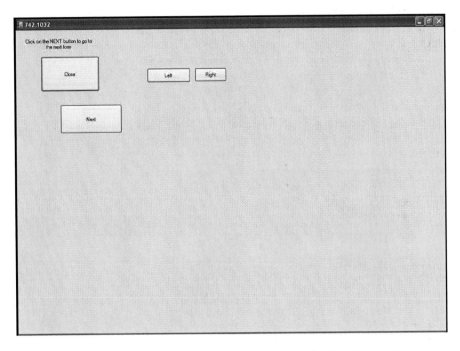

Figure 2.3 displays an example of using Labels for the display of instructions.

Array

Button Array

So far we have worked with single objects (forms and Buttons). Now we will create what is called a control array. A control array is a group of more than one object (such as a Button or Label) that controls a similar function in your program. For example, if you have three Buttons that a subject could click on to indicate a preference among three options, much less code would be needed if we created a control array than if we put three separate buttons on the screen and typed similar code underneath each of those buttons.

Open the VB 2005 Solution Forms if it is not already open, and select lblInstructions from frmForm. Now select *Edit* and then *Copy* from the main menu. Go to frmForm2 and select *Edit* and then *Paste* from the main menu. Now we have duplicated the same Label on two different forms with duplicate names. We can have duplicate objects with the same names because they are on separate forms. This is because they are really named *frmForm.lblInstructions* and *frmForm2.lblInstructions* (Note the period separating the form name and the label name is called "dot notation"). Yet, something different happens if we want two objects on the same form with the same name.

Create a new Button on frmForm and name the Button cmdLocation1. Change the text to *Top*. Now, select cmdLocation1, then select *Edit* and then *Copy*, and finally, *Edit* again and then *Paste* all from the main menu. Now we will have two Buttons that we want to call cmdLocation. So change the name of this second Button to cmdLocation2, and the text to *middle*. Select either of the cmdLocation buttons and repeat your earlier steps. The third button should be identical to the other two except it has the name of cmdLocation3, and a text of *bottom*.

To turn the three separate Buttons into a control array (in other words to link the click event of one to each other), you simply need to change a little existing code. Double-click on cmdLocation1 and go to the edit level. Note the line of code directly above your cursor:

```
Private Sub cmdLocation1_Click (...)
```

Notice at the end of this line of code it states:

```
Handles cmdLocation1.click
```

Just add the following code after cmdLocation1.click:

```
, cmdLocation2.click, cmdLocation3.click
```

Double-click on either of the other two cmdLocation Buttons and note that each cmdLocation button now handles all three Buttons.

Advantages of the Control Array

One benefit of this newly constructed control array is that you can reduce the amount of program code you use. Remember on frmForm the Buttons to change the alignment of lblInstructions? Under each Button you had to have a new line of code. With the array we can alter object properties with one line of code for all three cmdLocation Buttons.

To change the text displayed in our Label object when any one of our new cmdLocation Buttons is clicked, add the following code under any one of the three Buttons:

```
Dim buttonClicked as Button
buttonClicked = CType (sender, Button)
lblInstructions.Text= "You pressed" & buttonClicked.Text
```

Now when you press any cmdLocation Button, the text of that Button will be translated into the text property of the Label. Run the program and click on the different Buttons.

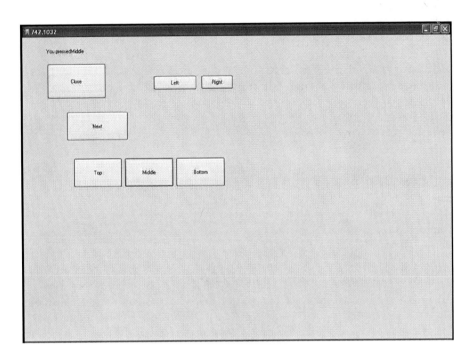

Figure 2.4 displays an example of using Command Arrays

Simple Audio

Beep

Sometimes it is good to have simple sounds incorporated into your program to get the users attention. There are several ways to do this. The easiest way to add a sound is to utilize the "Beep" function. This Beep is code that will tell VB 2005 to play the actual default sound your computer plays during the running of any windows application.

Let's add a new form to our existing project. Click on the *Add New Item* icon and notice that there are many types of Items we can add. However for now just click on *WindowsForm*. For now let's name the form frmForm3. While this is not that clever of a naming convention, it is consistent with the naming convention we have started. Change the text of frmForm3 to *Form 3*, and the Windows state to *Maximized*. Now we need to access frmForm3 from the main page, or from frmForm. Go to the frmForm and add a Button called *cmdForm3* and change the text to *Form3*. Double click cmdForm3 and enter the following three lines of code below Private Sub cmdForm3_Click():

```
Dim x as New frmForm3()
x.show()
me.Visible = False
```

Go back to frmForm3 and add a Button called cmdBeep, change the text to *Beep*. Double-click cmdBeep and add the following code below Private Sub cmdBeep_Click():

```
Beep
```

That's it. Just "Beep." Run the program, click on the *Form3* Button, and then click on the *Beep* Button.

Simple Graphics

Image Graphics

There are several ways to add graphics to your program. For now we will use the object called a PictureBox. Go to Form3 if you are not already there. Add a PictureBox to the form and call it imgForm3 for lack of a better name at this point. An outline of a box will appear on your form. Stretch it to whatever size you desire. Under properties find BorderStyle. Change the BorderStyle from *None* to *Fixed Single*. You will see your PictureBox take on new dimensions. Now find the Image property, double-click on the small box to the right of the image description, and browse your directory for any picture that you might like to put in the PictureBox. Many standard images can be found in your Windows directory. Chances are the PictureBox will not be the identical size as the picture you want to place in it. Therefore, BEFORE you add your picture to the PictureBox, change the *SizeMode* property to *StretchImage*. If you do this after you add your picture, it may not work. So again, change the *SizeMode* property of the PictureBox before you add your picture. Now the picture will fit, but it may be distorted because the aspect ratio (proportions) has changed. Select imgForm3 by clicking on it once. Try to resize the PictureBox by clicking and dragging on the blue resizing boxes in and out until you have the proportions that best accommodate your picture.

Adding a Graphic During Run Time(while the program is running)

A very useful feature of the PictureBox is that it will allow you to add or change the image within it during the running of the program. This is extremely beneficial if you are presenting a variety of stimuli to the subject across a series of trials and do not want the subject to see all of them at the onset of the experiment. Just think of the headache it would be if you needed to create a new PictureBox for every stimulus you had for your program.

First you need to figure out ahead of time what the path and file name are for the desired pictures. Lets say the picture is called *Picture1.bmp* and is located in the *c:\My Documents* directory. To work through this example, actually find an image on your computer, copy it to the *My Documents* directory, and rename it *Picture1.jpg*.

Add a new Button to Form3 called *cmdImage* and change the text to *New Image*. Locate cmdImage just below the PictureBox you previously added to your form. Double-click on the cmdImage and add the following code below Private Sub cmdImage_Click():

```
Dim path As String = "c:\My Documents\Picture1.jpg"
imgForm3.Image = Image.FromFile("c:\My Documents\
    Picture1.jpg")
```

Now run the program, go to Form3, and click on the New Image Button. Note that there is a space between the word *My* and the word *Documents*. If you do not add this space your program will not find the image. Also, keep in mind that if your image uses a capital letter or a space between a multiword picture name, you must have these same capitalization and spaces or VB 2005 will not be able to find the image file. Lastly, you must add the file extension to your picture's name. In the above example, we used a .jpg. You can also use GIF files and BMP files, which would result in .gif or .bmp file extensions respectively.

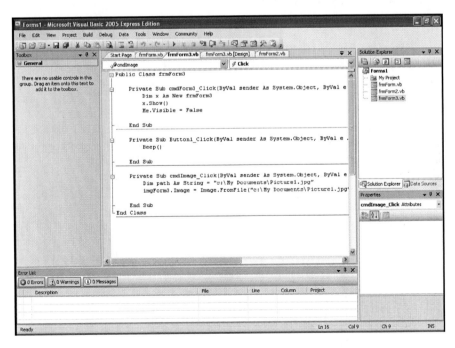

Figure 2.5 displays an example of code for incorporating graphics into an PictureBox

Adding Multiple Graphics During Run Time

For this exercise we will need to use a variable to keep track of the pictures. Double-click on Form3 and enter the edit mode. The left dropdown menu should say *frmForm3*. Click on this once, and select the *(frmForm3 Events)*. Type the following text *above* the Public Class frmForm3 code::

```
Option Explicit On
```

Then just below *Public Class frmForm3* type:

```
Dim vPicCount
```

The *v* will remind you later that this is a variable, or an entity that contains values. We will talk more about variables later, for now though simply understand that a variable keeps track of values that we can assign during programming, or the subject can generate and alter during run time. Under the same dropdown box, now select the *(frmForm3 Events)* option again. You will see that the default event that is associated with the form is *(Declarations)* (this appears in the right dropdown menu). Change this option to *Load*. The subroutine will look like this:

```
Private Sub frmForm3_Load()
End Sub
```

This means when the form loads, VB 2005 will do what ever is in the subroutine. Currently nothing is here. So when the form loads, it waits for the user to click on a Button to start some action. Yet, we want the form to do something, in this case load a picture, before the user even clicks on a Button. Therefore, we will have the form generate a value associated with our newly created variable and use that value to determine what type of picture will appear in the PictureBox. We will want the initial value of variable, vPicCount to equal 0. So type the following in this blank subroutine, directly under the text Private Sub frmForm3_Load().

```
vPicCount = 0
```

Now, when frmForm3 opens, the variable will be initialized to a value of 0. We also need to develop the following subroutine so we can cycle through three pictures (Picture1.jpg, Picture2.jpg, Picture3.jpg). Therefore, double-click on your cmdImage Button, and take a look at the following line of code you previously typed.

```
Dim path As String "c:\My Documents\Picture1.jpg"
imgForm3.Image = Image.FromFile ("c:\My Documents\
    Picture1.jpg")
```

This code calls one specific picture into the PictureBox at run time. Yet, now we want a variety of pictures to be displayed. Again, we will use pictures that are located in *c:\My Documents* directory. If you do not have at least three pictures in that directory, add them now, and change their names to Picture1, Picture2, and Picture3. Remember to note the file extensions.

What we want the computer to do is to show Picture1, then Picture2, then Picture3. To do this we need to learn to concatenate a string. This is actually very easy in VB 2005. Therefore, let's assume vPicCount has a value of 1 (vPicCount = 1), and if we do, the following sections of code are equivalent:

```
("c:\My Documents\Picture" & vPicCount & ".jpg")
```

```
("c:\My Documents\Picture1.jpg")
```

What this new, and somewhat different looking section of code says is, load a picture which has the first part of its name *Picture*, the second part of its name being equal to vPicCount (our new variable we created), and the last part of the name being the file extension (in this case a .jpg). Or in other words, load *Picture1.jpg*. If we increase the value of vPicCount by one (vPicCount = vPicCount + 1) then the following two sections of code are equivalent because now vPicCount = 2.

```
("c:\My Documents\Picture" & vPicCount & ".jpg")
```

```
("c:\My Documents\Picture2.jpg")
```

Because we want the picture to change each time we change the value of vPicCount, delete your previous code under the Button and type the following three lines of code directly under Private Sub cmdImage_Click():

```
vPicCount = vPicCount + 1
Dim path As String = ("c:\My Documents\Picture" &
    vPicCount & ".jpg")
imgForm3.Image = Image.FromFile ("c:\My Documents\
    Picture" & vPicCount & ".jpg")
```

Run the program, go to Form3, and click on New Image Button. Notice that when you passed the third picture (Picture3.jpg) and error message occurred because the was no Picture4 and you drove the computer crazy looking for it because it assumed there was a Picture4.

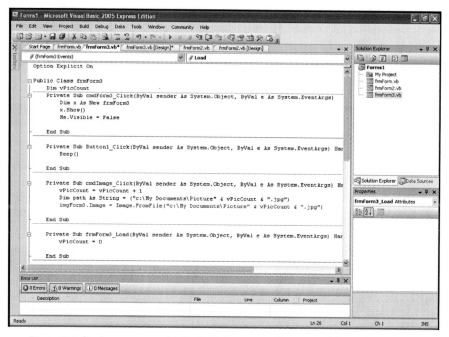

Figure 2.6 displays an example of code for incorporating sequential graphical images into a PictureBox.

There are two ways you can fix this run time error. The first is to tell the computer only increment vPicCount if it has a value below three (If vPicCount < 3 the vPicCount = vPicCount + 1). So add this line of code below vPicCount = vPicCount + 1.

```
If vPicCount < 3 then vPicCount = vPicCount +1
```

We don't want to run both lines of code that advance vPicCount so we want to *remark out* the old line. You do this by putting a 'in front of the old line. Notice how the old line turns a different color (probably green). The ' remarks out the line of code telling the computer to ignore it. *Remark out* is also very helpful if you want to put notes in your code so you remember what you were writing earlier. Just put the quotes at the front of anything you want to type in, and the computer will ignore it. Your subroutine should now look like this:

```
Private Sub cmdImage_Click()
'vPicCount = vPicCount + 1
If vPicCount < 3 then vPicCount = vPicCount + 1
```

```
Dim path As String = ("c:\My Documents\Picture" &
   vPicCount & ".jpg")
imgForm3.Image = Image.FromFile ("c:\My  Documents\
   Picture" & vPicCount & ".jpg")
End Sub
```

Run the program, go to form3, and click on the New Image Button. You should have solved the error problem now. Your pictures should change three times, and stay on your third one, no matter how many more times you click on *New Image*.

The Error Trapper

The other way to prevent the error message is to include an error trapper. While topics such as error trapping and debugging are usually held back until later chapters in programming books, it is important to get into the habit of using them in your programs. Many types of error trapping will be discussed later, we won't go into that much detail yet, and just show you the code. Note that you have to take the remark off of the old line that was originally causing the error and place a ' in front of the line of code starting with the *If* statement. For fun we will make the computer also Beep to let you know you have made an error, but the Beep is not required to make the error handler work. Therefore, rework your code under Private Sub cmdImage_Click() so that it looks like this:

```
Private Sub cmdImage_Click()
On Error GoTo Handler
vPicCount = vPicCount + 1
'if vPicCount < 3 then vPicCount = vPicCount + 1
Dim path As String = ("c:\My Documents\Picture" &
   vPicCount & ".jpg")
imgForm3.Image = Image.FromFile ("c:\My  Documents\
   Picture" & vPicCount & ".jpg")
Exit Sub
Handler:
Beep
Exit Sub
End Sub
```

Run your program. After you click on your *New Image* Button three times, all consecutive clicks will result in a Beep. This allows you to become aware that an error or incorrect value has been now associated with your variable.

Randomizing Picture Presentations

Sometimes you may want the order of pictures to be random. For example, if you are presenting a series of pictures to children and require them to respond on one Button if the picture is of a stranger and on another Button if it is of a friend/

family member. Here you probably do not want the list of pictures to be in a set repeated order. Randomization of pictures is quite easy to do in Visual Basic 2005.

VB 2005 has a random function (RND) that works off of the computer's internal clock. Unless you what to display the same random pattern each successive time you run the program (and you may) you have to *randomize* Visual Basic 2005 each time you start the program. To do this you use the RANDOMIZE function which is different from RND. Note that while the Randomize function can be added just about anywhere in the program, it is best to include it at the very beginning with the first form that is opened. So go to frmForm and double-click the form to go to the form editor. Select *frmForm* then *Load* from the drop down boxes at the top of the editor. Type the following code below Private Sub Form_Load().

```
Randomize
```

Now the program will use a new random pattern each time you run it. Go to frmForm3.

While serving a slightly different function from Randomize, the RND function also generates random values. Here though RND pulls a random number between 0 and 1 each time it is used. This seems rather useless, but it can actually add great possibilities to your program. To explore this simple process, add a new Button to frmForm3 and call it *cmdRandom* and change the text accordingly to *Random Number*. Double-click cmdRandom and add the following code to the subroutine:

```
me.text = Rnd
```

Run the program, go to frmForm3, and click on cmdRandom. Notice in the blue text bar above frmForm3 a small number with several significant digits appears. This is your random number. Now to incorporate this into our picture presentation, we need to get this number into a number between 1 and 3 so we can randomly display our pictures. Remember that RND makes numbers between 0 and 1. If we multiply 3 x 0 we get 0. If we multiply 3 x 1 we get 3. Now if we multiply 3 times a number between 0 and 1, we will get values between 0 and 3. To explore this change you code for cmdRandom to:

```
me.text = 3 * Rnd
```

Run the program. Notice that the numbers are like 0.33453, 2.6443, 1.73545 etc. While entertaining, we need integers like 1, 2, and 3 to correspond to our pictures. To make this occur, and change the code to generate whole number integers, simply type:

```
me.text = Int(3 * Rnd())
```

This tells the computer to round down the values to the nearest integer. Run the program and see for yourself.

We are now getting random values of 0, 1, and 2. To get values between 1 and 3 we simply need to shift the distribution by 1. To do this, change the code you have been working to look like this:

```
me.text = Int(3 * Rnd()) + 1
```

Run the program and see. Remember that we want to display a random picture in our PictureBox, and because we know the numbers will be between 1 and 3, we probably don't need our error trapper (but well keep it intact anyway). Instead of incrementing vPicCount each time we press the New Image Button as we did before, we can just assign it a random number. Remark out the old code vPicCount = vPicCount + 1 using the apostrophe. Make sure it turns green in color. Insert a new line of code to read:

```
vPicCount = Int(3 * Rnd()) + 1
```

Run the program and click on the New Image Button. You'll notice that sometimes when you click the Button, the image doesn't change. This is because the numbers are random and there is a one out of three possibility that the same number will come up consecutively. We have now created a small routine that will generate random stimuli presentations via clicking on a Button.

Timer

The Timer Object

In the previous section we worked with displaying graphics in a PictureBox when the subject pressed the New Image Button. Here one of three images appeared in a random order. There may be times when you want the images to appear "on their own" without having the subject be required to press a Button. This can be done using a Timer object. Note that VB 2005 also has a timer function that returns the current computer time. This is easily confused at first with the Timer object. We will use the computer time timer function later.

A Timer object can be found in the toolbox. Go to frmForm3 and add a Timer. Notice that there are very few properties associated with this very important object. Of these we are only going to use Name, Enabled, and Interval. Use the Name now by calling it *tmrPicture*. Enabled equals True means that the Timer is working. Enabled equals False means that it is turned off. The Interval property is used to tell the timer how often to display a new picture, or whatever task we assign it to do. The interval is measured in milliseconds so 1000 equals 1 second. Notice that there is no Visible property. The Timer is always invisible during run time.

Because we want the Timer to start when we tell it to, change the enabled property to false. Let's say we want to display a picture every 5 seconds. Change the interval property to 5000. Just as we had the code for the New Image Button execute the subroutine each time the Button was clicked, we want the Timer to execute the same command every 5000ms. Double-click on tmrPicture to open a new subroutine. Copy the code in the cmdImage subroutine and paste it into the tmrPicture subroutine you just created. Make sure you only copied the code and not the `Private Sub cmdImage_Click()` or the `End Sub` otherwise you will get an error. Now we need a way to start the Timer. Add a Button to frmFrom3, call it cmdStart and change the text accordingly. Double-click on the Button and add the following code in the subroutine:

```
tmrPicture.Enabled = True
```

Run the program. After you click on your new *Start* Button, your images will randomly appear in the PictureBox once every 5 seconds. Keep in mind you could get the same picture more than once in a row.

Random Timer Intervals

Suppose you want the pictures to be displayed at random intervals between 0 and 5000ms. This is easy to do because we just learned about how VB randomizes. To do this we simply need to add a line of code that changes the interval property each time the Timer displays the image.

Notice that we want the full range of values. If we just wanted discrete values of 0, 1000, 2000, etc. we need to include the INT for integer values, but we want the full range of values. This code has to be located below the new Timer interval to show the current interval value. Add this line of code under your Timer object.

```
tmrPicture.Interval = 5000 * Rnd
```

Your new tmrPicture subroutine should look like:

```
On Error GoTo ErrHandler
'vPicCount = vPicCount + 1
vPicCount = Int(3 * Rnd()) + 1
'If vPicCount < 3 then vPicCount = vPicCount + 1
tmrPicture.Interval = 5000 * Rnd
Dim path As String = ("c:\MyDocuments\Picture" &
    vPicCount & ".jpg")
imgForm3.Image = Image.FromFile
    ("c:\MyDocuments\Picture" & vPicCount & ".jpg")
Exit Sub
ErrHandler:
Beep
Exit Sub
```

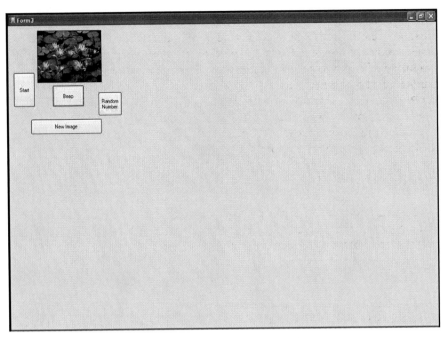

Figure 2.7 displays the lyaout of FrmForm3 during runtime.

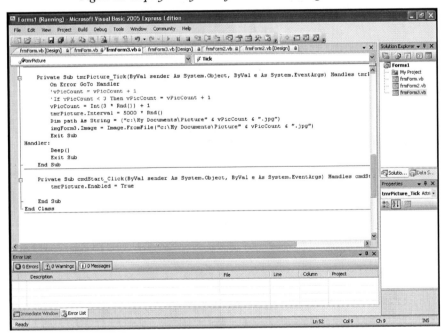

Figure 2.8 displays code incorporating a Timer to initiate random stimulus presentations.

In summary we have just created your first computer program. On one level this program does nothing more than a few interesting tricks. Yet on another level, this program contains much of the code you will use for most of the programs you will ever make in Visual Basic 2005. Study these little tricks closely, they will save you time, again and again.

Chapter 3: Schedules of Reinforcement

Overview

For the most part you have learned many of the necessary tools to prepare you to write some basic behavioral programs. There are some advanced topics you still might wish to learn that will be included in this chapter and others that will be discussed in detail later in the book. Let us begin by programming some simple schedules of reinforcement that you might wish to integrate into your research agenda. These are very simple examples, and might be useful for classroom demonstration. The programs themselves may not be ideal as stand alone programs, but they illustrate many concepts of Visual Basic 2005 that are critical for creating your own experiments.

In this chapter we will program the following schedules: 1) Fixed Ratio; 2) Variable Ratio; 3) Fixed Interval; and 4) Variable Interval. We assume that you are already somewhat familiar with the contingencies applicable for each schedule. If you are not familiar with these concepts you may want to refer to a textbook such as Learning (Catania, 1998) before beginning to write the following programs.

Fixed Ratio

Initial Preparation

For this program we want to display a reinforcer after the participant clicks on a Button a specified number of times. In this case the reinforcer will be a smiley face icon and points added to a cumulative total. *Note: We will use code that identifies our picture as "Face" but your picture can be anything you want.* Create a new Windows Application and name it FixedRatio. Now rename the form frmFR and save it as FR.vb. Add a Button called *butFR* and change the text to "…", a TextBox called txtFR, and an PictureBox called imgFR and place them on frmFR. Once you have placed the objects where you want them, you will need to change some of the properties of the objects. Use the properties window and change the following:

TxtFR's TextAlign Property to *Center*
ImgFR's Image Property to whatever picture, gif, jpg file you want.

Notice that imgFR resized to fit the icon. You may want the icon to be larger or smaller, so you will need to change imgFR or resize the image. To do this change imgFR's SizeMode property to *Stretch Image.*

Now we are ready to begin writing the code. There are several considerations we need to think about first. We have not specified how many clicks will be needed before the participant is reinforced. At this point we will have to change this value during programming, however later we will learn how to do this during runtime. Making such changes during runtime will allow experimenters or research assistants

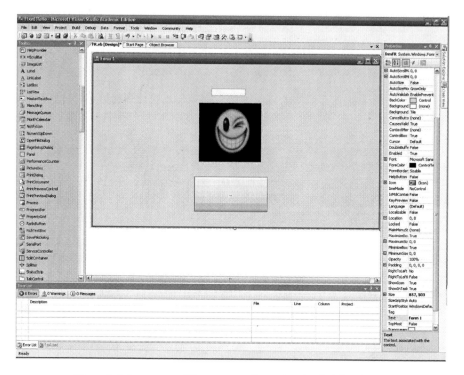

Figure 3.1 shows a possible screen configuration for the FR schedule.

to customize the program to the specific experimental condition without having to learn code or modify the actual program.

We must also think about things that were not specified such as how big do we want the PictureBox, Button, and TextBox objects? What color do we want the objects and the form? What do we want the text on the form and Button to read? When do we stop the program? Do we want to allow the participant to be able to terminate the program? How long is imgFR displayed when it appears? Should it remain on for a specific amount of time or when the participant next clicks on butFR? How many points do we award for the reinforcement? There are probably a dozen other things that you haven't thought about just yet. The point is that as the programmer, you have to make many decisions that are often taken somewhat for granted at the initial phase of designing an experiment. For now, you can decide how you want to address these questions.

Change your objects to the sizes and colors you want. Keep in mind your preferences at all stages of programming. We believe it is best to write these ideas down before beginning to write the program. While you may not have all the specifications up front, the more you can do initially, the better. See how the simple FR schedule quickly becomes quite complex?

Appearance During Run Time

Now consider what do we want the participant to see when the program begins? Probably butFR and txtFR, while imgFR should be invisible. In this case, you will need to change imgFR Visible Property to *False* in the property window. What do we want displayed in txtFR? Should txtFR be blank, have a value of *0*, or a value of *1*? Let's change txtFR's text property to *0* and run the program. So when the program begins the participant should see butFR and txtFR with the value of *0*. When you click on butFR nothing happens. That is to be expected, because there is no code written under the Button just yet. Now, end the program. The first thing you may have noticed is that your window state property of your form is not maximized. To have your schedule program encompass the entire screen, change the WindowState property to maximized.

Using Variables to Create a Point Counter

Next double-click on butFR so we can write some code. Move the cursor above the `Public Class frmFr` code and type the code:

```
Option Explicit On
```

We will need to keep track of the number of clicks so we will need a variable to store this value. Under the line Public Class frmFR, type:

```
Dim vCount
```

This will declare the variable. The *v* is just a naming construct we use to let us know that Count is a variable. Visual Basic 2005 does not require it. The name vCount is not a magical name that counts things either. We could have called our variable vPotato, or simply Moose. The name is up to you. We prefer to use a theme of prefexes that designate what the types of variables are along with names that are somewhat programatically relevant. The choice is yours though. Now, when the participant clicks on butFR we will need to advance vCount by one. Therefore, under Sub butFR_Click() type:

```
vCount = vCount + 1
```

This literally means make vCount equal vCount plus one. Now we need to tell the computer to display imgFR and advance txtFR's. Let's decide on 5-points after 10 clicks have been made on butFR. Utilizing these values, on the next line type:

```
If vCount > 9 Then
imgFR.visible = True
txtFR.Text = txtFR.Text + 5
```

An "End If" line of code should have been automatically added after the last line you typed. If not, add it manaully. Now run the program and start clicking. If all goes well on the 10th click, imgFR is displayed and txtFR is increased by 5 points. Nothing happens as planned on the 20th click and it is difficult to keep counting to see what click number you are on. So we still have some work to do. Our image remains on the screen, our counter is now adding by five, and things appear to be getting out of control. End the program.

To begin fixing these flaws, often called "bugs" in the world of programming, under the line vCount = vCount + 1 type:

```
me.Text = vCount
```

This will keep track of the number of clicks we make on our Button in the top or text part of our form. When the program is finished we can just remark out this line of code with the ' key or even delete it because we don't want the participants to see it during run time. Now we have to figure out how to reinforce every 10th click. We just need to reset the value of vCount each time we reinforce by typing the following code just below the code to display the image (imgFR.Visible = True):

```
vCount = 0
```

Now run the program. You will see that vCount is resetting after the 10th click and txtFR is advancing by 5 each 10th click, by viewing the values displayed in the Form's text.

Turning On and Off an Image

While our point counter is working just fine, imgFR stays on all of the time once it appears. There are several things we can do at this juncture. First, we could set up a Timer so imgFR disappears after a given interval. Second, we could make imgFR disappear after butFR is clicked. Or third, we could have the participant click on imgFR to make it disappear. Let's decide on the third option. Now, when imgFR appears, butFR should disappear. And when imgFR is clicked on it disappears and butFR appears. Under the code to make imgFR.Visible = True, type:

```
butFR.Visible = False
```

Next select imgFR from the leftt drop down box and click from the right drop down box at the top of the editor to open the *Click* subroutine. Under Sub imgFR_Click() type:

```
imgFR.Visible = False
butFR.Visible = True
```

Run the program. It should now work just fine.

Terminating the Program

The final line of code that we might need is one that automatically terminates the program. Let's just decide for now that we want the program to end after 10 reinforcements. There are several ways we can do this. We know that after 10 reinforcements the value of txtFR will be 50. So when txtFR = 50 we can end the program. But what if we change the number of points awarded? Then we would have to remember to change the cutoff point. Another way is to divide the total points by the pay off and if that value equals 10 then we can end the program. For now let's decide on terminating when txtFR = 50. Just below the *End If* statement in the butFR_Click() routine type:

```
If txtFR.Text > 49 Then End
```

Now, since 50 is greater than 49, the program will end once the subject obtains 50 points. Run the program. You can experiment with the program by changing the reinforcement schedule and see if it still works. For example, you might try adding an *Exit* command Button and the *End* statement so the participant can terminate the program. Try changing other object properties and program parameters.

Don't forget to remark out the me.Text = vCount line of code when you run the program for a real participant. This was only used during programming to allow us to check that the variables we created were working properly.

Disabling a TextBox from User Input

One possible kink in your well-designed program is the fact that your participant may "cheat" and change the value of your TextBox, hence changing when the program ends, their points, and giving you a bunch of grief. You can fix this problem by clicking once on the TextBox, and changing the property *Enabled* in the property toolbox from *True* to *False*. Your problem should now be solved.

Variable Ratio

Initial Preparation

Let's suppose you want to make a program with a Variable Ratio schedule of reinforcement. For the variable ratio we want reinforcement to occur after an average number of clicks. To do this we need to specify a range of values and then find a random number between those values before the reinforcer is produced. This program is very much like the Fixed Ratio program. We can recycle some of the code for our new project. First we need to save the work we have done thus far. Click on "File" in the upper left of your screen and select "Save All." In the resulting dialog box choose a location to save the project and click on "Save." We now have our progress saved so that we may reuse it for our new project. Create a new project and name it *Variable Ratio*. Move your cursor to the Solution Explorer where the forms are listed and right click the mouse on the highlighted text of the Variable Ratio Project to view a popup menu. Select *Add*.

error: no form! → change the name ~~right~~ *double click* ~~properties~~ *Change Startup form*

Figure 3.2 displays the code for developing a fixed ratio schedule of reinforcement.

Then click on *Add Existing Item*. Next, from the browser locate and select FR.vb, then click on the open button. You should see frmFR added to your list of forms. We have no use for the default form1 so locate your mouse over form1 in the Solution Explorer and right click. Select *delete* from the popup menu. Now only frmFR should remain in the Solution Explorer. You might think about changing the PictureBox image for your new schedule.

Editing an Existing Form

We also want to make some changes to FR.vb so it can become a variable ratio, but we don't want these changes to be shown when we run the fixed ratio program. So we need to change the name of the form. Locate your cursor over FR.vb in the Solution Explorer and right click. Select the rename option, and change the name to *VR.vb*. This will create a new form to be used in the VR project, and keep your frmFR form in tact. Any changes we make will not affect the other program. Finally change the name property of VR.vb to frmVR and run the program.

Changing Object Names

We now need to rename txtFR to txtVR; butFR to butVR; and imgFR to imgVR. Changing the names of these items in the designer mode should have automatically updated the names of the items in the code in the edit mode. In past versions of

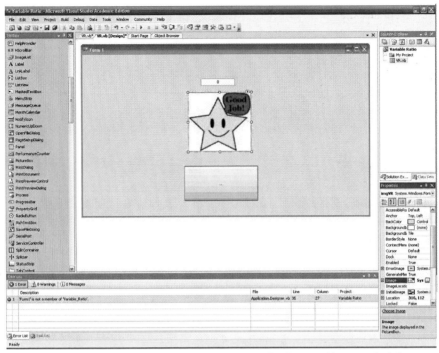

Figure 3.3 shows a possible screen configuration for the variable ratio schedule.

visual basic you would be required to manually edit the names of all items at both the design and edit modes. This is a new feature to Visual Studio 2005 that saves a lot of time and cuts down on a lot of potential sources of error in adding items from existing projects. Enter the edit mode and make sure that the names of the items in the code reflect the changes you made at the design level.

You may notice that while the names of the items were changed in the code, the names of the items in the subroutines titles were not changed. You will need to make these changes manually. In the *Private Sub butFR_Click()* subroutine change the text, *butFR_Click()* to *butVR_Click()* and in the *Private Sub imgFR_Click()* subroutine change the text, *imgFR_Click()* to *imgVR_Click()*. Make these changes, and then run the program. It should work just like the FixedRatio program, which is good at this point.

Using Random Numbers

We still need to make the schedule a variable ratio. Because we are going to use a random number we have to tell the computer to randomize the number strings each time the program is run. This is done by double-clicking on the form to enter edit mode and opening a new frmVR_Load subroutine. Under Sub frmVR_Load type:

```
Randomize
```

Each time the form is loaded the number string is randomized. Next we need to write a subroutine independent of any one object to find a random number according to our specifications. To do this, at the bottom of all text (above "End Class") in the editor type:

```
sub rand_number
```

and press return. Something called a subroutine will automatically be created for you.

Subroutines

A subroutine is a section of code that performs an action like generating random numbers, writing to file, displaying images, etc. This same code could be located under a Button or other similar objects, but if we want the action to occur at various times during the program, a subroutine allows us to call that action without retyping the code under every different Button or object. After you hit the return key you should see the following text in the editor (you don't need to type it, VB.2005 has done this for you already):

```
Sub rand_number()
End Sub
```

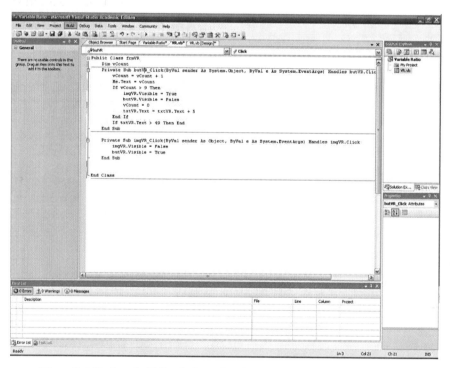

Figure 3.4 displays the Edit window after changing the FR code to the VR code.

The underscore in the subroutine name is just a construct that tells us rand_number is a stand-alone subroutine. The creation of this name and underscore within the subroutine is for our convenience to keep track of our work and make it more readable later on. However, a specific name or the underscore symbol is not required by VB. A subroutine can be called anything you like. Some programmers never even use subroutines. While we didn't either in our early programming days, we learned the hard way that subroutines are a very wise method to organize code.

Generating Numbers

Now we need to define the range of integer values. Let's say 10 plus/minus 3 so we will have a range of 6, or in other words a VR10 with a range of 7 to 13. We need a new variable to hold the random number, so near the top of the editor under your last Dim vCount line of text type:

```
Dim vRand
```

Now under Sub rand_number() type:

```
vRand = Int(Rnd * 7) + 7
```

This code tells the computer that you want to generate an integer (Int) value. It also states that you want the random value between 0 and 1 that the Rnd function will generate to be multiplied by 7. This will give you a value of 0, 1, 2, 3, 4, 5, or 6 because the Int function always rounds down to the next integer value. We then add 7 to the integer value to shift the distribution into the desired range between 7 and 13 inclusive. Now we can generate a value between 7 and 13 every time we call on this subroutine. Let's generate a value for vRand when we load the form. To do this type the name of the subroutine inside the frmVR_Load () subroutine, on the next line following *Randomize*, type:

```
rand_number
```

Now when the program starts we will have a new random number. We also need a new random number after each reinforcer is delivered so next type the name of the random subroutine just below the line of code in your Button that sets vCount = 0:

```
rand_number
```

Because we want the reinforcement to occur each time vCount=vRand we have to change the following code

```
If vCount > 9 Then
```

to
```
If vCount >= vRand Then
```

We may also want to see what vRand equals during the program development. We still want to see the number of clicks so we have to change the following code:

```
'me.Text = vCount
```
to
```
me.Text = vCount & ", " & vRand
```

This code will display the two values separated by a comma and a space. Before Testing the program to make sure that the changes are working properly, we still need to set frmVR as the Startup form for the project. Click on *Project* at the top of the screen and choose the *Variable Ratio Properties...* option. Locate the Startup form drop down box and change the option from *Form 1* to *frmVR*. Run the program. It should run fine. The first number displayed in the Form Text is the number of clicks you are making on the Button. The second number is the random number that the computer generated first upon loading the form, and afterwards each time the reinforcer image is clicked. Now go ahead and experiment by changing object properties and program parameters.

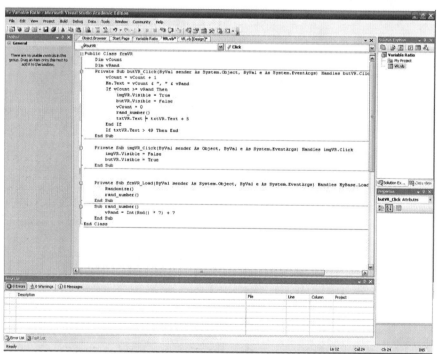

Figure 3.5 shows the final code to create a variable ratio schedule of reinforcement.

Fixed Interval

Initial Preparation

For the fixed interval schedule we need to display a reinforcer on the first click after a fixed period of time has elapsed. So each time the participant clicks on a Button, the program needs to check to see if that predetermined amount of time has passed before it displays the reinforcer. This program is very similar to the FixedRatio program so let's recycle frmFR again. To do this, create a new project and change the name to *Fixed Interval*. Add FR.vb and remove form1 as detailed in the Variable Ratio section. Change the name of the form to *frmFI*. Right click on FR.vb in the Solution Explorer and change the text to FI.vb. Click on the Fixed Interval project in the Solution Explorer to highlight it. Now right-click and select *Properties*. Change the Startup Object to *frmFI*. Save both the new form and your new project by holding down the Ctrl+Shift keys and pressing the "S" key.

As before, rename the objects txtFR to txtFI, imgFR to imgFI and butFR to butFI in the properties window. Now change the respective routine names in the editor too. Run the program. It should still work on the fixed ratio schedule; therefore we have some changes in the code to make. One of the first modifications might be to change the image in the PictureBox.

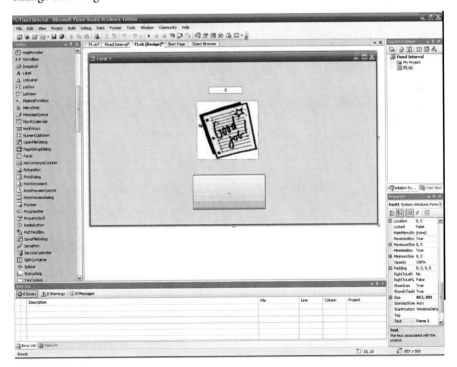

Figure 3.6 shows a possible screen configuration for the fixed interval schedule.

The Timer and If-Then Statements

Each time we click on butFI we want the computer to check and see if the predetermined amount of time has passed. VB.2005 has a function called *Timer* (not to be confused with the Timer object). Timer returns a value based on the amount of time elapsed according to the computer clock. The actual value is not important because we are only interested in the difference of time between two sampling periods. Thus if we store the timer value at time1 and subtract that value from the timer value at time2 (time two will be larger) then we can ask if that value is greater than the allocated time interval. We will see how that is done using VB.2005 code.

First we need a new variable called vTime so add a line of code below Dim vCount to read:

```
Dim vTime
```

Move the cursor down to the frmFI_Load subroutine and insert the following code to set the initial time.

```
vTime = Microsoft.VisualBasic.Timer
```

Although we will not be counting the number of clicks we will keep the vCount and associated code for use later on. We have to decide on the value of our fixed interval. Let's say 15 seconds. Now change the existing conditional code located under your butFI Button

```
If vCount > 9 Then
```
to
```
If Microsoft.VisualBasic.Timer - vTime > 15 Then
```

We also need to reset the timer value when the participant clicks on imgFI. Insert the following code into the imgFI_Click() subroutine:

```
vTime = Microsoft.VisualBasic.Timer
```

We additionaly want to display the amount of time passed in the form test so change the existing code

```
'me.Text = vCount
```
to
```
me.Text = Microsoft.VisualBasic.Timer - vTime
```

Run the program and it should work.

Rounding Time and Numbers to Whole Integers

Notice the time values written to the form text. They are written up to the 14ᵗʰ decimal point. You can change these to whole numbers by editing the text code to read

```
me.Text = Int(Microsoft.VisualBasic.Timer-vTime)
```

Experiment on your own with changing object properties and program parameters.

A Shorthand Shortcut

You may have started to become irritated with the repeated typing of long lines of code such as Microsoft.VisualBasic.Timer. Luckily for you, VB thought you might too. So, to create a shorthand for this line of code, typ the following text below the Option Explicit On:

```
Imports VB = Microsoft.VisualBasic
```

Now replace your long line of code with the shorthand: VB. This comes in quite handy as the programs become larger.

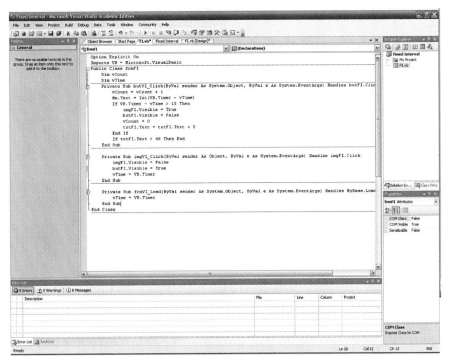

Figure 3.7 displays the code for creating a fixed interval schedule of reinforcement.

Variable Interval

Initial Preparation

The variable interval is similar to the fixed interval with the exception that the reinforcer is delivered on the first click after an average of a specified amount of time passes. The Variable Ratio program has the variable subroutine so let's recycle that program, but we will still use some of the code from the Fixed Interval program. So create a new project and name it Variable Interval. Add VR.vb, rename it VI in the Solution Explorer Window and change its name in the Properties Window to frmVI. Delete Form 1 and change the Startup form to frmVI as we did for the pervious schedule programs. Change the names and respective code of the objects to imgVI, txtVI, frmVI, and butVI. Change the startup object to frmVI. You might also want to change the picture in your image box. Run the program. The program should work like it did for the variable ratio.

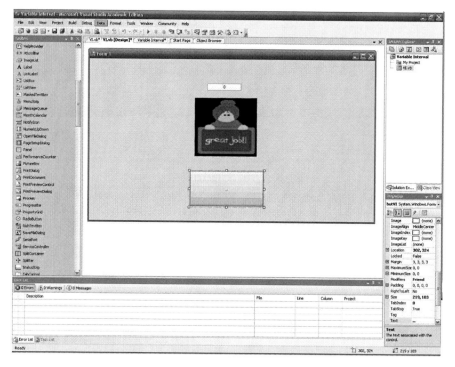

Figure 3.8 shows a possible screen configuration for the variable interval schedule.

Now we need to change some code. Under Option Explicit On, add the following code:

```
Imports VB = Microsoft.VisualBasic
```

Now under Dim vRand type:

```
Dim vTime
```

Here again, we are creating the new variable vTime. Now add the following code below the rand_number code in the Private Sub frmVI_Load() routine:

```
vTime = VB.Timer
```

You should also add this same code at the end of the imgVI subroutine (yet before *End Sub*.) This will result in the computer resetting the time interval when the program starts and also when the participant starts a new trial by clicking on imgVI.

Shifting Variable Range Distributions

We now have to determine the VI range. Let's say 15 seconds plus/minus 5 seconds. We need to change the existing code

```
vRand = Int(Rnd() * 7) + 7
```

Since the range is now 10, we need to change the 7 to a 11 and because the lowest number will be 5, we need to shift the distribution by that amount. Change the new code to read:

```
vRand = Int(Rnd() * 11) + 5
```

Next we have to change our conditional if statement to determine if the correct passage of time has occurred. We need to change the statement:

```
If vCount >= vRand Then
```

Rather than counting clicks, we need to find the difference between time1 and time2 by subtracting vTime from the timer function. The new line of code should read:

```
If VB.Timer - vTime > vRand Then
```

And of course we will want to see what values the program is using while we are programming, so we can change

```
me.Text = vCount & "," & vRand
to
me.Text = VB.Timer - vTime & " ," & vRand
```

Run the program. Experiment with changing object properties and program parameters.

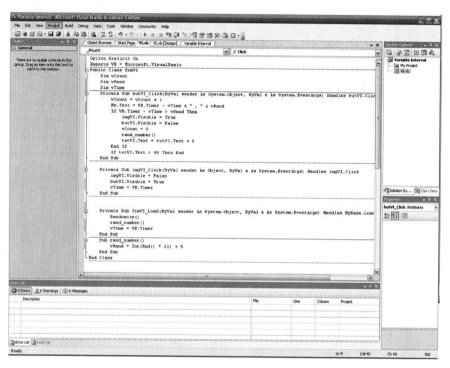

Figure 3.9 shows the code necessary to create the Variable Interval schedule.

Reference

Catania, A. C. (1998). *Learning*. Prentice Hall: New York.

Chapter 4:
Control Objects

Thus far this book has taken you through some of the basic examples of how to use some of the available tools in Visual Basic 2005. In chapter 2 we learned how to place control objects such as textboxes, labels, picture boxes, and buttons on forms as well as how to adjust and utilize some of their associated properties and events. In chapter 3 we explored a bit more thoroughly how to utilize some of these controls as well as the necessary code to create a program that could deliver reinforcers based upon specific schedules of reinforcement.

As we have progressed thus far it may have become readily apparent to you that these programs can get very complicated very quickly. As this book progresses we will show you how to create programs with multiple forms capable of passing information between them. However prior to that it may be prudent to demonstrate how we can maximize the amount of information presented on a single form while reducing the amount of code and effort necessary to interact with all items. This chapter will demonstrate for you how to use some new controls that you may find very useful down the road. While not a stand alone demonstration of a program that will allow you to explore a specific research question, it will serve to help build your familiarity and skills with new controls.

Container Controls

One way we can make positioning and interacting with objects on forms a bit easier is to include them in some type of container control. A container is just what it sounds like. It is a control that will contain other controls. VB 2005 offers several types of containers including Panels, GroupBoxes, SplitContainers, TabControls, TableLayoutPanels, and FlowLayoutPanels. All have subtle and not so subtle differences in properties and potential uses, but all serve the same function of housing other controls within a form. Let's look at an example of how to use the simplest of these containers, a Panel.

Open up Visual Basic and create a new windows application. Name the application, "Panel Demonstration". Change Form1's name to frmDemo, and set the WindowState property to Maximized. You may also need to change the project's properties to make frmDemo the startup form. Also go ahead and resize the form to give yourself a larger area to work with. Your form should now look like Figure 4.1.

Place a PictureBox on the form, change the name to "imgOne", and change its SizeMode property to "StretchImage". Also change imgOne's Image property to whatever image you would like. Now, select imgOne, and with your right mouse button, copy and paste the PictureBox onto the form to create a second PictureBox that is identical to imgOne. Rename the second PictureBox, "imgTwo", then

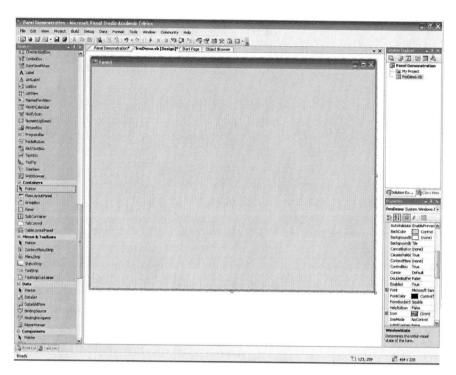

Figure 4.1 shows initial setup of frmDemo.

reposition it alongside imgOne, and change imgTwo's Image property to some other image of your choosing. Note that by copying the already created imgOne rather than just adding another PictureBox from the toolbox, imgTwo will have the same properties as imgOne. This may seem like an insignificant thing, but when creating forms with multiple instances of the same types of objects with the same properties this will save you time and aggravation.

Let's also place a Label on the form, change its name to "lblInstructions", its Autosize property to 'False", its TextAllign property to "MiddleCenter", and its Text property to "Please select one of the images below by clicking on it with your mouse.". Reposition lblInstructions above the two images. You may also want to adjust the font size and type to suit your tastes. Your form should now look like Figure 4.2. From the instructions placed on the label it should be clear that we want something to happen when the user clicks on one of the images. To start, let's do something simple, such as hiding the images.

From the design level of the form, double click on imgOne. This should create a "Click" routine for the first image. Let's include some code to hide both images. Under "Private Sub imgOne_Click()" type the following code:

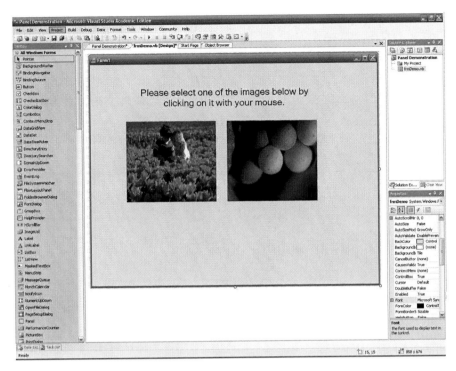

Figure 4.2 shows frmDemo with 2 PictureBoxes and Label.

```
imgOne.Hide()
imgTwo.Hide()
```

Now return to the design level of the form and double click on imgTwo. Copy and paste the code you just wrote into the "Private Sub imgTwo_Click()" routine. Now run the program. If all went well you should see the two images on the screen below the instructions, and when you click on either image, they both should disappear. Now Stop the program and return to the design level of the form.

We now have a very simple program that presents two images and then hides them both when either one is clicked with the mouse. To accomplish this took only 4 lines of code. This may seem not seem like much, but imagine if you were presenting a larger array of 10-20 images. This would then require 10-20 lines of code under a click routine for each separate image, resulting in 100-400 lines of code total. While in this simple type of example the code could simply be copied and pasted into each routine, it is still quite a large amount or work. One way we can cut down on the total amount of coding is to place these images on a Panel, and when an image is clicked on, we can simply hide the containing Panel instead of all of the images.

From the Toolbox menu on the left of the screen select a Panel object, and with your mouse, click and drag it over all of the items we have placed on frmDemo thus far. Change the Panel's name to "pnlContain". You should see the new Panel outlining the two images and the label as in Figure 4.3.

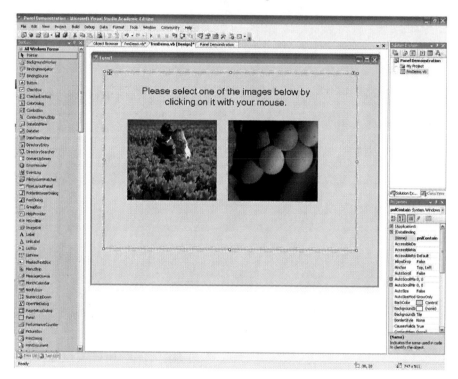

Figure 4.3 shows frmDemo with a Panel containing all objects

Try repositioning and resizing pnlContain on the form with your mouse. Note that all of the items are now linked to the panel and move with it as you reposition it, and as you resize the panel they remain locked in position no matter how small you make the Panel. This aspect of containers can make them quite useful when you have a number of items arranged in a specific manner on a form and need to reposition all of them in some way. If these items are arranged on a Panel, only the Panel needs to be repositioned. However, it can also create a problem as we will demonstrate here.

Click on pnlContain to select it and then hit your "Delete" key. What happens is that not only is the Panel deleted, but all of the controls contained within it are as well. Before you get too frightened about losing what you're done so far, locate the "Edit" tab on the menu strip at the top of the screen. Click on "Edit" and then select the "Undo" option. All of your items should now be back on the screen.

We added pnlContain to cut down on the amount of code used so let's edit the code we have written so far. Double click on one of the PictureBoxes to return to the code level of the form, then select the code we typed previously under "Private Sub imgOne_Click()" and delete it. Type the following line:

```
pnlContain.Hide()
```

Now copy the code you just typed and replace the code under "Private Sub imgTwo_Click()" with the new code. Now run the program. Note that as before when you click on the images they both disappear, only now we've accomplished the same feat with half of the code. Also note that now the Label we included for instructions also disappears. This is happening because just like the images we placed lblInstructions on the panel as well. You might not want the Label to be hidden when the images are clicked so let's move it off of the panel.

Stop the program and return to the design level of the form. To move lblInstructions off of pnlContain and still have room at the top of the form you may need to experiment a bit with resizing and repositioning the Panel and the two images contained within it. Once you have lblInstructions off of pnlContain and positioned above it (See Fig 4.4) we can explore another aspect of using container controls.

With your mouse resize pnlContain so that the top of the Panel reaches the top of frmDemo. Notice how now lblInstructions appears to float in front of the Panel and the two PictureBoxes contained within. This occurs because when multiple objects are placed on a form or container and share some overlapping location on that form or container, they exist in layers. In this case the Label object is currently on the front layer, with the Panel and the objects contained within it being treated as one object on the back layer. We can change the order of these two objects and send them to either the front or back layers. Click on lblInstructions to select it then right click your mouse. From the resulting options select "Send to Back". The Label should now be located behind the Panel. Click on pnlContain to select it then resize it back below the level of lblInstructions.

You now have some basic experience with the simplest of container controls, the Panel. Many of the other container controls share similar properties and can be used in much the same way, and we would suggest that you experiment a bit with the other types to come up with some ideas of how they might be useful.

MenuStrips and Message Boxes

At this time let's explore another type of control object that you can use that can both save a lot of space on your form as well as make your programs look more like the programs you use in your everyday computing. Visual Basic offers a tool for creating your own menu bars across the top of forms, just like the menu bars that you see across the top of your Visual Basic program or any other Microsoft program that you utilize on a day to day basis. In the toolbox on the left of your screen locate the MenuStrip item. Select it and place it on frmDemo.

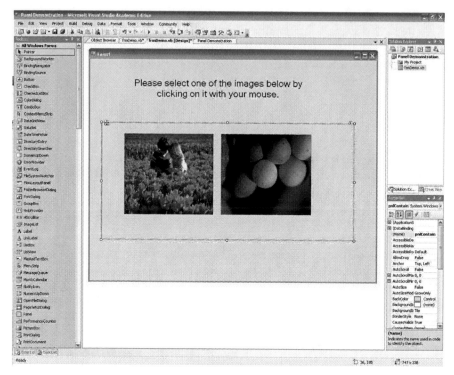

Figure 4.4 shows frmDemo with Panel only containing 2 PictureBoxes.

You should now see a light gray box across the top of your form with an off white box on the left with the text "Type Here" as displayed in Figure 4.5. Click on this white box with your mouse. Notice when you do so that you can now not only type in text into that box, but that now two more boxes are created, one to the right and one below. From this MenuStrip we can create entire tree structures of options across the top of the screen with sub options below which can contain their own sub options. Ultimately, we want to include several options on this form. We might want to include a general options tab that would allow us to perform certain actions such as changing the color of the form or the panel we've included as well as the images contained within the two PictureBoxes. We might also want to include an "Exit" tab that would allow us to end the program.

Click on the white box to select it and then type "Options". In the new white box to the right type "Exit" then click somewhere on the form so that the MenuStrip is no longer selected. As can be seen in Figure 4.6 you should now have both an "Options" and an "Exit" tab across the top of your form.

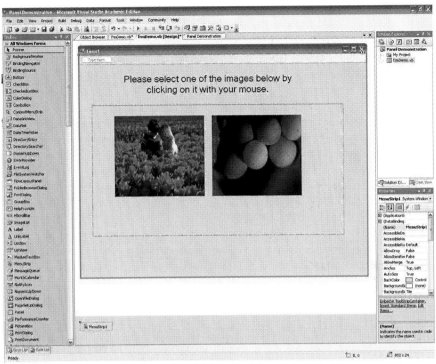

Figure 4.5 displays the addition of a MenuStrip to frmDemo.

Figure 4.6 displays MenuStrip with "Options" and "Exit" tabs

Now, double click on the "Exit" tab. This should have opened a new click routine in the code level of the form, named "Private Sub ExitToolStripMenuItem_Click()". We can now place code in this routine that we want executed whenever you click on the "Exit" tab. Below the text "Private sub ExitToolStripMenuItem_Click()" type the word "End" and run the program. With the program running click on the "Exit" tab. This should close the program.

While convenient, including something like the "Exit" menu item in a working program that your research subjects might interact with could be problematic. It would be very easy if that option were available at all times for whoever was using the program to prematurely exit before the entire program was complete. Many programs that you interact with in everyday computer usage try to keep you from making such errors by warning you that your actions might be accidental or premature while giving you the option of going through with them or not. They accomplish this through the use of Message Boxes which pop up on your screen to give you more information about what your actions will do to the program, while at the same time giving you the option of following through with them or not. Visual Basic allows you to create custom Message Boxes to accomplish these same functions.

Return to the single line of code we typed below "Private sub ExitToolStripMenuItem_Click()" and delete the text "End". Type in the following code:

```
Dim i as Integer
i = MsgBox("Are you sure you wish to exit?",
   MsgBoxStyle.YesNo + MsgBoxStyle.Information +
   MsgBoxStyle.SystemModal, "Message Box")
If (i = MsgBoxResult.Yes) then
End
End if
```

The preceding code should open a Message Box which will ask you whether or not you wish to exit the program, while also presenting you with two buttons with the options of "Yes" and "No". When you click on "Yes" the program should end, and when you click on "No" the Message box should close and your program should still be running. Run the program and see how it works. When you click on the "Exit" tab, you should see the Message box as displayed in Figure 4.7. Go ahead and click on "Yes" and we can begin examining how to include some other options.

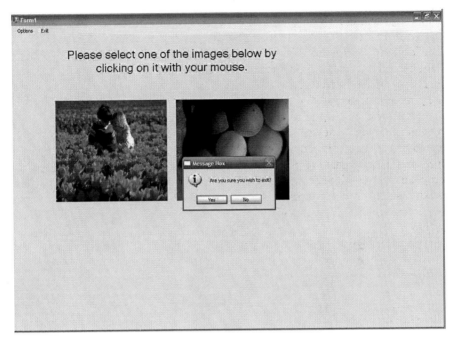

Figure 4.7 displays functioning Message Box.

Color Dialogs

One of the potential options we discussed adding previously was building in the option of changing the color of the form during runtime. Visual Basic offers you a tool that would allow users of your program to select from a collection of colors. This tool is called a ColorDialog. Return to the design level of frmDemo and locate the ColorDialog tool in the toolbox on the left of the screen. Select the ColorDialog and add it to your form. Notice how it jumps off of the form and is placed below the form as seen in Figure 4.8. Change the ColorDialog's name property to cdlogForm.

Now that we have the ColorDialog in our program we need to add in the option to change both the color of the form and the Panel. Click on the "Options" tab on the MenuStrip we added to the form. In the white box below the text "Options", type in the text "Change Color". There should also now be a white box to the right of the "Change Color" box. In this type the text "Form". This should have also created another white option box below the one in which we just typed the text "Form". In the box below "Form" type the text "Panel". You should now have a tree structure of options that looks like figure 4.9. Double click on the "Form" option. This should open a "Click" routine in the code level of the form for this option.

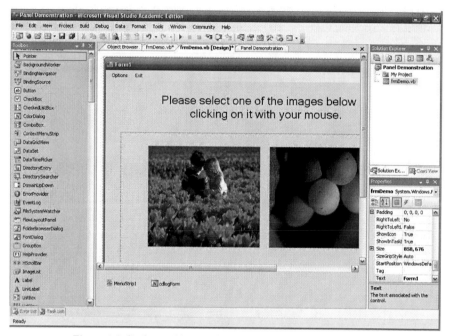

Figure 4.8 displays addition of ColorDialog control to frmDemo.

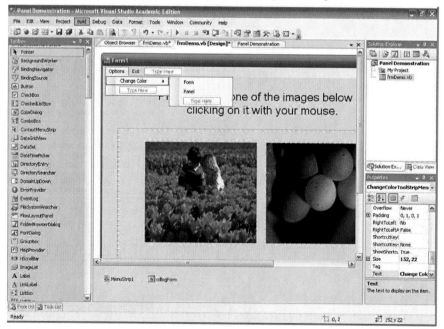

Figure 4.9 displays the expansion of tabs below the "Options" tab in the MenuStrip.

When the user clicks on the "Form" option, we want the ColorDialog we added to the form to open up and present them with different color options. To accomplish this we need to type the following code into the "Private Sub FormToolStripMenuItem_Click()" subroutine.

```
If cdlogForm.ShowDialog = Windows.Forms.DialogResult.OK
    Then
Me.BackColor = cdlogForm.Color
End if
```

Now run the program. When you click on the "Options" tab at the top of the screen, the "Change Color" option should appear with a black arrow to its right. When you click or hover over this option with your mouse you should see both the "Form" and "Panel" options we added previously. Click on the "Form" option with your mouse and a ColorDialog box should appear like that seen in Figure 4.10. Select from any of the colors available and click the "OK" button at the bottom of the dialog box. Your entire form should now be the selected color.

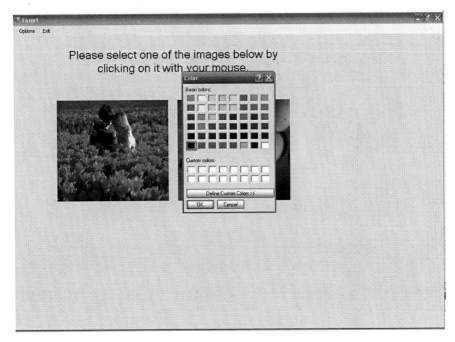

Figure 4.10 displays a functioning ColorDialog control.

We also wanted to build in the ability to change the color of the Panel we added previously. Stop the program using the "Exit" tab and return to the design level of the form. Double click on the "Panel" option that we added under "Options" previously. This should open a new "Click" routine in the code level of the form. Under "Private Sub PanelToolStripMenuItem_Click()" type the following code:

```
If cdlogForm.ShowDialog = Windows.Forms.DialogResult.OK
    Then
pnlContain.BackColor = cdlogForm.Color
End If
```

Run the program once again and click on the "Options" tab then click on the "Panel" option under the "Change Color" option. As with the form this should open the ColorDialog we added to the program. Pick a color and click on "OK". Your panel should now have a different background color than your form as in Figure 4.11. You can close the program with the "Exit" tab and we will explore some other options.

Figure 4.11 displays the panel with a new color setting supplied by the ColorDialog control.

Open File Dialogs

Earlier we stated that we might want to include options for selecting the pictures in the two PictureBoxes on our form. One way we can accomplish this is through the use of an OpenFileDialog. You may already be quite familiar with OpenFileDialogs. You use them every time you open a document in Microsoft Word or any other common program you interact with everyday. These dialog boxes allow you to search through the file structure on your computer to locate a file you wish to open. They also generally limit the type of files displayed to be those of the type that can be opened in whatever program you are using.

In this case since we wish to build in the functionality to insert an image into the PictureBoxes on our form, we would need to use an OpenFileDialog which limits our choices to image file types that will work with the PictureBox control in Visual Basic (i.e. .jpg, .jpeg, .tiff, .gif, .bmp, and .png files). Return to the design level of frmDemo. In the toolbox on the left of your screen you should be able to locate the OpenFileDialog tool. Select it, add it to the form, and change its Name property to "ofdlogPicture".

We now have an OpenFileDialog control on the form, so we need to add options under the "Options" tab in the MenuStrip we added to allow us to select images for the two PictureBoxes on the form. Click on the "Options" tab on the MenuStrip at the top of our form. In the white box below the text "Change Color" type in "Change Image". This should have also opened up another white option box to the right of the text you just typed. In this box type "Image 1". There should also now be anther white option box below the text "Image 1". In this box type "Image 2". Your form should now look like Figure 4.12.

Figure 4.12 displays the addition of the OpenFile Dialog and expansion of the "Options" tabs.

What we want to happen is that when whoever is using the program clicks on either the "Image 1" or "Image 2" tabs, our OpenFileDialog box will open and allow the user to search for an image file on their computer. To accomplish this we will need to create a "Click" routine for each of these options. Double click on the text "Image 1" to open a "Click" routine at the code level of the form. Under the text "Private Sub Image1ToolStripMenuItem_Click()" type the following code.

```
ofdlogPicture.InitialDirectory = "C:\"
ofdlogPicture.Filter = "Images|*.jpg;*.jpg;*.bmp;*tiff;
    *.png;*.gif"
If ofdlogPicture.ShowDialog =
    Windows.Forms.DialogResult.OK Then
imgOne.Image = Image.FromFile(ofdlogPicture.FileName)
End If
```

What the preceding code does is set the initial directory on the user's computer in which the OpenFileDialog begins searching to the users "C" drive. It also sets the type of files to be displayed to only those that may be imported into a PictureBox control. The code then opens the OpenFileDialog to allow the user to search for an image, and once an image has been selected and the user clicks on the "OK" button in the dialog box, it sets the image property of imgOne to the picture selected. Run the program and see if everything works as described.

Assuming that everything worked as described be can move on to adding the same code for the second image. Stop the program and return to the design level of frmDemo. Double click on the "Image 2" tab on the form's MenuStrip to create a new "Click" routine. Copy the code we typed in the "Private Sub Image1MenuStripItem_Click()" routine and paste it under the text "Private Sub Image2MenuStripItem_Click()". We need to change one line of code in order to place the image selected with the OpenFileDialog into imgTwo. Change the text "imgOne.Image" to "imgTwo.Image". Your code should look like that in Figure 4-13. Now run the program again. You should be able to freely change the images in both imgOne and imgTwo. Exit the program and we will work with a final type of dialog box.

Save File Dialogs

One final option that we might want to include in this program is the ability to save the images we place in the two PictureBoxes to a location on the computer of our choosing. We can accomplish this with another type of dialog box that you may be familiar with from using other Microsoft programs in your day to day life, the SaveFileDialog control. This type of control works much like the OpenFileDialog. It opens up to let the user choose a location in their computer's file structure to save a file. It also let's one choose a name for the file to be saved under.

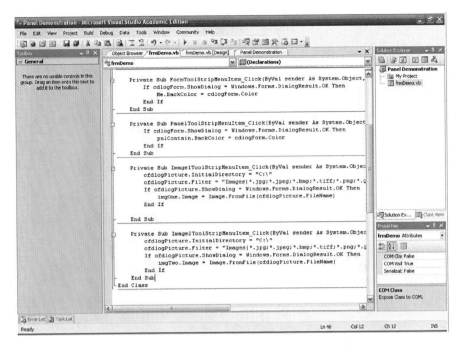

Figure 4.13 displays the code for the "Image 1" and "Image 2" menu items.

To begin with you need to return to the design level of frmDemo. In the toolbox on the right of the screen locate the "SaveFileDialog" control. Select it, place it on the form, and change its "Name" property to "sfdlogPicture". We now need to add options to our MenuStrip at the top of the form to allow users of the program to save images. Click on the "Options" tab on the MenuStrip at the top of the form. In the white box below the text "Open Image" type "Save Image". Add two options to this new option tab named "Image 1" and "Image 2". Your form should now look like Figure 4.14.

As with the OpenFileDialog we want the user to be able to open the SaveFileDialog when they click on the "Image 1" and "Image 2" tabs under the "Save Image" option. Double click on "Image 1" to open a new "Click" routine. Under the text "Private Sub Image1ToolStripMenuItem1_Click()" type the following code:

```
sfdlogPicture.InitialDirectory = "C:\"
sfdlogPicture.Filter = "Images|*.jpg;*.jpg;*.bmp;*tiff;
    *.png;*.gif"
sfdlogPicture.FileName = "Image 1.jpg"
If sfdlogPicture.ShowDialog = Windows.Forms.DialogResult.OK
    Then
imgOne.Image.Save(sfdlogPicture.FileName)
End if
```

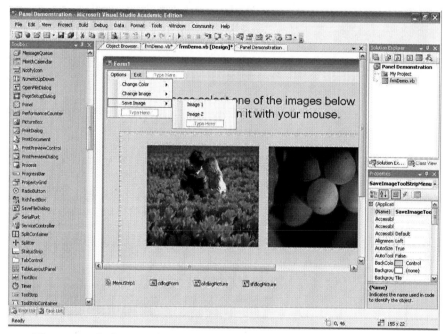

Figure 4.14 displays the addition of the SaveFile Dialog and the expansion of the "Options" tab of the MenuStrip.

Return to the design level of the form. Click on the "Options" tab on the MenuStrip at the top of the form then on the "Save Image" tab to open the "Image 1" and "Image 2" options. Double click on the "Image 2" tab to create a new "Click" routine. Copy the code we just entered into the "Private Sub Image1ToolStripMenuItem1_Click()" routine and paste it under the new "Private Sub Image2ToolStripMenuItmes1_Clic()" routine. We need to change two lines of code to get this to save the image in imgTwo. In the third line of code change the text "Image 1.jpg" to "Image 2.jpg" and in the next to last line of code change the text "imgOne.Image" to "imgTwo.Image". Your code should look like that in Figure 4.15. Run the program. When you click on either "Image 1" or "Image 2" in the "Save Image" options you should get a dialog box as seen in Figure 4.16.

The initial file name for the image you are about to save is either set to "Image 1" or "Image 2", however you can change this to whatever you might wish to name the image you are saving. Save the image then exit the program and go to the location on your computer in which you saved the image to ensure that everything went according to plan.

You now have some basic experience dealing with several new types of controls. You may be asking yourself "What was the point of learning about these controls? I would never want a research subject messing around with saving files or changing colors." While this may be the case you will find that as the programs you build get bigger and more complex, your will need to build more flexibility into them. In

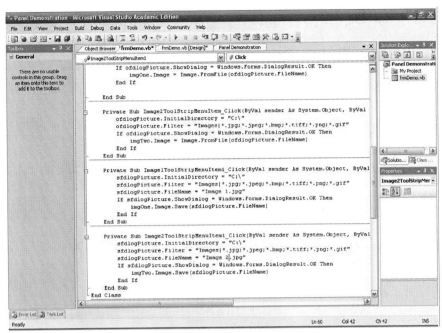

Figure 4.15 displays the code for the "Image 1" and "Image 2" tabs under the "Save" option.

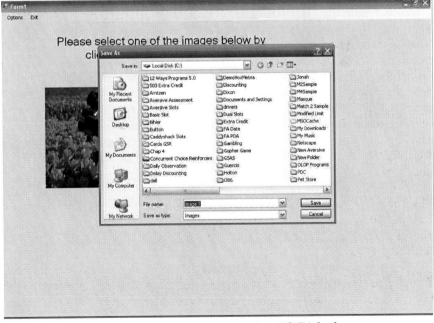

Figure 4.16 displays a functioning SaveFile Dialog box.

many of the programs described in this text, changes in the methodology of your study would require editing the program's code for most every type of change. Anticipating where changes may occur in the future and building in some flexibility will save you extra time and aggravation down the road.

While you may never want a research subject to interact with a file or color dialog box, you yourself may want to. As your programs become larger and more complex, learning how to build in forms that only you, the experimenter, interacts with to change options and save files will be extremely useful. In many of the programs we have created to study various aspects of human behavior it has been very useful to build forms that let us set the parameters for a given study, then save those parameters to a file. Later that file may be loaded when the program is run for another participant and the program can then set these parameters from the file. This allows us to change the parameters or to store multiple files of parameters which might be loaded depended on the variation of a study you wish to conduct. Many of the controls described in this chapter are essential for accomplishing these actions.

Chapter 5: Advanced Topics

Overview

Chapter 5 is designed to get you acquainted with some of the more advanced features of Visual Basic 2005 and their application within multimedia. While we use the term "advanced" this does not mean it will require more skill or computer saviness than what was necessary to complete previous chapters. What we mean by "advanced" is that Chapter 5 will allow you to enhance your program in many desirable ways beyond simple parameters. For example, what if you want to add your own voice to the program? Or, what if you want your get your data to write to a text file or a spreadsheet? Or, what about using a video clip as a stimulus? All of these questions will be answered in Chapter 5.

Variable Types

Visual Basic 2005 has the ability to use several variable types such as Variant, Binary, String, Integer, Short, and Long. We have already been using some variables in our Visual Basic 2005 programming, namely Integers. In some program languages it is critical to accurately define the variable you will be using in your program. Not so with Visual Basic 2005. Visual Basic 2005 allows the user to define a variable as a Variant. Variants can later be assigned by Visual Basic 2005 to a variety of variable types depending on how they are being used in the program. Binary variables can hold a value of 0 or 1 only. String variables are used to hold non-numeric values such as letters or letters and numbers combined. Integer variables are numeric, but round down any decimal value. However, Short and Long variables will hold decimal values.

Variable types are assigned when the variable is declared. We have already declared variables in our previous schedule of reinforcement programs. To declare a variable we use the Dim statement. For example to declare a variable called vStop to hold an integer value, you simply would type the line:

```
Dim vStop as Integer
```

If we wanted vStop to hold a string of characters, we would declare the variable by typing:

```
Dim vStop as String
```

And so on. The default for Visual Basic 2005 is Variant. If a variable is not declared, Visual Basic 2005 will assign it as Variant by default. Remember this point. Declaring your variables incorrectly will often result in your program not running correctly.

Minmizing Typos

Another problem with variables is that we often misspell them when we are programming. For example if you accidentally typed *vStob* rather than *vStop* the program would not do what you wanted it to and it could cause you to waste a considerable amount of time trouble shooting and debugging your program. The last thing you want to add to your list of chores is spell checking your entire program. One way to prevent this is by using the *Option Explicit On* statement at the top of each form.

Levels of Variables

Perhaps the most important issue regarding variables in Visual Basic 2005 is the variable hierarchy. Variables can be Public, Form Level, or Local. Variables can be declared in a Module, at the top of the form, and within a subroutine. Depending on where you declare your variable some may take precedence over others. Generally, variables in the module take precedence over variables declared at the form level. Variables at the form level generally take precedence over variables declared at the subroutine level. The best way to deal with these issues at present is to avoid using the same variable names. Also, variables used at the subroutine level cannot be used at the form level. And variables used at the form level are difficult to use at the module or multiform level. We have been using the construct of assigning a *v* to our form level variables. For example *vStop*, *vGo*, and *vCount*. You might want to use the letter *p* to indicate global or module level variables. For example *pStop*, *pGo*, and *pCount* to make completely different variables but with similar names. For variables declared only in the subroutines, also called the local level, you might want to use the simple algebraic variables such as x, r, and i. If you follow these simple constructs you will be able to keep better track of your variables and others will be able to follow your code if they happen across it at a later date.

The choice of variable type is an important issue in programming as the type of variable you assign will determine how much space the computer assigns or reserves for that variable. While Visual Basic 2005 is very tolerant, and computers are faster and more efficient every year, the type of variable you use is not that much of a concern when designing simple programs. Yet as you construct larger projects or if you decide to develop commercial programs, variable declaration can become very important.

The last issue you may wish to consider when constructing variables is if they should hold values across forms. One application this may occur with is a point counter. If you have multiple forms, yet wish the subject to retain his/her current point total across those forms (as when switching from Phase 1 to Phase 2 of an experiment) the variable will need to be Public in order for Visual Basic 2005 to retain the relevant information. In this case, do not declare your variable on the form, but rather declare it in a module as will be discussed in Chapter 8.

Input/Output – Reading and Writing Data from Text Files

Input Files

We have already discussed how to get data from the participant through the keyboard using frames and textboxes. Another way to enter data is by using text files. This allows us to create a program parameter before running the program, and the computer will simply access this set of parameters during run time, and adjust the experiment accordingly.

Create a new standard Windows Project and name it *Variable*. Rename the form *frmVariable* and change the text property to *Variable*. Now we need to create a text file. Microsoft provides a text editor called *NotePad* with its software. If you have *NotePad*, open it using the Windows® start button usually located at the lower left of the monitor. Select the *Programs* option, next select *Accessories*, and finally *NotePad*. With *NotePad* open type the number 10 then press *Enter* to write on a new line. Type the number 55, then on a new line type 23. Save the file on the C-Directory as *C:\Variable.txt* and close *NotePad*.

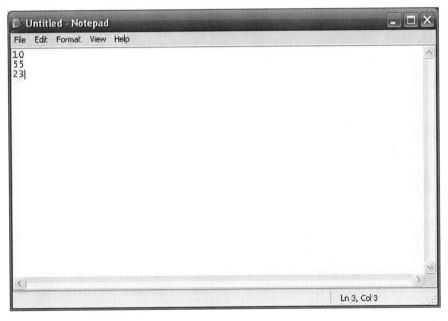

Figure 5.1 shows the input file for the Variable program.

Return to project *Variable* and change the WindowState property to *Maximized*. Afterwards, open the VB.NET code editor by double-clicking on your form. What we want to do is read each line of *Variable.txt* to a variable. So to do this we must first declare a variable that will hold the data found in our *Variable.txt* data file. In the editor, place the cursor above all existing code. Then type:

```
Option Explicit On
```

Next reposition the cursor below the line of code "Public Class frmVariable" and type:

```
Dim vReadFile as Integer
```

This will declare a variable vReadFile as an Integer to declare the variable. Under the frmVariable_Load() subroutine type:

```
FileOpen (1, "c:\Variable.txt", OpenMode.Input)
```

This tells the computer the name and location of the file to open, that the file will be used to read from as input and that from now on we will refer to that file by its alias "#1." From now on we refer to the file Variable.txt as #1 (BTW: we could use any name for an alias) when we are programming. We now need some code to read in a line from the text file and assign it to vReadFile. We also need to assign the code to an event. Let's use a Timer object to accomplish this task.

Add a Timer to frmVariable, rename it *tmrVariable*, change the Enabled property to *True*, and change the interval property to 5000 (ms) so that every 5 seconds it will read in a new number. Double-click in tmrVariable to enter edit mode. Type the following code into the timer subroutine.

```
Input (1, vReadFile)
me.Text = vReadFile
```

This will allow the program to read the first line and then to display that value in the text section of our form. Change your window state property of your form to *Maximized*. Now run the program after you change the Startup object. Notice that every 5 seconds (5000ms) a new number is displayed until the end of the file is reached and then we get an error message.

End of File Statements

We could have included an error handler to eliminate our error message, but there is a better way to do this with the End of File (EOF) statement and an If / Then statement. Therefore, add the additional code under your Timer object after Private Sub tmrVariable_Timer() so the entire subroutine lookks like this:

```
If Not EOF(1) Then
Input (1, vReadFile)
```

```
me.Text = vReadFile
Else
File Close (1)
End
End If
```

Notice too that we have added a line of code to close the input file when the EOF is reached. Run the program. Your error should disappear, and the program should end at the end of file.

Output Files

Now, suppose we want to write values to a different text file. In other words, we want an output file that writes some type of data to it. Say we want to read a value in from *Variable.txt*, multiply it by 10 and divide it by 2, then write the output to a file called *TimesFive.txt*. First we would have to open *TimesFive.txt* and then each time vReadFile is updated, that value is read into an equation and then written to *TimesFive.txt*.

To open the output file type the following line in the frmVariable_Load() subroutine:

```
FileOpen (2, "c:\TimesFive.txt", OpenMode.Output)
```

You can put this code above or below the other open statement.

Notice that we are having the computer open a file that currently does not exist on our computer. This was done purposely. VB.NET will create the file the first time we run the program. The next step is to make the calculation after it is read from *Variable.txt*. To do this, type the following code below the Input (1, vReadFile) line in the tmrVariable subroutine:

```
x = vReadFile * 10 / 2
```

To get the value of x to write to *TimesFive.txt,* type the following code on the line immediately below equation we just wrote:

```
WriteLine (2, x)
```

Because we are using a variable in the subroutine, we must declare it at the beginning of the subroutine by typing:

```
Dim x
```

Now include a close statement for file #2 under the existing Close #1 statement by typing the following:

```
FileClose (2)
```

The timer subroutine should look like this:

```
If Not EOF(1) Then
Dim x
Input (1, vReadFile)
   x = vReadFile * 10 / 2
   Write (2, x)
me.Text = vReadFile
Else
FileClose (1)
FileClose (2)
End
End If
```

Run the program. When the program ends, open *TimesFive.txt* using the *NotePad* text editor. You should see three lines with 50, 275, and 115. Close *NotePad*.

Now suppose you want to write the input values vReadFile to *TimesFive.txt*. To do this, change the Write (2, x) statement to:

```
WriteLine (2, vReadFile, x)
```

Run the program and then open *TimesFive.txt* using *NotePad*. Notice that the program added a comma between each value. Most importantly, notice that the old information in the file has been overwritten! This is because output files are always overwritten each time they are opened. To instruct VB.NET to append the new data below the existing data, change the open statement for the output file to read:

```
FileOpen (2, "c:\TimesFive.txt", OpenMode.Append)
```

Here the Append text is replacing the Output text. Append and Output are two different types of data file writing procedures and you can select between them depending on your research purposes. Run the program. Open *TimesFive.txt* using *NotePad* and notice that the new values have been appended to the file.

Adding a Header to Your Data File

When you append data to a file, it is a good idea to divide the output by using headers. Headers usually contain information about the program, the programmer, and the data. Below is an example of a header that might be found in a program. Add the following code in the Private Sub frmVariable_Load ( ) under the two FileOpen statements.

```
WriteLine (2, "*************************************")
WriteLine (2, "This program was written by: (Put your name
    here)")
WriteLine (2, "The date is", Date.Now)
WriteLine (2, "*************************************")
```

The Date.Now function will return the current date and time to your computer. Make sure you include the appropriate quotation marks. Make sure this code is located below the open statement for file 2. Also make sure you use commas in the header after the file alias, and that you use quotes before and after Text or Literals. Run the program and then open the output file. The header separates your data sets and provides you with additional information.

Just as we combined Literals with other types of information, we can combine our output with literals. For example, change your output code under the Timer to:

```
WriteLine (2, "Input = ", vReadFile, "Output = ",x)
```

Try running the program now. Notice that Visual Basic 2005 maintains the comma between the literal and the input/output values. This is a good thing. Some programs such as Microsoft Excel can import data and use the commas to separate individual fields. If you were to import TimesFive.txt there would be four separate columns. There should be two columns with numbers and two columns with the literals.

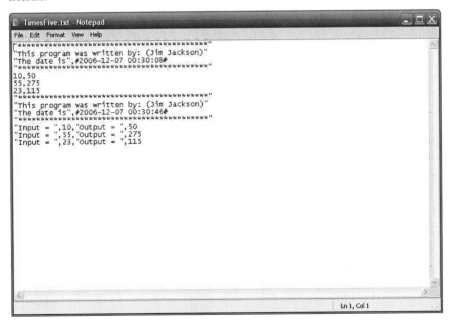

Figure 5.2 shows the output file for the Variable program.

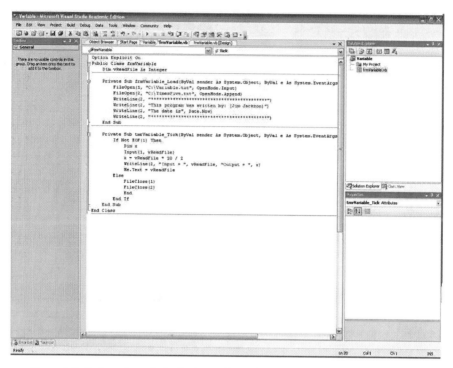

Figure 5.3 displays the code for frmVariable with input and output file information.

Multimedia Control (AxMediaPlayer)
and Common Dialogue Control

Overview

So far we have shown you how to add sound to the programs using the Beep function and how to add pictures to the programs using the PictureBox object. Visual Basic 2005 has advanced abilities to play sound files such as .wav and to play animated graphic files such as .avi or .mpeg. In this next section we will write a program to open a sound file and play it using the Windows Media Player. To use the Windows Media Player object you MUST have a SOUND CARD.

Create a new project and name it *Multimedia*. Rename the form to *frmMultimedia*, change the text property to *Multimedia*, and change the WindowState to *Maximized*.

Adding the Windows Media Player Object

If your toolbox does not contain the Windows Media Player object (most of them will not), you can add it by clicking the "Tools" option in the menustrip at the top of the screen. From the available options click on the "Choose Toolbox Items..." option. This should open a dialog box with two options, .NET Framework Components and COM Components. Click on the "Com Components" tab and

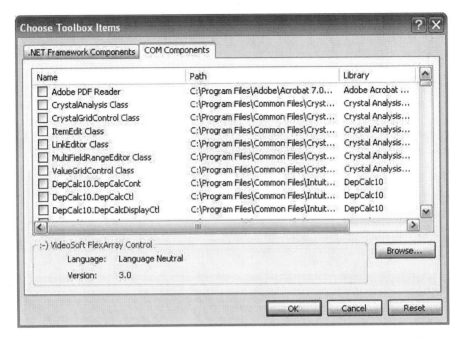

Figure 5.4 displays the customize toolbox menu for adding components to the toolbar.

locate and check the box to the left of "Windows Media Player". Click OK to make it appear in the toolbox.

If your computer does not have an option for Windows Media Player Control, you will need to click on the *browse* button. You will be sent to the windows system files. Now, locate the file name

```
c:\Windows\System32\msdxm.ocx
```

Once done, click, add. The Windows Media Player Control should now be an option for you to add. If for some reason your system files do not include msdxm.ocx, you will need to obtain the file via the Microsoft web site or from a friend.

Now double-click on the Media Player object to add it to the new project. Change the Media Player Visible property to *False* and the Name to *wmp1*.

Adding the Microsoft Common Dialogue Control

In order to select an audio file to play, we will need to add an OpenFileDialog Object. This Object will be already located in your toolbox by default. When you attempt to place it on your form, it will drop below much like the Timer object does. Now rename the OpenFileDialog1 control, *ofdMultimedia*.

We will also need to add a TextBox object named txtMultimedia, and a Button named butMultimedia. Change the text in butMultimedia and txtMultimedia to "....".

We will need to write some code to activate the OpenFileDialog object to butMultimedia so that we can browse for .wav files. Double-click butMultimedia and add the following code under Private Sub cmdMultimedia_Click()

```
ofdMultimedia.ShowDialog()
txtMultimedia.Text = ofdMultimedia.FileName
```

Now we need to add another Button. Do so, and rename it butPlay. Also change the text to *Play*.

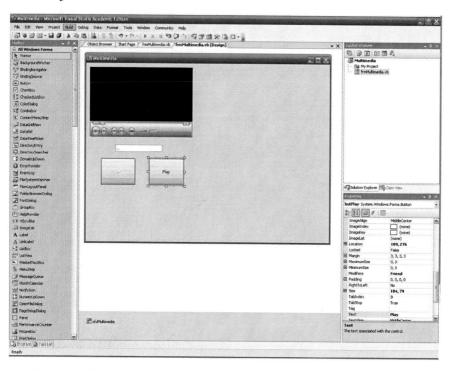

Figure 5.5 displays a possible screen configuration for the Multimedia application.

Next we need to enter the following under the butPlay_Click() subroutine to play our .wav selection: (note there is a number 1 after the word wmp – not a letter L).

```
wmp1.URL= txtMultimedia.text
wmp1.Ctlcontrols.play()
```

Now move the cursor to the top of the Edit menu and type:

```
Option Explicit On
```

Run your program, click on the "..." Button and browse for a media file. Now you should have a program that, during run time, allows you to select an audio or video file of various formats including .wav, .mid, .avi, etc., with one button, and play that .wav file with another button.

Figure 5.6 shows the window for choosing your multimedia during runtime application.

Experimenter Selected Media Files

Another method of playing media files that is useful when doing research is for the files to be pre-selected before runtime. This way a subject would simply click on a button, and it would result in the playing of the media file. Such files may serve as either discriminative or consequential stimuli. To do this, we will need to modify the current program. Add a new Button. Leave it named as Button 1. Under Private SubButton 1_Click ( ), type:

```
wmp1.URL= "c:\windows\media\Chimes.wav"
(note: you can put any media file directory and name you
    want here)
wmp1.Ctlcontrols.play()
```

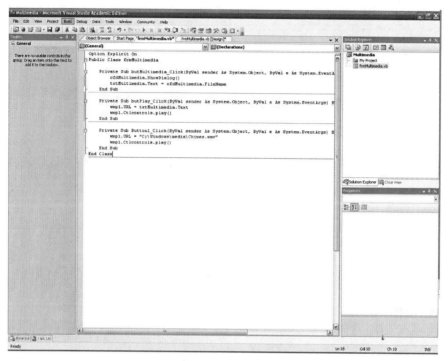

Figure 5.7 displays the code for creating a Multimedia program.

Your program now will contain features that you no longer need. Like the TextBox and the Button with the "…" text, and the Button with the "Play" text. Actually, if you click on these Buttons during runtime, you may get error messages. So, just click on these two Buttons and txtMultimedia when the program is not running and hit delete. They disappear. Go into the edit mode and delete their associated code. Now you should be left with only your new Button1 that plays your favorite .wav file, the Windows Media Player, and the ofdMultimedia.

If you want more than one Button to play media files, say one per Button, you can repeat the above steps x more times. Now, create two new Buttons, and copy the code from Button1 to the new buttons. Change the .wav file for each of the Buttons and you are done.

There are many features for the Windows Media Player and we cannot cover them all here in this book. We recommend you consult the VB 2005 language reference guide included with the program for more features. There are also many very sophisticated commercially available visual basic books on game programming. When you use the Windows Media Player to play media files, the code above is generally sufficient. In later chapters we will write code for complex matching-to-sample programs that will use the Windows Media Player in a slightly different way.

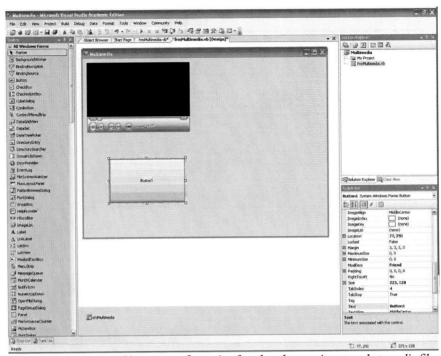

Figure 5.8 shows a possible screen configuration for when the experimenter selects media files.

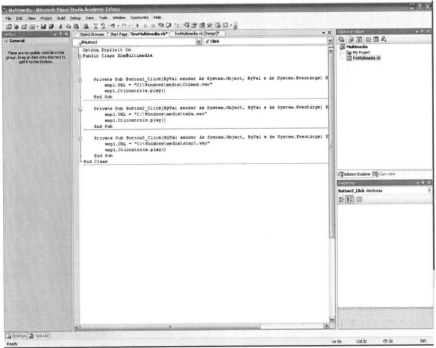

Figure 5.9 shows the code for creating 3 Buttons that play different sounds.

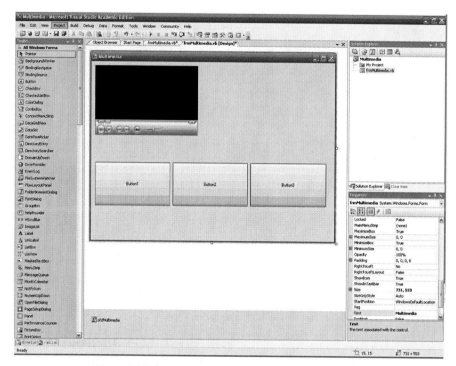

*Figure 5.10 shows a screen configuration for the 3 Buttons
that play different sounds.*

Chapter 6:
Behavior Observation and Data Recording

Overview

The Human Observer

Until now this book has dealt with the designing of human operant experiments that consisted of both the computerization of the apparatus and the data collection system. It has been assumed that the setting of your experiment is a laboratory room equipped with a computer and monitor that the subject interacts with. Yet, the purpose of this chapter is to teach you how to create a stand-alone data collection program that would be useful for the observation of human behavior in natural or applied settings.

Many times the preparations we design for research are not capable of incorporating into a computer interface. Much of the applied behavior analytic research occurring today does not lend itself to total atomization. For example, one can not provide attention or extinction to a subject via the computer interface. One can not conduct a descriptive or functional analysis by placing a client displaying any one of a variety of problematic behaviors on the computer. The recording of these naturally occurring behaviors such as aggression, verbal abuse, depression, or self-stimulation can not be captured automatically by the computer because the subject is not directly interacting with the computer. The only way such behaviors can be recorded is via the human observer with the subject's interaction in a naturalistic environment. Many times this human observer records data on these types of behaviors using a pencil and paper. There are many parameters of data collection that might be recorded including response frequency, latency, intensity, duration, or topography. While pencil and paper systems work well when observers are well trained, they are often time consuming, and labor intensive. Many companies offer their own version of an automated data collection system to aid the human observer in his/her data collection activity. Yet, these systems cost money, are static in nature, and may become obsolete before justifying the price paid.

Many excellent resources exist for behavioral psychologists interested in learning more about data collection (c.f. Bellack & Hersen, 1998). Those readers interested in learning more about the utility of automated data collection systems may wish to explore Kahng and Iwata (1998). For a step by step programming guide to handheld computerized data collection use Microsoft Visual Tools for the Pocket PC, see Dixon, (2003).

In this chapter we will incorporate some of the earlier techniques of file inputting and outputting, variable creations, and using multiple forms to create a user friendly, very dynamic data collection system. With the examples in this chapter you should be able to collect a wide range of data in a variety of ways in a very short time period. The biggest benefit of designing such a system is that it allows for you the human observer to customize your system to the specific experiment or clinical observation at hand.

Control Panel

Form Interface

A simple yet efficient means of constructing a control panel is by using a separate form with Buttons serving as options to link various types of data collection together in one program. For example, you may wish to have a data collection system that can be used for duration and latency recording, yet also incorporate the ability to collect frequency type data. Here we would create a separate form for each type of data collection and link the various types of data collection together via the control panel.

To begin creating this control panel, open VB.2005 and create a new project. Name the project "Data Collection". Change the name of the form to "frmControl", change the text to "Control Panel". In this chapter's example we will create a system that will collect duration/frequency, time sampling, frequency, and descriptive analysis data. Therefore, add four separate Buttons to frmControl and change their text to correspond to the four types of data collection. Also change their names from Buttons1-4, to butDuration, butTS, butFreq, and butDA.

You might also wish to add a simple greeting or brief instruction onto the control panel form. Therefore, add a Label, change the name to lblInstructions, and change the text to "Welcome to the Data Collection Assistant. Please select the type of data you would like to record from the options below." Alter the font properties for a better design, especially AutoSize to equal False.

Now that your control panel template is in an appropriate layout, a few lines of simple code will take the user to their desired type of data collection. Yet, before we create these code links of hiding one form and displaying another, let's create the actual various data collection forms.

Duration and Latency Recording

Form Overview

Insert a new Windows form into your project and rename it frmDuration. Add a Label to the form that displays to the user that this is the correct form for collecting duration and latency data. Change the name of the Label to lblInstructions and change the text to "Duration and Latency Recording."

Starting and Stopping Timers

The most basic components of this form consist of two Buttons that will start and stop the computer timers when clicked, which will generate the duration and latency data. Therefore add two Buttons separately to your frmDuration and change their names to butStart and butStop, and their text property to "Start" and "Stop" respectively. Because you will want the user to see the actual duration and latency

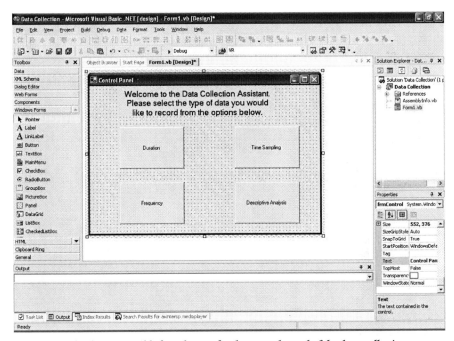

Figure 6.1 displays a possible form layout for the control panel of the data collection system.

values as they are generated, add two TextBoxes and change their names to txtDuration and txtLatency. Change their text property so they are blank. You may also wish to add a Label above each TextBox so the user easily identifies them. Therefore, add two Labels and change their names to lblDuration and lblLatency and position them directly above their associated TextBoxes. Also change their text property to *Duration* and *Latency* respectively.

Note there is a tool in the toolbox called a *Panel*. Add this tool to your form and initially cover all of your existing Buttons, Textboxes, and Labels with it. Next, with the right mouse button, click on the panel and select *Send to Back*. Finally change the BorderStyle property of the Panel to *Fixed Single*.

Identifying and Creating an Output File

Because many different users might use the data collection program in a variety of situations, it makes a lot of sense to allow the user to specify the name and location of the data output file. There are many ways to do this, yet a very simple way is via a TextBox the user inputs the file name and extension. Therefore, simply add a TextBox and change the name to txtFile. Change the text property to "Enter your data file here." To further aid the user in entering the data file name and location, add a Label directly to the left of this TextBox, change the name to lblFile, and change the text to "What data file do you want to create? Ex. a:\john.txt."

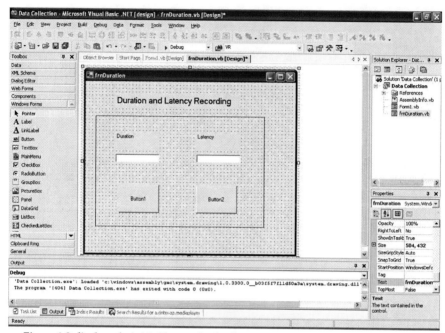

Figure 6.2 displays the initial layout for the duration and latency data collection form.

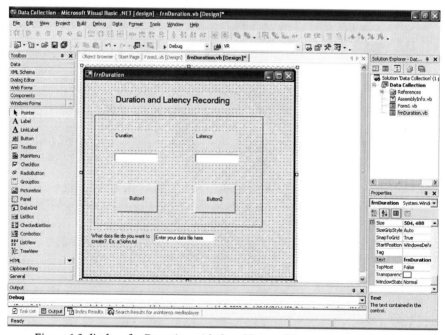

Figure 6.3 displays frmDuration with the addition of the user output file objects.

Reducing Errors

It is often the case that programs are designed less than "fool proof" for a user. This means that users might click on a wrong Button or select an incorrect option and crash the program. Take for example the current form. If the user clicks on butStart before selecting an output file, duration data will be computed; yet it will not be recorded into a file for later analysis. One way to minimize the risk of run-time errors on the part of your user is to make possible incorrect response options invisible or disabled until the "optimal" time for them to be available to the user. With this form, the optimal time for the user to click on butStart is after a data output file has been specified. Therefore change the *Enabled* properties of butStart and butStop to *False*. Add a new Button, change the name to butBegin, the text to *Begin*, and place it next to the TextBox txtFile. This Button will kick in the data output file and change your butStart and butStop enabled properties to *True*. To do this, add the following code under the butBegin Button:

```
butStart.Enabled = True
butStop.Enabled = True
butBegin.Visible = False
FileOpen (2, txtFile.Text, OpenMode.Append)
```

Using TextBoxes to Track Client and Staff Names

If a relatively small number of users will be using the data system, or if you wish to track the user of the system for a given time period, you may wish to incorporate additional TextBoxes into your program. In the case of our data collection system let's assume we want to track user name and client name. The latter referring to the person we are collecting data on. To incorporate the TextBoxes for these purposes, add one to your form from the toolbox. Change the name from Textbox1 to txtClient and the text to blank. Now add a second TextBox and change the name to txtStaff and the text to blank. Next add Labels above these TextBoxes to orient the user as to their function. Name these two labels lblStaff and lblClient, change their text properties accordingly,and position them directly above their corresponding TextBoxes.

Lastly add a new Button somewhere towards the bottom of the form that will allow the user to terminate the data collection program. Change the name of this Button to butEnd and the text to *End*.

Linking the Form Functions Together

Because the user will only need to write the client name and staff name once to file, this information would be best generated via butBegin. This Button is present upon the form loading, and since it disappears after it is clicked (via the "butBegin.Visible = False" code) it will only write this information once. Therefore, add the following line of code under the butBegin Button after the previously written code.

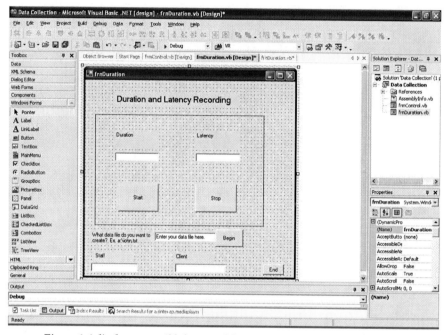

Figure 6.4 displays a possible layout of the Duration form for data collection.

```
WriteLine (2, txtStaff.Text, txtClient.Text)
```

In order for the computer to generate duration and latency measures when the butStart and butStop buttons are clicked by the user, Visual Basic's *Timer* function will need to be used. The Timer function is a command of code that captures the clock time of your computer. Unfortunately this clock time is a number corresponding to the *number of seconds after midnight*. This time is pretty irrelevant for most programming purposes. Yet, there is an easy transition of this value into a meaningful number. By capturing the clock time at point A, and again at point B, we can then subtract value at point A from the value at point B and obtain the difference in seconds. Using this conceptualization, the time from clicking on the start Button to clicking on the stop Button can create a *duration* measure. Therefore, add the following code under butStart:

```
WriteLine (2, txtDuration.Text, txtLatency.Text)
vTime1 = VB.Timer
txtLatency.Text = VB.Timer - vTime3
```

What the above code does is first write the current time and date to the data output file followed by the time values placed in the txtDuration and txtLatency TextBoxes. The first time this Button is clicked, these values will be blank. Yet, using the next line of code, this will soon change. vTime1 = VB.Timer places the current computer clock time into a variable called vTime1. This value will be held until the butStop Button is clicked to compute duration. The third line of code places the current computer clock time minus the value of a variable called vTime3. vTime3 will be 0 upon the first run through of the subroutine because it will be created upon clicking on the butStop Button to compute latency. As a result, this value will be simply the computer clock time and will appear in txtLatency.

In order to capture latency we need to obtain a value for vTime3. We also need to calculate the time from the clicking of butStart to butStop, or duration. Therefore, add the following code under butStop:

```
vTime2 = VB.Timer - vTime1
txtDuration.Text = vTime2
vTime3 = VB.Timer
```

What the above code does is calculate a value for vTime2 which will be placed in txtDuration. vTime2 is based on the current computer clock time minus the clock time when the butStart Button was clicked (i.e. vTime1). The next line of code places this value in txtDuration. The third line of code creates a value for vTime3. This value is used as described above for computing latency. Before running the program and testing your code writing skills, remember to declare your vTime1, vTime2, and vTime3 variables under the Public Class frmDuration section of the editor. To do so, type the following code:

```
Dim vTime1
Dim vTime2
Dim vTime3
```

Next place the cursor above all existing code and type:

```
Option Explicit On
```

Finally type the shorthand recognition for the VB.Timer code directly under Option Explicit On:

```
Imports VB = Microsoft.VisualBasic
```

An Exit Option

In addition to ending your program, the butEnd Button should close the data output file. This will allow for subsequent users to run the program and create their own data file without the difficulty possibly encountered if a previous file is still open. Therefore add the following code under butEnd:

```
FileClose(2)
End
```

The last step to complete is to link frmDuration to the control panel (frmControl). To do this add the following code to frmControl's butDuration:

```
Dim x as New frmDuration()
x.Show()
me.Visible() = False
```

Run the program and check your progress.

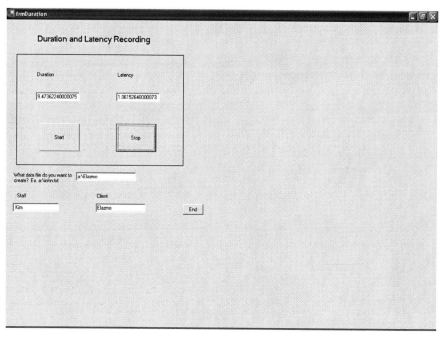

Figure 6.5 displays the run time display of frmDuration.

Time Sampling Recording

Form Overview

Insert a new Windows form into your project and rename it frmTS. Change the text property to frmTS. Add a Label to the form that displays to the user that this is the correct form for collecting time sampling data. Change the name of the Label to lblInstructions and change the text to "Time Sampling Recording." Alter font and TextAlign properties for a more custom look.

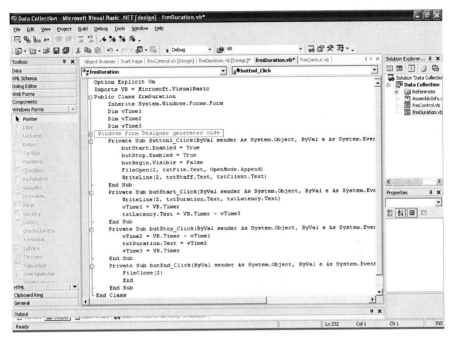

Figure 6.6 displays the programming code of frmDuration.

The most basic components of this form consist of an output data file TextBox, a TextBox indicating the duration of time between samplings, and responses for the user to select from during these time samplings.

Create the output file by adding a new TextBox and changing the name to txtFile. Change the text to blank. Next place a Label to the left of txtFile named lblFile and change the text to "Enter your data file here."

Time sampling data collection requires specific intervals of time to elapse before the user records a response indicating that the behavior has occurred during the last interval of time or that the behavior is occurring right now (as in the case of momentary time sampling). In order for Visual Basic 2005 to "prompt" the user following the elapsing of certain intervals of time, we will need to use the Timer object. The Timer object is different from the timer function described earlier which only aquires the current computer clock time. The Timer object is in essence a counter that will perform a variety of actions upon its enabling. What we want this object to do is prompt the user to make a response following the elapsing of an interval of time. Therefore, add a Timer object from the toolbar and place it on your form. Note that it drops below the form. This is fine because the Timer is invisible during runtime. Change the name to tmrInterval and its enabled property to *false*. While we could pre-set the interval of time during the programming process by changing tmrInterval's interval property to X, it would make more sense to allow the user to do this during run time. As a result, the time interval could vary across each running of the program.

Timer Customization

To allow for the customization of the Timer's interval, add a new TextBox, change the name to txtInterval and leave the text property blank. Next add a new Label box, change the name to lblInterval, and the text property to "Time Interval (sec)." The txtInterval will allow the user to input a desired time interval for their recording purposes and the lblInterval will orient that user to the TextBox. In order for the Timer object to obtain the value entered into the TextBox, as well as for Visual Basic 2005 to create the data file specified in txtFile, we need an event to happen. As before in the previous form we will have the user click on a Button to activate these parameters. Add a new Button, change the name to "butBegin" and the text to "Begin." Place the following code under butBegin:

```
butBegin.Enabled = False
FileOpen (2, txtFile.Text, OpenMode.Append)
WriteLine (2, Date.Now, txtInterval.Text)
vInterval = txtInterval.Text
tmrInterval.Interval = vInterval * 1000
tmrInterval.Enabled = True
```

This code first disables the butBegin Button so that this data is only generated once. Second, it opens/creates the text file that is specified in txtFile for Append. Third, it creates a variable entitled vInterval and makes its value equal to the value inputted into txtInterval. Fourth, it alters the tmrInterval interval property to equal the value of vInterval multiplied by 1000. This calculation is done because values entered into txtInterval are in milliseconds and the computer needs to recalculate them into seconds. Lastly, the tmrInterval is enabled, or turned on. Now that it is turned on, we need to make it do something once the interval has elapsed.

Because we just created a variable entitled vInterval this will need to be declared on the form so that VB.2005 recognizes it. Therefore, type the following code under the `Public Class frmTS` section of the editor:

```
Dim vInterval
```

Now at the top of the editor type:

```
Option Explicit On
```

Timer Prompted Responding

Let's move forward by having the user make one of two response options after the interval has elapsed. A *yes* or a *no* response regarding the occurrence of a behavior. We will want the computer to record the response, and reinitiate the Timer so that the interval will start over again. Begin by adding two new Buttons, and changing

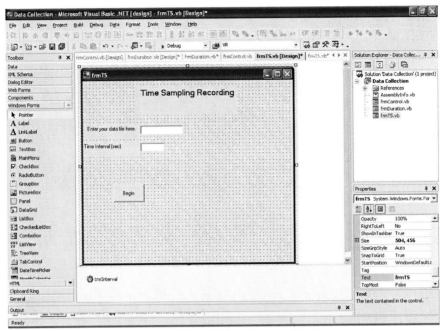

Figure 6.7 displays a possible graphical layout of the data output file,
Timer object, and "Begin" Button.

one's name to butYes and the other's name to butNo. Now change butYes's text to *Yes* and butNo's text to *No*.

Standing alone these Buttons could have a variety of meanings to the user of the program. This is good because many types of questions could be posed, allowing for a more diverse program. For example one may wish to assess "Is the behavior of interest occurring right now?" or "Has the behavior of interest occurred since the last interval?" or even "Has the behavior become more severe since the last interval?" To orient the user to the specific functions of the butYes and butNo Buttons, add a Label object, change the name to lblPrompt, and change the text to your desired question. For purposes of this example, let's make the text read "Is the behavior occurring right now?" Change the visible property to *False* because we will want the prompt to be displayed only following the completion of the tmrInterval's interval. Go ahead and also change butYes and butNo's visible property to *False* because we do not want the user to click on them immediately when the form loads.

To link the *Yes / No* Buttons to the behavior of the Timer, display lblPrompt, as well as have appropriate responses write to the data file, add the following code under butYes:

```
WriteLine (2, "yes")
tmrInterval.Enabled = True
lblPrompt.Visible = False
```

```
butYes.Visible = False
butNo.Visible = False
```

And the following code under butNo:

```
WriteLine (2, "no")
tmrInterval.Enabled = True
lblPrompt.Visible = False
butYes.Visible = False
butNo.Visible = False
```

Lastly, add the following code under tmrInterval:

```
Beep
lblPrompt.Visible = True
butYes.Visible = True
butNo.Visible = True
tmrInterval.Enabled = False
```

Let's start with the code under the Timer. The first line simply generates an audible tone for the user to orient himself/herself to the fact that it is now time to record data. The second line makes the lblPrompt object visible. The next two lines make the *Yes* and *No* response options visible. The last line turns the Timer's enabled function to *False*. In other words, it stops the Timer.

The code under the *Yes* and *No* response option buttons do a variety of similar things. First, they write to the data output file either an actual *Yes* or a *No* textual response. You may wish to add to this line of data by including time and date (using the Date.Now functions described above), or the number of intervals that have elapsed from the beginning of the data collection session (using a variable that adds by one each time the timer interval has completed). Next the code tells VB.2005 to make the lblPrompt visible property *False* as well as the butYes and butNo buttons. These properties are changed so that the prompt is not always displayed on the computer screen and so that responses are not made on the Yes and No buttons prior to the completion of the next interval of time. Finally, the last line of code restarts tmrInterval to start the beginning of the next interval.

As with the Duration form, add an *End* Button to terminate data collection, along with the necessary code to link frmTS to the control panel. To do the latter, add the following code under frmControl's butTS:

```
Dim x as New frmTS()
x.Show()
me.Visible = False
```

Run the program and check your progress.

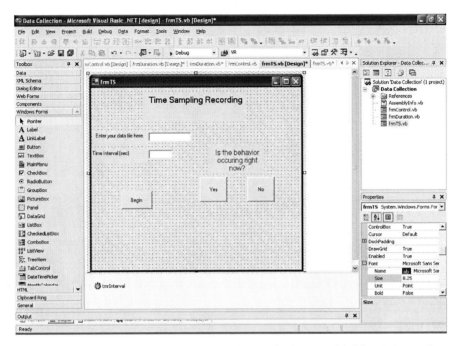

Figure 6.8 displays the status of the form following the elapsing of the Timer's interval.

Frequency Recording

Form Overview

Insert a new Windows form into your project and rename it frmFrequency. Add a Label to the form that displays to the user that this is the correct form for collecting frequency data. Change the name of the Label to lblInstructions, change the text to *Frequency Recording*, and alter font and TextAlign properties.

The most basic components this form consists of are a series of Buttons that add occurrences of targeted behaviors when clicked upon. This is easily accomplished with Buttons and corresponding variables. While you could already craft such a form incorporating the existing information found in this chapter, let's add some additional sophistication to the program via a data input file.

Data Input File

Using a data input file for observational recording allows for any variety of parameters to be loaded into the computer program during run time instead of being manually entered by the user. The input file can save time as well as add a greater degree of diversity into your data collection program. Take for example our current frequency data collection form. A user may wish to track the frequency of a variety of target behaviors of a given client. Yet, that user might work with 10 or so different

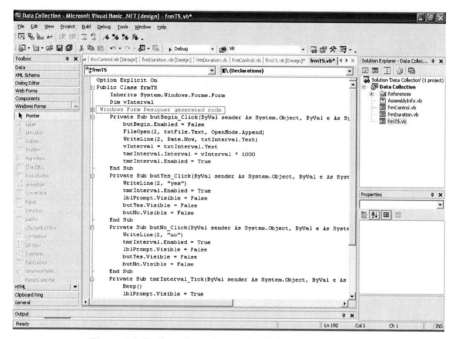

Figure 6.9 displays the majority of code found under frmTS.

clients each with their own set of targeted behaviors. The amount of time spent inputting each client's information increases along with the number of clients. Designing a data collection system that can handle such changing demands on the user is paramount.

To incorporate the input data file into our program, add a TextBox, change the name to txtInput and leave the text property blank. Next add a Label to the left of the TextBox, change the name to lblInput and the text to "Enter data file to input here. Type directory, data file, and extension. Ex. c:\pete.txt." This is a rather long Label text, but it crucial that the user input this specific information in order for the program to access his/her data file correctly.

We will also need a Button to create the event which accesses the data file and brings that information into Visual Basic 2005. Therefore, add a Button, change its name to butDatain an its text to "Load Data File." Place the following code under butDatain to open the desired data file:

```
FileOpen (1, txtInput.Text, OpenMode.Input)
```

Designing the Input File

Next we need to determine what type of information we would like to store in our data input file, and create the corresponding objects and code in Visual Basic 2005 to interact with that information. For purposes of illustration, let's say we

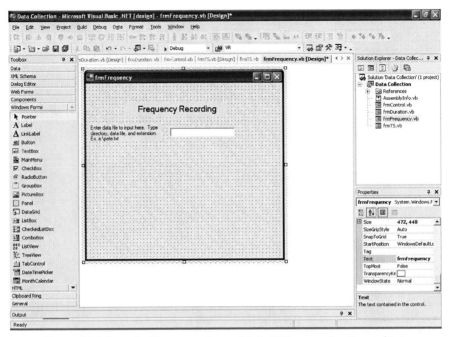

Figure 6.10 shows frmFrequency along with the lblInput and txtInput objects.

would like to have the client's name and up to six targeted behaviors stored in our data file. This will require that we have information separated by commas in our data file such as: "Pete, physical-aggression, SIB, hair-pulling, threats, request, in-seat." Create such a file yourself by opening Microsoft Notepad or Wordpad, which come standard with Microsoft Windows, type the above sequence, and save it as a text file named "pete.txt" to your c-drive. Make sure you add the "-" between words for a multiple word behavior like *hair-pulling*. Close your text editor program and return to Visual Basic 2005.

Creating the Response Recorders

Because the data input file has the client's name and up to six identified behaviors to be frequency recorded, let's create a TextBox that displays client name and six Buttons to correspond to each of the behaviors. Start by adding a TextBox to your frmFrequency form, change the name to txtName, and leave the text property blank. Next add a Label, change the name to lblName, and change the text to "Client Name." Now add six separate Buttons to your form to correspond to the six target behaviors. Change their names to butBeh1 through butBeh6 and all their text to blank. Finally add six new Labels and place them directly above your newly added Buttons. These labels will be used to display the current frequency of each identified behavior. Change the names of these labels to lblBeh1 through lblBeh6 . Do no change all their text to blank. Leave them labeled "Label1...Label6." You might also change their BorderStyle property to "Fixed Single".

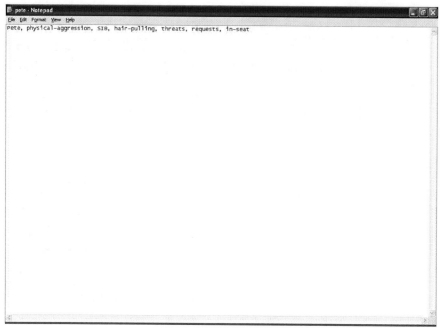

Figure 6.11 shows the correct format of the pete.txt data input file.

Customization for Less than X Response Options

Earlier we specified that the program would collect information on *up to* six targeted behaviors. If numbers less than six are found in the data file an error might occur during run time if certain precautions are not made. There are many ways to accomplish the safeguarding against such errors. A very simple way is to have a *dummy* target behavior that if placed in the input file corresponds to the absence of a target behavior. For example, the pete.txt file would now read: "Pete, physical aggression, SIB, x, x, x, x." Here the dummy target behavior is x, indicating that there really are only two behaviors we wish to record for Pete: physical aggression and SIB. Using these dummy behaviors, we can alter the properties of the butBeh3-butBeh6 buttons so that they do not record any information when clicked upon. Let's begin this process by adding the following code to the "butDatain" Button under the pervious code:

```
Input (1, vName)
Input (1, vB1)
Input (1, vB2)
Input (1, vB3)
Input (1, vB4)
Input (1, vB5)
Input (1, vB6)
```

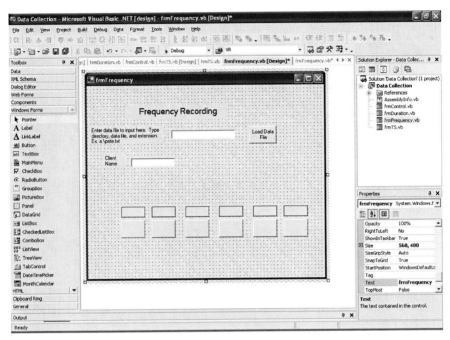

Figure 6.12 shows a possible layout of the newly added command buttons and labels.

```
txtName.Text = vName
butBeh1.Text = vB1
If vB2 = "x" Then
butBeh2.Enabled = False
Else
butBeh2.Text = vB2
End If
If vB3 = "x" Then
butBeh3.Enabled = False
Else
butBeh3.Text = vB3
End If
If vB4 = "x" Then
butBeh4.Enabled = False
Else
butBeh4.Text = vB4
End If
If vB5 = "x" Then
butBeh5.Enabled = False
Else
```

```
butBeh5.Text = vB5
End If
If vB6 = "x" Then
butBeh6.Enabled = False
Else
butBeh6.Text = vB6
End If
```

This code first loads the information found in the text input file into a series of seven variables. The first variable is called vName and the following six are called vB1-vB6 (short for behaviors 1-6). Remember that you need to declare such variables under the `Public Class frmFrequency` section of the editor with:

```
Dim vName, vB1, vB2, vB3, vB4, vB5, vB6
```

At the top of the editor add:

```
Option Explicit On
```

After loading the information found in the text file into these variables, VB.2005 places the first variable's text into txtName. Next it places the second variable's text (the first target behavior) into the text of butBeh1. Afterwards it checks to see if there are any more behaviors that are to be recorded. It does so by checking to see if the variable has a value of x. If it does, it disables the corresponding butBeh Button, but if not, it places that information into the text of butBeh Button and leaves the enable property equal to true. This last series of steps is repeated for the remaining four variables (vB3-vB6).

Variables to Track Frequency

Now with the input file information properly loaded into the Buttons, we are ready to link the Buttons (butBeh1-6) to variables that will keep track of behavior frequency. What will be necessary here are a series of integer variables, each corresponding to a target behavior that increases in value each time the butBeh Button is clicked by the user. To create this series of integer variables, add the following code in the `Public Class fromFrequency` section of the editor:

```
Dim vFB1, vFB2, vFB3, vFB4, vFB5, vFB6 as Integer
```

Here each vFB corresponds to each behavior that will be recorded. Next, add the following code under each of the corresponding butBeh Buttons changing the lblBeh and vFB numbers with each:

```
vFB1 = vFB1 + 1
lblBeh1.Text = vFB1
```

You should now have the necessary code for frequency counts of up to six independent behaviors.

Handling Recording Errors

While this last code adds the total frequencies of each behavior as desired, it is quite plausible that the user will make a mistake, click on the wrong button, or double-click and add too many instances of a behavior than desired. There are many ways we could handle this problem, from simply flagging the error in the text file, to subtracting an instance of behavior using code like: vFB = vFB - 1 . The option is up to you if the possibility of error seems important enough to safegauard your program against. Let's attempt to solve the problem in a pretty straightforward way via an error button.

Begin by adding a new Button, renaming it butError, and changing the text to *Error*. Next create a new variable called *vError* by adding the following code to the `Public Class frmFrequency` section of the editor:

```
Dim vError
```

Using the vError variable we can control the behavior of the vFB1 – vFB6 variables to either add one or subtract one when the butError Button is clicked. To do this we can make the value of vError equal to one when it is clicked on and then

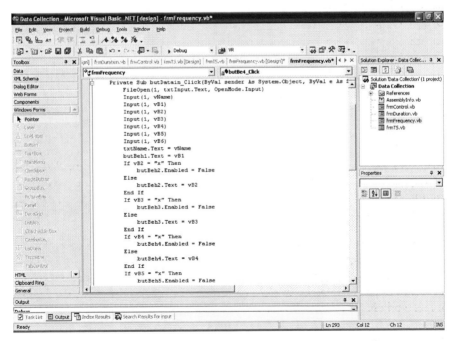

Figure 6.13 displays highlights of the necessary code to record behavior frequency.

use an If-Then-Else statement under each butBeh Button to add or subtract 1 from the corresponding vFB. Begin by adding the following code under butError:

```
vError = vError + 1
```

This code will add a value of 1 to the vError variable. Next go ahead and add the following code under each of the butBeh Buttons before the existing vFB1-6 = vFB1-6 + 1 code. Remember to change the FB(number):

```
If vError = 1 Then
vFB1 = vFB1 - 1
vError = 0
Else
```

Finish this If-Then-Else statement with the required *End If* following the previously existing vFB1-6 = vFB1-6 +1. Delete the automatic entry of End If that is placed after the Else. Your finalized subroutine should look like the following for butBeh1 and change only in the 1-6 value across your other butBeh Buttons:

```
If vError = 1 Then
vFB1 = vFB1 - 1
vError = 0
Else
vFB1 = vFB1 + 1
End If
lblBeh1.Text = vFB1
```

This additional code creates a means for errors to be corrected before they are written to file. By turning vError's value to 1, any subsequent click on a butBeh Button will subtract 1 from the current value of vFB. This is what the "If vError = 1" code will do. Immediately after this subtraction, vError is changed back to 0. Now if any additional clicks are made on butBeh buttons, 1 will be added to the total vFB variable, as before. Subtractions will only occur if vError is turned back to 1 by clicking on butError.

Data Output Using Timers

Next we need to deal with data collection output. Because we are collecting frequency data, the easiest way to handle this is for all accumulated frequencies to write to file when the data collection session is over. While this will accomplish a macro analysis of frequency, a user may wish to see subtle changes in frequencies as the session progresses. To do this we can incorporate a Timer object that automatically writes data to file every time that Timer's interval has elapsed. By making the interval repeat over and over again at a pre-specified time period, we will be able to have moment-by-moment frequency data for our subject.

Begin by adding a new Timer object to your form and changing the name to tmrData. Because we do not want the timer to kick in upon form load, change the enabled property to false. Add the following code under the tmrData subroutine:

```
WriteLine (2, vFB1, vFB2, vFB3, vFB4, vFB5, vFB6)
```

This code will simply write the values of our six behaviors to the data file. Along with the addition of this timer, we need to add code to open the data file we wish to write to. Plus, since we do not want to write data until the session actually begins, we need to have the user initiate the beginning of the session. As before, this task is easily accomplished via a Button.

Add a new Button to your form, change the name to butBegin, and the text to *Begin*. Add the following code under this Button:

```
tmrData.Enabled = True
WriteLine (2, vFB1, vFB2, vFB3, vFB4, vFB5, vFB6)
```

Now the Timer will write to file following the completion of the pre-specified interval placed in its interval property. Plus, frequency data for all six variables will write to file immediately upon initiating the program. Obviously, these values should initially be 0.

As before in our frmDuration and frmTS forms, we will want the user to control the name and location of the data output file. Add a TextBox, change the name to txtDataout, and leave the text property blank. Next, add a Label to the left of this TextBox, change the name to lblDataout, and the text to "Enter data file to OUTPUT here. Type directory, data file, and extension. Ex. c:\firstsession.txt." Change the AutoSize property to False.

To add user control over the interval of time between data recording to the output file, simply add a TextBox, change its name to txtInterval, and leave the text blank. Now add a Label to the left of this TextBox and change the name to lblInterval and its text to "Write data every X seconds." Alter the code under the butBegin Button to read:

```
tmrData.Interval = txtInterval.Text * 1000
tmrData.Enabled = True
FileOpen (2, txtDataout.Text, OpenMode.Output)
WriteLine (2, Date.Now, "data records=",
     txtInterval.Text)
WriteLine (2, vB1, vB2, vB3, vB4, vB5, vB6)
```

This code first takes the value entered in txtInterval, multiplies it by 1000 (to get seconds), and places it in the interval property of tmrData. Now the data file will write every time this interval elapses. Next, the code kicks in the timer or turns it on with *Enabled = True*. The code then opens or creates the data file in the directory

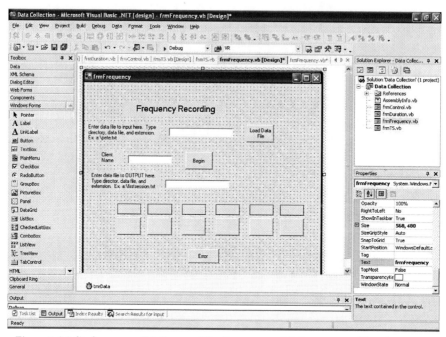

Figure 6.14 displays a possible layout of frmFrequency with data output file information.

and with the name specified in the txtDataout TextBox. After the file is open, the time and date are written followed by noting what interval of time was specified in txtInterval. Lastly, the values of all the vB1-6 variables are written to the text file.

Before we finish up here though, think about how you will get the program to stop writing data to file. This task could be accomplished via an *Exit* button containing *FileClose(2)* code. Yet, the same function is possible with the addition of another Timer, one that would keep track of session length. This feature will also ensure that data are not recorded for longer periods of time than desired. Keeping session length exactly the same interval may be critical for comparisons across sessions.

To accomplish this feat, just add another TextBox and Timer. First, add the TextBox, change the name to txtSession, and leave the text blank. Second, add a label, change the name to lblSession, and the text to "Session Length." Now add the Timer and change the name to tmrSession. Place the following code under the new Timer to close the program, plus write the data to file one last time:

```
WriteLine (2, vFB1, vFB2, vFB3, vFB4, vFB5, vFB6)
End
```

To hook up the desired session length to this timer, add the following code under butBegin:

```
tmrSession.Interval = txtSession.Text * 1000
tmrSession.Enabled = True
```

That should do it. Add another Button to prematurely terminate the session called butEnd and add the code:

```
End
```

Finally, add the following code to frmControl's butFreq Button to link this form to your control panel:

```
Dim x as New frmFrequency()
x.Show()
me.Visible = False
```

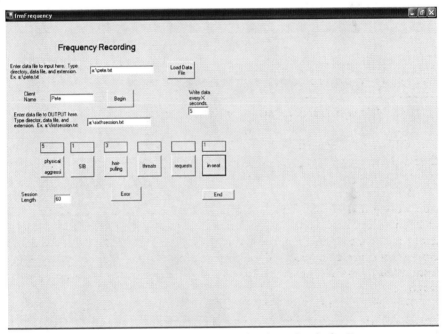

Figure 6.15 shows the resulting final graphical interface for frmFrequency.

Descriptive Analysis Recording

Form Overview

Insert a new Windows form into your project and rename it frmDA. Add a Label to the form that displays to the user that this is the correct form for collecting Descriptive Analysis data. Change the name of the Label to lblInstructions and change the text to "Descriptive Analysis Recording." Also change the Font and TextAlign properties to suit your style.

The most basic components of this form consist of a series of ComboBoxes that contain a list of options for the user to select from regarding antecedents, behaviors, and consequences. This is easily accomplished by adding three separate ComboBoxes to frmDA and changing their names to cbAnt, cbBeh, and cbCon. Next change the text property of each of these boxes to *Antecedent, Behavior,* and *Consequence* respectively.

ComboBox Items

To add options to the cbAnt, double-click on the *Item* property of the box in the properties window. Double-click on the (collections)... text and a little blank box will appear. Type your first possible antecedent here and press enter. You will have to repeat this step for each additional antecedent. Once done, click on cbBeh and do the same for behaviors. Finally, click on cbCon to add options to the

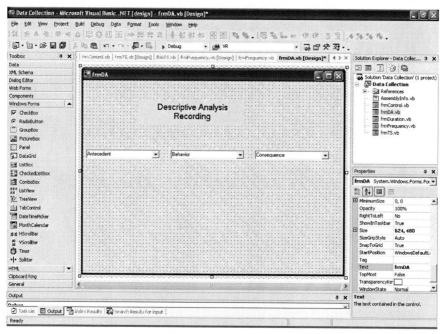

Figure 6.16 displays a possible layout of frmDA.

consequence ComboBox. Predetermining these options will reduce the amount of effort your data recorder would need to emit to type all this information in by hand. A great feature of the Combo Box is that if an option is not provided, the user could actually type in a customized novel option during the running of the program. Planning ahead for the most probable response options will keep this activity to a minimum.

A few other features we will need to add to this form to make it functional are a TextBox specifying where the data output file will go and a Button that writes the ComboBox information to that file. First, add the TextBox, change the name to txtData, and leave the text blank. Next, add a Label to the left of this TextBox, change the name to lblData, and the text to "Data File Name: ex. c:\mary.txt." Now add a Button directly below the txtData object that opens / creates the text file. Change the name of this Button to butBegin and the text to "Begin." Place the following code under the butBegin button:

```
FileOpen (5, txtData.Text, OpenMode.Append)
butBegin.Visible = False
```

This code will first open or create the data file, and second remove the butBegin Button so that it does not accidentally get clicked on again.

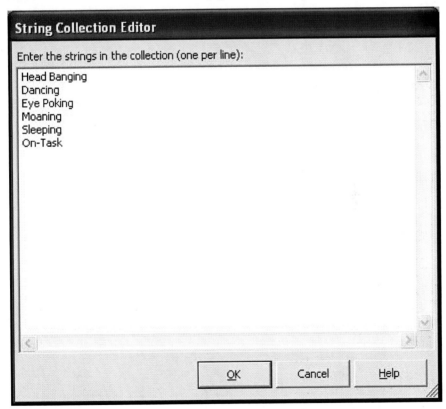

Figure 6.17 shows how the items are added to the ComboBoxes.

The last step for this form is to add another Button, this time to record the options selected in the ComboBoxes to the data output file. To accomplish this, add a Button, change the name to butRecord, and the text to "Record Information." Under this command button, add the following code:

```
WriteLine (5, Date.Now, cbAnt.Text, cbBeh.Text,
     cbCon.Text)
```

With this code, your form for Descriptive Analysis should be functional. Keep in mind you might want to add TextBoxes for client and staff names, a Timer for session length, or an End Button.

Link the frmDA to your frmControl by placing the following code under frmControl's but DA button:

```
Dim x as New frmDA()
x.Show()
me.Visible = False
```

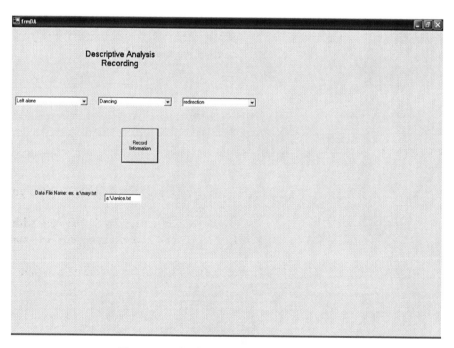

Figure 6.18 displays frmDA during run time.

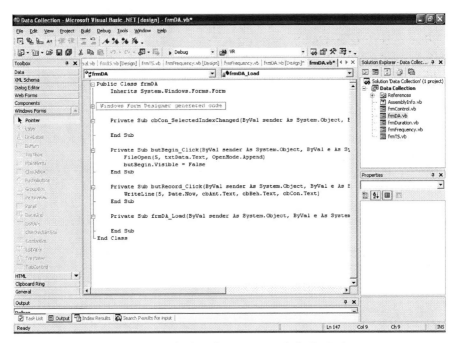

Figure 6.19 displays the necessary code for frmDA.

Our computerized data collection program should be complete. Run the program and check your progress. There are endless additional features that could be added to the program. Hopefully we have provided you an example that demonstrates the diversity in data collection options Visual Basic 2005 has to offer, and the framework for designing your own optimal program.

References

Bellack, A. S., & Hersen, M. (1998). *Behavioral assessment* (4th Ed). New York: Allyn & Bacon.

Dixon, M. R. (2003). Creating your own portable data collection system with Microsoft Embedded Visual Tools for the Pocket PC. *Journal of Applied Behavior Analysis.*

Kahng, S., & Iwata, B. A. (1998). Computerized systems for collecting real-time observational data. *Journal of Applied Behavior Analysis, 31*, 253-261.

Chapter 7: Matching to Sample

Creating a Stimulus Equivalence Program

A research preparation often used in behavior analysis to study human language and concept formation is called "matching to sample." In a matching to sample procedure, one stimulus, called the sample, is usually presented at the top of the computer screen while two or more stimuli, called comparisons, are presented directly below the sample. The subject is either shaped or instructed to make a "match" between the object at the top of the screen with one at the bottom of the screen. This is technically called conditional discrimination learning. The matching to sample preparation is useful for teaching colors, words, or identity relations among stimuli, and can be used for more complex learning preparations such as stimulus equivalence. In this latter type of matching to sample preparation, certain relations between the sample and the comparison stimuli are trained via differential reinforcement for correct responses, while other novel stimuli relations are simply tested without reinforcement to assess if they have "emerged" from a specific training history. For more information about research using the Match to Sample procedure to examine stimulus equivalence see Green and Saunders, (1998).

Assuming a general understanding of the methodology, here is what a basic outline for a matching to sample program used for stimulus equivalence research might consist of:

1. Create the stimulus classes with three member classes (3 classes) for a total of nine stimuli. Label each class A, B, and C. Label each specific stimulus A1, A2, A3, etc.
2. Arrange stimuli placement on the computer screen (with PictureBoxes) for the sample and comparison stimuli.
3. Program A-B conditional discrimination training. Start with a block of 18 trials, but make the trial number into a variable to allow for customization of the number of trials later on if desired. Ensure that all stimuli are displayed 6 times as samples in a random sequence. Ensure that all comparison stimuli are also randomized in terms of their placement.
4. Develop protocol to check if a response criterion has or has not been met. Initially set criteria at 16 out of 18 trials in a given block of trials. Create a variable that will add trial numbers until it gets to 18 and then at that time check to see if the number correct is 16 or greater. If so, go on to the next type of training (A-C), if not send back to restart A-B training with another block of 18 trials. As with the number of trials, make the criterion a variable to allow for customization.
5. Program A-C conditional discrimination training. Use the same methods as above for randomization and criterion. If responding is less than

specified criterion, repeat this phase, and do not go back to A-B training.

6. Program Mixed A-B / A-C training. Simply mix the types of trials from A-B and A-C together. Start off with 36 trials and a criterion of 32. If criterion is met, go on to testing phases. If criterion is not met, repeat only this phase.

7. Program various tests for derived relations in the absence of any type of reinforcement.

    a. Reflexivity test of A-A, B-B, and C-C relations. Start with 27 trials containing 3 presentations of each sample but allow for customization.

    b. Symmetry test of B-A and C-A relations. Start off with 36 trials containing 18 presentations of B-A and 18 presentations of C-A each but allow for customization.

    c. Transitivity test of B-C relations. Start with 18 trials of B-C presentations with each B stimulus serving as a sample 6 times for but allow for customization.

    d. Equivalence test of C-B relations. Start with 18 trials of C-B presentations with each C stimulus serving as a sample 6 times for but allow for customization.

8. Create programming routine to write a various amount of information to a data file on every trial. This information will include sample stimulus, comparison stimulus selected, correct comparison (if not selected), and response time from sample presentation to comparison selection.

While this is a list of what the program must do, there is more than one way to make it do these things. We have decisions to make about the look and feel of the program and we have to anticipate the research needs that are not outlined above. For example, do we need a control panel? Are there any additional parameters the researcher will want to change? What would these be? Are there any object properties the researcher will want to change during run time? What would these be? Are there going to be instructions to the participant? If so will the instructions be in the beginning of the program, at the end, or both? By now you might be able to anticipate these questions and others, plus you might even be able to respond to these questions using your programming ability.

Rather than using a control panel we will design this program so the researcher can pass parameters and object properties to the program during run time using an input file, similar to the input files designed in Chapters 5 and 6.

Program Requirements

1. Creating the Stimuli

You as the programmer will first need to decide what the stimuli will be. Common forms of visual stimuli may be arbitriay shapes, pictures of faces, or drawings of objects. Auditory simuli could also be utilized, by adding .wav or MP3 files. In this chapter's example, we will stick with all visual stimuli. Because you may wish to add, delete, or modify stimuli at a later date, we will design this program to allow stimuli parameters to be loaded during run time via a data input file. This is a nice feature, because it lets the user change stimuli prior to the program running without modifying any existing computer code to do so.

At this point, open a text editor such as NotePad, and create a new text file, call it M2S.txt (for Match to Sample) and save it in the directory where you will store the program files you are about to write. Your current text file will be blank. That is ok for now. Let's also create a directory structure of "c:\programming\M2S" and put the blank text file there. Close NotePad.

The program requirements above note that the stimuli should consist of three 3-class members. Therefore, you will need nine image files: A1, A2, A3; B1, B2, B3; C1, C2, C3. For programming purposes the images can be of anything, but it is easier for now during program construction if you make your own images as simple letters and numbers using the Paint program provided with Windows. This will allow for you to pre-test the program without having to recall which abstract stimuli were related to each other. When the program is completed, you can easily replace these "test" stimuli with actual stimuli.

Locate the Paint program and open it on your computer. Once the Paint program is open, select *Image* then *Attributes* from the main menu. Change the width and height to 75 pixels. You can then use the text tool to type *A1* and save it as *a1.bmp* in the same directory as your text file (c:\programming\M2S). This way the image will literally be that of *A1*. Again, using the image of A1 will allow you to track the program when you are writing it. Now create the other eight images and save them to the same directory. Close Microsoft Paint.

2. Configure the Forms

The next programming requirement refers to arranging the stimuli configuration. We have some decisions to make about the number of form(s) we will want to use for the program. Open Visual Basic 2005 and create a new project named M2S and change the location of the project to your c:\programming\M2S directory. Let's make the first form of this project an instructions form. Change the name property to *frmIns1*, the WindowState to *Maximized*, and the form Text to *Instructions*. Add a Label named *lblIns1* and size lblIns1 to fit the form based on how detailed you instructions may be. You may have to make adjustments after you run the program and see how everything lines up during run time. Add a Button and change the Name property to *butBegin*, and change the Text property to *Begin*.

Go back to NotePad and reopen M2S.txt. On the first line of the document type the line:

```
INSTRUCTIONS, This is where the instructions will go.
```

Note: type your instructions on the same line. Do not start a new line or press the ENTER button until you have completed your instructions. Also make sure the word *Instructions* is in all capital letters.

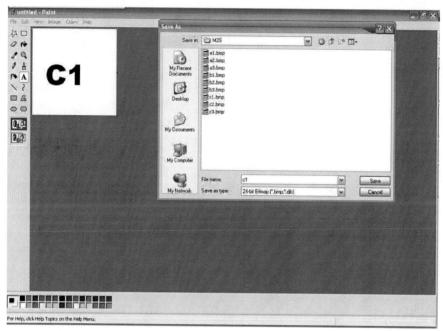

Figure 7.1 displays the C1 stimulus being created in Microsoft Paint.

Your text file should look like this:

```
INSTRUCTIONS, This is where the instructions will go.
```

Save and close the M2S.txt text file. *frmIns1* will be the first form to open, therefore we need to tell this form to open the input file M2S.txt when it is loaded. Also, we want it to read in the instructions, and display those instructions lblIns1. Double-click on the form, not on the Label or the Button, enter the edit mode, and type the following code in the Private Sub frmIns1_Load subroutine:

```
FileOpen(1, "C:\programming\M2S\M2S.txt",
OpenMode.Input)
Input(1, vHeader)
Input(1, vInstructions)
lblIns1.Text = vInstructions
```

Notice that we are using C:\programming\M2S to tell the computer to look for the text file in the same directory as the application or program. Because we are using this directory, all of the files used for this program have to be located in that same directory. We also need to declare two variables, vHeader and vInstructions. Under Public Class frmIns1 in the VB 2005 editor, type:

```
Dim vHeader As String
Dim vInstructions As String
```

And above the line Public Class frmIns1, type the following:

```
Option Explicit On
```

Run the program after you change the Startup object. You should see the instructions.

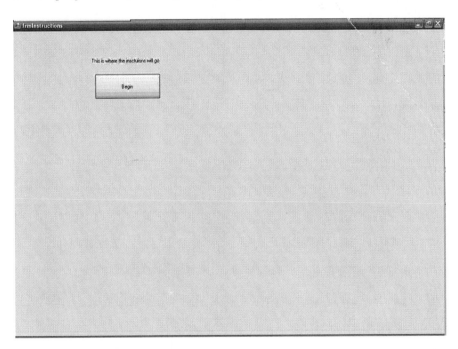

Figure 7.2 shows the instructions screen for the M2S program.

We now need to create a form for the main program. Add a new form by selecting *Project* and then *Add Windows Form* from the Main Menu. Change the name property to *frmM2S*, make the Text blank. Change the WindowState to *Maximized*. This form should load after the participant reads the instructions. To do this, go to frmIns1 and double-click on *butBegin* to enter edit mode. In the butBegin_Click subroutine type:

```
Dim x As New frmM2S
x.show()
me.Hide()
```

Run the program to make sure the change worked. Remember that by opening a new form before closing an old form prevents flicker. Close the program and go back to frmM2S. We now need to add PictureBoxes for the stimuli to appear in during run time. Specifically, we need one box for the sample stimulus and three boxes for the comparison stimuli. Add a PictureBox, change the name property to *picM2S0* and set the SizeMode property to StretchImage. Make the height and size property equal because the images that were designed in the Paint program were square.

Now make a control array by adding three more PictureBoxes. You should now change the suffixes of the three added PictureBoxes to picM2S1, picM2S2, and picM2S3. Make *picM2S0* the sample stimulus by placing it at the top of the screen, and make the others sample stimuli by placing them below the sample stimulus. We now need to link up the four picM2S PictureBoxes together into an array. This process is identical to the procedure used in Chapter 2. Start by double-clicking on picM2S0 and enter the edit mode. At the end of the line Private Sub picM2S0_Click(ByVal sender As System.Object, ByVal e As System.EventArgs) Handles picM2SO.Click add the following additional code:

```
,picM2S1.Click, picM2S2.Click, picM2S3.Click
```

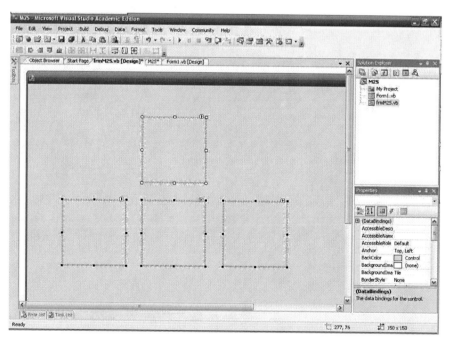

Figure 7.3 displays the screen layout with PictureBox arrays.

3. Training w/ Reinforcement

Recall that the type of reinforcement was not specified in the above outline. Reinforcement may take the form of points added to a counter, an audible noise, or a visual display of a smiley face. Let's use audio clips for reinforcement because the creation of a point counter was discussed in previous chapters. Let's have a relatively positive sounding audio clip for a correct response and a negative sounding audio clip for an incorrect response. The audio files should be brief so the participant does not have to wait for them to finish playing before making the next response.

For purposes of illustration, let's use "c:\windows\media\chimes.wav" for correct responses and "c:\windows\media\chord.wav" for incorrect responses. (Note: If your computer does not have these files in this specific directory you will need to use other files. For simplicity of following along with this chapter's example, you should create files with these names in this directory). Since the researcher may want to change the audio files later down the road or across sets of participants, let's add a few lines to our text file to say where the .wav files are located. Therefore, at the bottom of the M2S.txt file type:

```
CORRECT, "c:\windows\media\chimes.wav"
INCORRECT, "c:\windows\media\chord.wav"
```

Make sure that you capitalize the letters in your file names and directories where appropriate.

Let us next consider the following distribution of stimuli combination for A-B training where the first letter/number represents the sample stimulus and the three subsequent letter/number combinations represent the comparison stimuli: A1 - **B1**, B2, B3; A2 - B1, **B2**, B3; A3 - B1, B2, **B3**. As you can see, there are three basic combinations with the correct answers indicated in **bold**. Although the requirements from the above outline called for 18 trials, let's just start with three to make sure everything works. Therefore, add the following lines to your text file:

```
TRIAL1,A1,B1,B2,B3
TRIAL2,A2,B2,B1,B3
TRIAL3,A3,B3,B1,B2
END,,,,
```

The text file should now look like:

```
INSTRUCTIONS, This is where the instructions will go.
CORRECT, "c:\windows\media\chimes.wav"
INCORRECT, "c:\windows\media\chord.wav"
TRIAL1, A1,B1,B2,B3
TRIAL2, A2,B2,B1,B3
```

```
TRIAL3,  A3,B3,B1,B2
END,,,,
```

Here the text TRIAL indicates a new trial. The number represents the trial number. The first stimulus represents the sample and will be loaded into picM2S0. The next stimulus represents the correct answer and will be loaded into picM2S1. And the other two stimuli will be loaded into picM2S2 and picM2S3 respectively. END,,,, signals the end of the trials (the four commas are used for place holders). Save the changes to M2S.txt, and go back to edit mode of frmM2S.

You will need to generate a number of string variables in order for VB 2005 to recognize this input file information and convert it into code. Therefore, declare the following variables as String vHeader, vPos, vNeg and declare a variable array called vStimuli(0 to 3) as String by typing the following code under Public Class frmM2S:

```
Dim vHeader As String
Dim vPos As String
Dim vNeg As String
Dim vStimuli (3) As String
```

And above the line Public Class frmM2S, type the following:

```
Option Explicit On
```

Now go back to the form design mode of frmM2S and double-click on the form. Under the Private Sub frmM2S_Load subroutine, we need to read in the name of the reinforcement stimuli by adding the following lines of code:

```
Input(1,  vHeader)
Input(1,  vPos)
Input(1,  vHeader)
Input(1,  vNeg)
```

The code for the reinforcers is in place, but we still need to read in additional stimuli information. The vStimuli variable needs to hold four values and these values of vStimuli can correspond with the suffix values of the picM2S PictureBoxes for simplicity. Since we want all this information to load into the program immediately upon the form loading, and not wait for the participant to respond first, all this information must be inputted during the *form load*. To do so, just create a subroutine called *Load_Stimuli*. Do this by typing:

```
Sub Load_Stimuli()
```

A new subroutine will be created called *Load_Stimuli*. In this subroutine type:

```
Dim i
Input(1, vHeader)
Input(1, vStimuli(0))
Input(1, vStimuli(1))
Input(1, vStimuli(2))
Input(1, vStimuli(3))
For i = 0 To 3
picM2S0.Image = Image.FromFile("c:\programming\M2S\" &
    vStimuli(0) & ".bmp")
picM2S1.Image = Image.FromFile("c:\programming\M2S\" &
    vStimuli(1) & ".bmp")
picM2S2.Image = Image.FromFile("c:\programming\M2S\" &
    vStimuli(2) & ".bmp")
picM2S3.Image = Image.FromFile("c:\programming\M2S\" &
    vStimuli(3) & ".bmp")
Next i
```

The subroutine will read the stimuli values (A1, B1, etc.), append the file path to the beginning of the file name, and then add the file type (.bmp). The program then assigns the new values to the PictureBoxes using the For/Next statement. To have the program call on the subroutine, add the following code at the end of the Form_Load() Subroutine (before the *End Sub* of course):

```
Load_Stimuli
```

You may have noticed that as the program is currently designed, the correct response is always placed in the first position of the comparison row. This will be altered shortly. Also, note that in the case of our first trial, *B1* should be the correct response. However nothing happens when we click on *B1* just yet. We need to hook up the audio files. To do so add the Windows Media Player to frmM2S, set the Visible property to *False* and change the name to *wmp1*. Refer to Chapter 5 if you do not recall the specific steps for adding the Windows Media Player.

Double-click on one of the PictureBoxes to start a subroutine in edit mode. When the participant clicks on the PictureBox with the suffix value of 1 (the correct answer) we want the computer to play vPos. When the participant clicks in a PictureBox with the suffix value of 2 or 3, we want to play vNeg. We can accomplish this using an *If Then - Else* statement. Under the picM2S0_Click() subroutine type the following code:

```
Dim buttonClicked As PictureBox
buttonClicked = CType(sender, PictureBox)
```

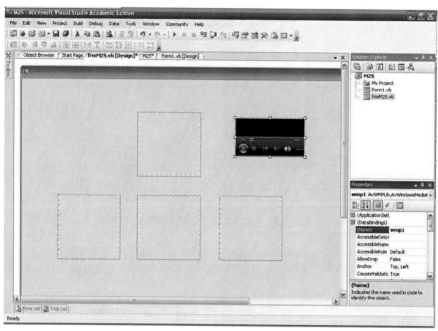

Figure 7.4 shows a screen configuration of the PictureBoxes and Windows Media Player.

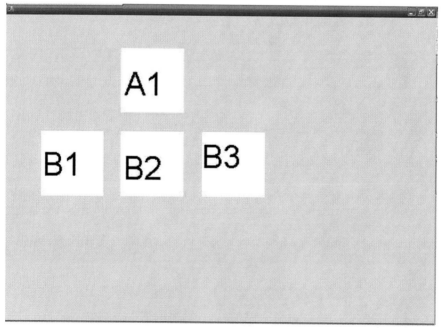

Figure 7.5 shows the PictureBoxes during runtime with stimuli loaded.

```
If buttonClicked.Name = picM2S1.Name() Then
wmp1.url = vPos
wmp1.Ctlcontrols.Play()
Else
If buttonClicked.Name = picM2S2.Name() Or
   buttonClicked.Name = picM2S3.Name Then
wmp1.url = vNeg
wmp1.Ctlcontrols.Play()
End If
End If
```

Here is how the code works. First this code keeps track of which Button was clicked using the buttonClicked variable and CType command. Once it stores the specific Button name (vM2S(0-3)) that was clicked, it checks to see which of the "If-Then-Else" conditions has been satisfied. If picM2S1 was clicked, it opens the Media Player and plays the positive .wav file we placed in the text file. If picM2S1 was not clicked, the code checks to see if either picM2S(2 or 3) was clicked. If so, the negative .wav file. If picM2S0 is clicked, nothing happens, which is good since, this is the sample stimulus.

Let's take this a step further. After we click on the comparison stimuli, we want the next trial to appear. To do this we just need to call on the Load_Stimuli() subroutine we created. Add the following line of code at to the end of both sections of the If-Then-Else code:

```
Load_Stimuli
```

The new subroutine should look like the following:

```
Dim buttonClicked As PictureBox
buttonClicked = CType(sender, PictureBox)
If buttonClicked.Name = picM2S1.Name() Then
wmp1.url = vPos
wmp1.Ctlcontrols.Play()
Load_Stimuli()
Else
If buttonClicked.Name = picM2S2.Name() Or buttonClicked.Name
   = picM2S3.Name Then
wmp1.url = vNeg
wmp1.Ctlcontrols.Play()
Load_Stimuli()
End If
End If
```

Run the program again. Notice that the stimuli changes after each response. We only have three lines of stimuli, thus the program ends abruptly because it has reached the end of the text file. This will be changed when we add more lines of stimuli configurations to the input file.

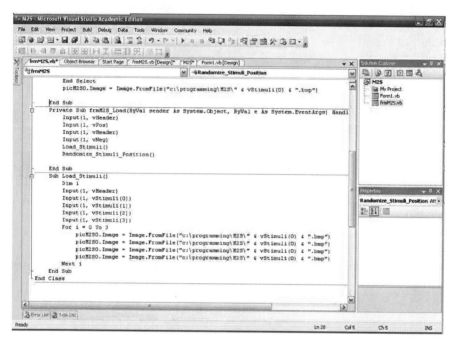

Figure 7.6 shows the code for loading the different trials into the M2S program.

We still haven't finished all of the requirements of #3 in the earlier outline, but we are making progress. The stimuli still need randomized placement across trials. This is rather easy because we know how to generate a random string of three numbers without replacement. So type the following anywhere in the text editor:

```
Sub Randomize_Stimuli_Position()
```

This will create a new subroutine called Randomize_Stimuli_Position. Under this new routine now type:

```
Randomize()
Dim r
r = Int(6 * Rnd() + 1)

Select Case r
```

```
Case 1
picM2S1.Image = Image.FromFile("c:\programming\M2S\" &
   vStimuli(1) & ".bmp")
picM2S2.Image = Image.FromFile("c:\programming\M2S\" &
   vStimuli(2) & ".bmp")
picM2S3.Image = Image.FromFile("c:\programming\M2S\" &
   vStimuli(3) & ".bmp")

Case 2
picM2S1.Image = Image.FromFile("c:\programming\M2S\" &
   vStimuli(3) & ".bmp")
picM2S2.Image = Image.FromFile("c:\programming\M2S\" &
   vStimuli(1) & ".bmp")
picM2S3.Image = Image.FromFile("c:\programming\M2S\" &
   vStimuli(2) & ".bmp")

Case 3
picM2S1.Image = Image.FromFile("c:\programming\M2S\" &
   vStimuli(2) & ".bmp")
picM2S2.Image = Image.FromFile("c:\programming\M2S\" &
   vStimuli(3) & ".bmp")
picM2S3.Image = Image.FromFile("c:\programming\M2S\" &
   vStimuli(1) & ".bmp")

Case 4
picM2S1.Image = Image.FromFile("c:\programming\M2S\" &
   vStimuli(1) & ".bmp")
picM2S2.Image = Image.FromFile("c:\programming\M2S\" &
   vStimuli(3) & ".bmp")
picM2S3.Image = Image.FromFile("c:\programming\M2S\" &
   vStimuli(2) & ".bmp")

Case 5
picM2S1.Image = Image.FromFile("c:\programming\M2S\" &
   vStimuli(3) & ".bmp")
picM2S2.Image = Image.FromFile("c:\programming\M2S\" &
   vStimuli(2) & ".bmp")
picM2S3.Image = Image.FromFile("c:\programming\M2S\" &
   vStimuli(1) & ".bmp")

Case 6
picM2S1.Image = Image.FromFile("c:\programming\M2S\" &
   vStimuli(2) & ".bmp")
```

```
picM2S2.Image = Image.FromFile("c:\programming\M2S\" &
    vStimuli(1) & ".bmp")
picM2S3.Image = Image.FromFile("c:\programming\M2S\" &
    vStimuli(3) & ".bmp")
End Select

picM2S0.Image = Image.FromFile("c:\programming\M2S\" &
    vStimuli(0) & ".bmp")
```

There are three parts to this subroutine. First, we use the Randomize statement to generate a string of random numbers to be used in during running of the program. Second, we declare the variable r to use to hold the random number we generate on each trial. Third, we generate a random number between 1 and 6. The reason for the 1 to 6 range is because there are 6 possible combinations of comparison stimuli arrangements. They are B1, B2, B3; B1, B3, B2; B2, B3, B1; B2, B1, B3; B3, B1, B2; and B3, B2, B1. Using the random number placed into the variable "r", we can create a Select Case statement to distribute the stimuli into their respective PictureBoxes. Because vStimuli(0) is always the sample, and our sample stimulus in the data file will always be listed first, we can just have one line of code that always puts vStimuli(0) into picM2S0 and not repeat it throughout each Select Case.

To link this subroutine up to the program, add the following text at the end of the Private Sub frmM2S_Load() (i.e. below Load_Stimuli()):

```
Randomize_Stimuli_Position()
```

Also place this code below the Load_Stimuli()line found in the two different locations the Private Sub picM2S0_Click subroutine. Placing the code here allows for a new random number and stimuli positioning to occur each time a comparison stimulus is clicked upon.

Run the program and check your progress.

Fixing One Problem Often Creates a New One

You may have noticed that now that you solved the randomization problem, you created another problem. The Media Player now plays vPos every time you click on picM2S1 regardless if this is the correct response or not. This is not good and will need to be fixed.

To fix this problem we need to create a variable that can be used to track where vStimuli(1) is no matter where our random number generator places it. Once we know where vStimuli(1) is, we can check to see if it is sitting in the PictureBox that the participant just clicked on. Two things need to happen here. First, we need to place a value in this new tracking variable when the stimuli are loaded into the PictureBoxes. Second, we need to edit the Media Player code to play the vPos .wav file only if our tracking variable is a specific value. Let us start by creating a new variable called vTrack. Declare this variable under the Public Class frmM2S section by typing:

```
Dim vTrack
```

Add the following line of code at the end of the Select Case 1 section of the Randomize_Stimuli_Position()subroutine:

```
vTrack = 1
```

This code will inform Visual Basic 2005 that vStimuli(1) is sitting in the first comparison position (i.e. picM2S1). The new Select Case 1 section of code should look like:

```
Case 1
picM2S1.Image = Image.FromFile("c:\programming\M2S\" &
    vStimuli(1) & ".bmp")
picM2S2.Image = Image.FromFile("c:\programming\M2S\" &
    vStimuli(2) & ".bmp")
picM2S3.Image = Image.FromFile("c:\programming\M2S\" &
    vStimuli(3) & ".bmp")
vTrack = 1
```

Add the following line of code at the end of the Select Case 2 section of the Randomize_Stimuli_Position()subroutine:

```
vTrack = 2
```

Add the following line of code at the end of the Select Case 3 section of the Randomize_Stimuli_Position()subroutine:

```
vTrack = 3
```

Add the following line of code at the end of the Select Case 4 section of the Randomize_Stimuli_Position()subroutine:

```
vTrack = 1
```

Add the following line of code at the end of the Select Case 5 section of the Randomize_Stimuli_Position()subroutine:

```
vTrack = 3
```

Add the following line of code at the end of the Select Case 6 section of the Randomize_Stimuli_Position()subroutine:

```
vTrack = 2
```

The logic should be easy to follow by this time. Now the code to kick in the Media Player needs to be altered. Begin by editing the line of code which currently states:

```
If buttonClicked.Name = picM2S1.Name Then
```

to read

```
If buttonClicked.Name = picM2S1.Name And vTrack = 1 Or
    buttonClicked.Name = picM2S2.Name And vTrack = 2 Or
    buttonClicked.Name = picM2S3.Name And vTrack = 3 Then
```

This is all one long line of code but it is not as scary as it might seem. This code is nothing more than a giant If-Then statement that can be satisfied in three different ways. Because this statement takes care of playing the vPos .wav file if the conditions are satisfied, anything else should kick in the vNeg .wav file. Therefore, delete the line of code which currently states:

```
If buttonClicked.Name = picM2S2.Name Or buttonClicked.Name
    = picM2S3.Name Then
```

and the corresponding *End If*.

One last problem that has now arisen is that without this line of code, clicks on picM2S0 (the sample stimulus) can kick in the next trial. We do not want this to happen. Actually we never want anything to happen when a participant clicks on picM2S0. To remove anything ever occurring when picM2S0 is clicked, simply remove the section of code:

```
picM2S0.Click
```

from the first line of the Private Sub picM2S0_Subroutine. The edited first line of this subroutine should now read:

```
Private Sub picM2S0_Click(ByVal sender As System.Object,
ByVal e As System.EventArgs) Handles picM2S1.Click,
picM2S2.Click, picM2S3.Click
```

Run the program and check your progress. Everything should work fine up to this point. As a matter of fact, as the program stands, you have a working conditional discrimination computer program.

A "Debriefing" Form

Once you finish the three trials the program ends abruptly. This is because we are not taking advantage of the END,,,, command in the text file. Let's make it so that when the program reads the END,,,, command it shows a final form with some debriefing information. Add a new form, change the name property to frmIns2, change the text property to *Thank You*, and change the WindowState to maximized. Add the following text below the "Input(1, vStimuli(3))" line in the Load_Stimuli() subroutine on frmM2S:

```
If vHeader = "END" Then
Dim x As New frmIns2()
x.Show()
Me.Close()
Else
```

Add the following line after the "Next i" line in that same subroutine:

```
End If
```

and delete the automatically added *End If* that was inserted above *For i=0 to 3*. Also edit your M2S.txt file so the last line reads:

```
END, A1,A1,A1,A1
```

The entire Load_Stimuli () subroutine should look as follows:

```
Dim i
Input(1, vHeader)
Input(1, vStimuli(0))
Input(1, vStimuli(1))
Input(1, vStimuli(2))
Input(1, vStimuli(3))
If vHeader = "END" Then
Dim x As New frmIns2()
x.Show()
Me.Close()
Else
For i = 0 To 3
picM2S0.Image = Image.FromFile("c:\programming\M2S\" &
    vStimuli(0) & ".bmp")
picM2S1.Image = Image.FromFile("c:\programming\M2S\" &
    vStimuli(1) & ".bmp")
```

```
picM2S2.Image = Image.FromFile("c:\programming\M2S\" &
    vStimuli(2) & ".bmp")
picM2S3.Image = Image.FromFile("c:\programming\M2S\" &
    vStimuli(3) & ".bmp")
Next i
End If
```

The commas served us well earlier, but now we need to put actual stimuli in these place holders to avoid getting an error when we run the program. This is just another little picky aspect of Visual Basic 2005. While the A1 stimuli are never actually seen by the participant (or you while you test the program), they need to be "virtually" placed into the Load_Stimuli () subroutine before frmM2S can shut itself down (i.e. Hide). You can try running the program without the four A1s just for fun to see the error that would occur.

So far we have developed the program to read instructions and present them to the participant. Open .wav files and play them differentially for correct or incorrect responses. Read in stimuli trials and randomize placement of the comparison stimuli, and display an instruction screen when the trials have been complete.

Requirement #3 specifies that each sample is presented 6 times, a total of 18 trials. As with most of the programming decisions, there are several ways to accomplish this requirement. For now let's just enter all 18 trials by cutting the three existing trials in M2S.txt and pasting them back in 5 times. Obviously you could make different arrangements of trial sequences, but just stick to this cut and paste method now for illustrative purposes. Change the number in the TRIAL header to increment up to 18. Save the changes to the text file. Your text file should now look like this:

```
INSTRUCTIONS, This is where the instructions will go.
CORRECT, "c:\windows\media\chimes.wav"
INCORRECT, "c:\windows\media\chord.wav"
TRIAL1,  A1,B1,B2,B3
TRIAL2,  A2,B2,B1,B3
TRIAL3,  A3,B3,B1,B2
TRIAL4,  A1,B1,B2,B3
TRIAL5,  A2,B2,B1,B3
TRIAL6,  A3,B3,B1,B2
TRIAL7,  A1,B1,B2,B3
TRIAL8,  A2,B2,B1,B3
TRIAL9,  A3,B3,B1,B2
TRIAL10, ·A1,B1,B2,B3
TRIAL11, A2,B2,B1,B3
TRIAL12, A3,B3,B1,B2
TRIAL13, A1,B1,B2,B3
```

```
TRIAL14, A2,B2,B1,B3
TRIAL15, A3,B3,B1,B2
TRIAL16, A1,B1,B2,B3
TRIAL17, A2,B2,B1,B3
TRIAL18, A3,B3,B1,B2
END, A1,A1,A1,A1
```

```
Untitled - Notepad
File Edit Format View Help
INSTRUCTIONS, "This is where the instructions will go."
CORRECT, "c:\windows\media\chimes.wav"
INCORRECT, "c:\windows\media\chord.wav"
TRIAL1, A1,B1,B2,B3
TRIAL2, A2,B2,B1,B3
TRIAL3, A3,B3,B1,B2
TRIAL4, A1,B1,B2,B3
TRIAL5, A2,B2,B1,B3
TRIAL6, A3,B3,B1,B2
TRIAL7, A1,B1,B2,B3
TRIAL8, A2,B2,B1,B3
TRIAL9, A3,B3,B1,B2
TRIAL10, A1,B1,B2,B3
TRIAL11, A2,B2,B1,B3
TRIAL12, A3,B3,B1,B2
TRIAL13, A1,B1,B2,B3
TRIAL14, A2,B2,B1,B3
TRIAL15, A3,B3,B1,B2
TRIAL16, A1,B1,B2,B3
TRIAL17, A2,B2,B1,B3
TRIAL18, A1,B3,B1,B2
End, A1,A3,A1,A1

                                                            Ln 21, Col 21
```

Figure 7.7 displays the Notepad document with all 18 trials.

Try running the program and see if it goes through all 18 trials. As you may have guessed, you could enter as many trials as you wanted. The program will continue to display the stimuli until it reaches the END,,,, command.

Keep in mind that we wanted to randomize the presentation of the trials each time the program runs. Right now the trials are being presented in the order that we wrote them in the input file. While randomization may be important here, other times when you may be assessing behavior across a sequence of specific contingency arrangements the existing code would do fine. Randomization of these trials can be a bit tricky, but we know how to make a random string of number between 1 and 18. We also know about variable arrays and how they can hold multiple amounts of information.

Basically we need to create something programmers often call a "lookup table" for our stimuli trials. For example, once we generate a random string of numbers from 1 to 18 (that correspond to our trial types), we can look at the first number and then display the stimuli in that particular row. So if the first number was 7, then we would display the stimuli listed in TRIAL7 of our data input file. If the random number generated was 11, we would display the stimuli listed in TRIAL 11, and so on.

What would be useful here is something called a two dimensional array. VB 2005 has the capability to use multidimensional arrays, but they are difficult keep track of, therefore we recommend using a two dimensional array and only when needed. The two dimensional array can be read like a spreadsheet that has rows listed from 0 to 17 and columns listed from 0 to 3.

We will also need to modify our code by declaring a two dimensional array to hold the trial information. Then we need to have VB 2005 read in the information from the text file stopping at the END,,,, command. Also, we need to create a random string of numbers from 1 to 18 including a one dimensional array to hold these values. Lastly we will need a third variable to keep track of the trial we are on. Once all 18 trials have been displayed, the program needs to end or goes on to the next task.

Before we begin changing all this code in our M2S project, let's write a pilot program to see how this works. Creating small little side programs like this are helpful because they allow you to test new routines as well as not disrupt the existing and so far correctly working main program. When creating larger scale programs, the last thing you want to do is find out that the past five hours of programming does not work correctly, and you can not remember how to get back to the point that did work five hours ago.

Save your current project and open a new one called *Pilot*. Rename the form to *frmPilot* and change the location of the files to C:\programming. Change the Text property to *Pilot*, and change the WindowState to Maximized. Add a Label to frmPilot. Change the name and Text property to *lblPilot*, and the BorderStyle to *FixedSingle*. Copy and paste lblPilot to create the array. We need an array of 4, so paste the Label 3 times. Double-click on the first of your Labels, enter the Edit mode and add `Label1.Click`, `Label2.click`, `Label3.click` after `Handles lblPilot.click` as detailed earlier in this chapter for picM2S0-3. We will also need a Button to advance the trials. Add a Button to frmPilot, change the name property to *butNext*, and the Text property to *Next*. That should do it. Code is also needed to open the file and advance the trials. Then we need to read the trial information into a two dimensional array, and create a random string of numbers. This all has to happen before the form appears, so it needs be located in the Form_Load() subroutine.

But before we get there, let's declare the necessary variables. As mentioned earlier, a two dimensional array is needed to hold the trial information, Dim vTrials((18),(3)). Also a one dimensional array is needed to hold the random number string: Dim vRandNumber(18) As Integer, and we will need a variable to keep track of the actual trial number: Dim vCounter As Integer. Place all of this under the Public Class frmPilot statement by typing the following code:

```
Dim vTrials((18), (3))
Dim vRandNumber(18) As Integer
Dim vCounter As Integer
```

Now under the Form_Load() subroutine you will need to declare a couple of variables we will be using and add some code to open the text file. Go back to the frmPilot design window, double-click on the form, enter the edit mode and type the following after Private Sub frmPilot_Load()

```
Dim i, r, x, y
FileOpen(1, "C:\programming\M2S\M2S.txt", OpenMode.Input)
```

There are three rows of information we are not currently interested in, specifically that code pertaining to the instructions and the two .wav files. We can advance past these by entering the following code under the last line you typed:

```
For i = 1 To 3
Input (1, x)
Input (1, y)
Next i
```

Also, go back and edit your M2S.txt file so that the INSTRUCTIONS line only has 1 word ("This") after the word INSTRUCTIONS. You can change back your instructions to "This is where the instructions will go." later after finishing this little side Pilot project.

We now need to read in the next 18 lines containing trial information. We don't want to read in the header, so we will use the *x* variable as a place holder.

```
For i = 1 To 18
Input(1, x)
Input(1, vTrials(i, 0))
Input(1, vTrials(i, 1))
Input(1, vTrials(i, 2))
Input(1, vTrials(i, 3))
Next i
```

Finally, we need to generate our random numbers using the following code:

```
Randomize()
For i = 1 To 18
r = Int(18 * Rnd() + 1)
If vRandNumber(r) < 1 Then
vRandNumber(r) = i
Else
```

```
i = i - 1
End If
Next i
```

You may recall that this is the same type of randomization routine we explained in an earlier section of the book. The completed Form_Load() subroutine should look like this:

```
Dim i, r, x, y
FileOpen(1, "C:\programming\M2S\M2S.txt", OpenMode.Input)
For i = 1 To 3
Input(1, x)
Input(1, y)
Next i
For i = 1 To 18
Input(1, x)
Input(1, vTrials(i, 0))
Input(1, vTrials(i, 1))
Input(1, vTrials(i, 2))
Input(1, vTrials(i, 3))
Next i
Randomize()
For i = 1 To 18
r = Int(18 * Rnd() + 1)
If vRandNumber(r) < 1 Then
vRandNumber(r) = i
Else
i = i - 1
End If
Next i
```

Both arrays should now be loaded. Run the program and see if you have any errors. Nothing will happen if you click on the *Next* Button because we have yet to add some code. But the absence of errors means you have typed in the above code properly.

Stop the program and double-click on butNext to enter edit mode at the butNext_Click() subroutine. When we click on butNext, we can use an IF statement to ensure we don't advance past the 18th trial, as well as keep track of the trial number. We can also watch the trials advance using me.Text = vCounter. Add the following four lines of code under *butNext* to load the trial information in the Labels:

```
If vCounter < 18 Then
vCounter = vCounter + 1
```

Figure 7.8 shows the code for frmPilot.

```
me.Text = vCounter
lblPilot.Text = vTrials(vCounter, 0)
Label1.Text = vTrials(vCounter, 1)
Label2.Text = vTrials(vCounter, 2)
Label3.Text = vTrials(vCounter, 3)
End If
```

Run the program and see if it works. Notice that the trials are not yet randomized. To do this we need to make a small modification to the Label objects' vTrials(vCounter, 0) code. Specifically it needs to include our random number. Therefore, change the code to look like this:

```
If vCounter < 18 Then
vCounter = vCounter + 1
Me.Text = vCounter
lblPilot.Text = vTrials(vRandNumber(vCounter), 0)
Label1.Text = vTrials(vRandNumber(vCounter), 1)
Label2.Text = vTrials(vRandNumber(vCounter), 2)
Label3.Text = vTrials(vRandNumber(vCounter), 3)
End If
```

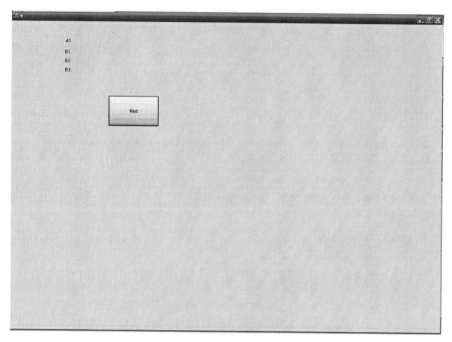

Figure 7.9 displays the Pilot program during runtime.

The trials should now be randomized because we are using the array with the random numbers to indicate which trial stimuli to use. It should work fine.

Now let's transplant the code back into the M2S project. Save the Pilot project and open the M2S project. Locate your mouse cursor in the Solution Explorer on the upper right of the screen, highlight M2S, and right-click to display the pop-up menu. Select *Add*, then *Add Existing Item*. Now select frmPilot from the Pilot directory. Note: Your frmPilot may still say *Form1*, depending on how you saved it initially. If it does still say *Form1* (you can check when the Pilot project is still open by looking in the Solution Explorer) you must first, reclose the M2S project, go back, open Pilot project and save frmPilot correctly. This will add the form to your project so you can copy and paste code as needed. We need to copy the code under the Form_Load() subroutine from frmPilot to frmM2S. The Form_Load() code in frmM2S is getting rather busy. We can make a subroutine with the code from frmPilot and then simply run the subroutine from the Form_Load() subroutine of M2S.

To start a subroutine, double-click on frmM2S to enter edit mode, move the mouse to the last line of the editor (before *End Class*), and type:

```
Sub Load_Random_Trials
```

Press the return key if you have not already done so. VB 2005 will make the subroutine for you. Copy and paste the code written in frmPilot under the Form_Load() subroutine into the Load_Random_Trials() subroutine. Now type the following below the Load_Stimuli code in frmM2S_Load() subroutine:

```
Load_Random_Trials
```

Remember that there was a For/Next statement in frmPilot to advance past the first three lines in the text file. This is no longer needed in the frmM2S project, so remark out the following four lines using the ':

```
'FileOpen(1, "C:\programming\M2S\M2S.txt", OpenMode.Input)
'For i = 1 To 3
'Input(1, x)
'Input(1, y)
'Next i
```

Now copy and paste all the code from under frmPilot's butNext to a new sub routine on frmM2S. Create this new subroutine by typing the following on the last line of the editor (before *End Class*):

```
Sub Show_Rand_Stim
```

Now place the code here. First, copy the code from frmPilot under butNext to this new subroutine. Next, move the vCounter = vCounter + 1 statement from the middle of the subroutine to the beginning of the subroutine. The subroutine should look like this:

```
Sub Show_Rand_Stim()
vCounter = vCounter + 1
If vCounter < 18 Then
Me.Text = vCounter
lblPilot.Text = vTrials(vRandNumber(vCounter), 0)
Label1.Text = vTrials(vRandNumber(vCounter), 1)
Label2.Text = vTrials(vRandNumber(vCounter), 2)
Label3.Text = vTrials(vRandNumber(vCounter), 3)
End If
End Sub
```

Next the program will need to read the trial information into the PictureBoxes and not the labels used when we built the little side program on frmPilot. Plus we will need to declare the variable vTrials that we used on frmPilot now on our frmM2S. First, copy the variables declared under Public Class in frmPilot to Public

Class in frmM2S. Since the two dimensional array (vTrials(18),(3)) will be replacing
the one dimensional array (vStimuli(3)), remark out the Dim vStimuli(3) by placing
an apostrophe before the line of code. Your new variable declarations on your
frmM2S should now look like this:

```
Dim vTrack
Dim vHeader As String
Dim vPos As String
Dim vNeg As String
'Dim vStimuli(3) As String
Dim vTrials((18),(3))
Dim vRandNumber(18) As Integer
Dim vCounter As Integer
```

Second, edit your Label code so that the data can be read into the PictureBoxes
instead. As your code currently stands, you have a Select Case that is being used to
generate random numbers for the random placement of comparison stimuli in
picM2S1-3, as well as the two dimensional array that holds and displays random
trials. You will be able to control for order and positioning effects of the comparison
stimuli by merging these two components together: the random trial presentations
coupled with random positioning of the comparison stimuli. To accomplish this
feat we need to change the stimuli presentation code under the Select Case. What
we can use here is the code from frmPilot's butNext Button that now resides in a
subroutine called Show_Rand_Stim. Let's combine the two by changing the code
under your Select Case statements to read the like the following:

```
Case 1
picM2S0.Image = Image.FromFile("c:\programming\M2S\" &
    vTrials(vRandNumber(vCounter), 0) & ".bmp")
picM2S1.Image = Image.FromFile("c:\programming\M2S\" &
    vTrials(vRandNumber(vCounter), 1) & ".bmp")
picM2S2.Image = Image.FromFile("c:\programming\M2S\" &
    vTrials(vRandNumber(vCounter), 2) & ".bmp")
picM2S3.Image = Image.FromFile("c:\programming\M2S\" &
    vTrials(vRandNumber(vCounter), 3) & ".bmp")
vTrack = 1
```

You should be able to see what we did here was replace the previous picM2S0-
3 = code that specified a specific stimulus from our recently deceased "vStimuli"
variable and replaced it with code that now specifies a stimulus that is selected
using our vRandNumber, vTrials, and vCounter variables we created on frmPilot.
Edit the remaining 5 Cases of this subroutine so that the entire subroutine looks
as follows:

```
Sub Randomize_Stimuli_Position()
Randomize()
Dim r
r = Int(6 * Rnd() + 1)

Select Case r
Case 1
picM2S0.Image = Image.FromFile("c:\programming\M2S\" &
    vTrials(vRandNumber(vCounter), 0) & ".bmp")
picM2S1.Image = Image.FromFile("c:\programming\M2S\" &
    vTrials(vRandNumber(vCounter), 1) & ".bmp")
picM2S2.Image = Image.FromFile("c:\programming\M2S\" &
    vTrials(vRandNumber(vCounter), 2) & ".bmp")
picM2S3.Image = Image.FromFile("c:\programming\M2S\" &
    vTrials(vRandNumber(vCounter), 3) & ".bmp")
vTrack = 1
Case 2
picM2S0.Image = Image.FromFile("c:\programming\M2S\" &
    vTrials(vRandNumber(vCounter), 0) & ".bmp")
picM2S1.Image = Image.FromFile("c:\programming\M2S\" &
    vTrials(vRandNumber(vCounter), 2) & ".bmp")
picM2S2.Image = Image.FromFile("c:\programming\M2S\" &
    vTrials(vRandNumber(vCounter), 1) & ".bmp")
picM2S3.Image = Image.FromFile("c:\programming\M2S\" &
    vTrials(vRandNumber(vCounter), 3) & ".bmp")
vTrack = 2
Case 3
picM2S0.Image = Image.FromFile("c:\programming\M2S\" &
    vTrials(vRandNumber(vCounter), 0) & ".bmp")
picM2S1.Image = Image.FromFile("c:\programming\M2S\" &
    vTrials(vRandNumber(vCounter), 3) & ".bmp")
picM2S2.Image = Image.FromFile("c:\programming\M2S\" &
    vTrials(vRandNumber(vCounter), 2) & ".bmp")
picM2S3.Image = Image.FromFile("c:\programming\M2S\" &
    vTrials(vRandNumber(vCounter), 1) & ".bmp")
vTrack = 3
Case 4
picM2S0.Image = Image.FromFile("c:\programming\M2S\" &
    vTrials(vRandNumber(vCounter), 0) & ".bmp")
picM2S1.Image = Image.FromFile("c:\programming\M2S\" &
    vTrials(vRandNumber(vCounter), 1) & ".bmp")
picM2S2.Image = Image.FromFile("c:\programming\M2S\" &
    vTrials(vRandNumber(vCounter), 3) & ".bmp")
```

```
picM2S3.Image = Image.FromFile("c:\programming\M2S\" &
    vTrials(vRandNumber(vCounter), 2) & ".bmp")
vTrack = 1
Case 5
picM2S0.Image = Image.FromFile("c:\programming\M2S\" &
    vTrials(vRandNumber(vCounter), 0) & ".bmp")
picM2S1.Image = Image.FromFile("c:\programming\M2S\" &
    vTrials(vRandNumber(vCounter), 2) & ".bmp")
picM2S2.Image = Image.FromFile("c:\programming\M2S\" &
    vTrials(vRandNumber(vCounter), 3) & ".bmp")
picM2S3.Image = Image.FromFile("c:\programming\M2S\" &
    vTrials(vRandNumber(vCounter), 1) & ".bmp")
vTrack = 3
Case 6
picM2S0.Image = Image.FromFile("c:\programming\M2S\" &
    vTrials(vRandNumber(vCounter), 0) & ".bmp")
picM2S1.Image = Image.FromFile("c:\programming\M2S\" &
    vTrials(vRandNumber(vCounter), 3) & ".bmp")
picM2S2.Image = Image.FromFile("c:\programming\M2S\" &
    vTrials(vRandNumber(vCounter), 1) & ".bmp")
picM2S3.Image = Image.FromFile("c:\programming\M2S\" &
    vTrials(vRandNumber(vCounter), 2) & ".bmp")
vTrack = 2
End Select
'picM2S0.Image.FromFile("c:\programming\M2S\" & vStimuli(0)
& ".bmp")
```

Now that we have capitalized on the code image location code used in Show_Rand_Stim, we can delete the following four lines and the If-Then statement:

```
lblPilot.Text = vTrials(vRandNumber(vCounter), 0)
Label1.Text = vTrials(vRandNumber(vCounter), 1)
Label2.Text = vTrials(vRandNumber(vCounter), 2)
Label3.Text = vTrials(vRandNumber(vCounter), 3)
```

We will no longer need the line of code used to display the trial count in the Text of frmPilot: me.Text=vCounter so delete that too. All that should now remain in Show_Rand_Stim is: vCounter = vCounter + 1. Because we want to activate the Show_Rand_Stim subroutine when the form loads and when the participant clicks on the PictureBox, add that line of code in both subroutines. In other words, add the following code BOTH in the Private Sub frmM2S_Load() and two places in Private Sub picM2S0_Click subroutine. Make sure you position this code between the Load_Stimuli() and the Randomize_Stimuli_Presentation() code in each location:

```
Show_Rand_Stim
```

Again, make sure the above code is positioned above Randomize_Stimuli_Presentation() and below the Load_Stimuli() lines.

Because we reconfigured the code to generate the presentation of stimuli in random order, you do not need the form to use the Load_Stimuli subroutine anymore. That subroutine would only load trials in the order they were written in the file. Therefore, delete that entire subroutine along with the Load_Stimuli code written under Private Sub frmM2S_Load() and Private Sub picM2S0_Click(). You could simply just remark out the above code too and get the same result.

One last revision needs to be made before we run the program and check to see if this big change actually will work. Now that the correct comparison stimulus is randomized, it does not always wind up being presented in picM2S1. Our code for playing our "reinforcing" .wav file assumes that it does. Therefore change the two lines of code which checks to see which picM2S Button has been clicked along with which vTrack value was generated by our Select Case to:

```
If buttonClicked.Name = picM2S1.Name() And vTrack = 1 Or
    buttonClicked.Name = picM2S2.Name() And vTrack = 2
    Or buttonClicked.Name = picM2S3.Name And vTrack = 3
    Then
```

and

```
Else
If buttonClicked.Name = picM2S2.Name() Or buttonClicked.Name
    = picM2S1.Name() Or buttonClicked.Name = picM2S3.Name
    Then
```

Add a final "End If" at the bottom of the subroutine.Run the program. That should take care of requirement #3 (Finally!). The resulting code of your frmM2S form should read as follows:

```
Option Explicit On
Public Class frmM2S
Inherits System.Windows.Forms.Form
Dim vTrack
Dim vHeader As String
Dim vPos As String
Dim vNeg As String
'Dim vStimuli(3) As String
Dim vTrials((18), (3))
Dim vRandNumber(18) As Integer
Dim vCounter As Integer
```

```
Private Sub picM2SO_Click(ByVal sender As System.Object,
    ByVal e As System.EventArgs) Handles picM2S1.Click,
    picM2S2.Click, picM2S3.Click
Dim buttonClicked As PictureBox
buttonClicked = CType(sender, PictureBox)
If buttonClicked.Name = picM2S1.Name() And vTrack = 1 Or
    buttonClicked.Name = picM2S2.Name() And vTrack = 2 Or
    buttonClicked.Name = picM2S3.Name And vTrack = 3 Then
wmp1.url = vPos
wmp1.Ctlcontrols.Play()
'Load_Stimuli()
Show_Rand_Stim()
Randomize_Stimuli_Position()
Else
If buttonClicked.Name = picM2S2.Name() Or buttonClicked.Name
    = picM2S1.Name() Or buttonClicked.Name = picM2S3.Name
    Then
wmp1.url = vNeg
wmp1.Ctlcontrols.Play()
'Load_Stimuli()
Show_Rand_Stim()
Randomize_Stimuli_Position()
End If
End If
End Sub


Private Sub frmM2S_Load(ByVal sender As System.Object,
    ByVal e As System.EventArgs) Handles MyBase.Load
Input(1, vHeader)
Input(1, vPos)
Input(1, vHeader)
Input(1, vNeg)
'Load_Stimuli()
Load_Random_Trials()
Show_Rand_Stim()
Randomize_Stimuli_Position()
End Sub

Sub Randomize_Stimuli_Position()
Randomize()
Dim r
r = Int(6 * Rnd() + 1)
```

```
Select Case r
Case 1
picM2S0.Image = Image.FromFile("c:\programming\M2S\" &
    vTrials(vRandNumber(vCounter), 0) & ".bmp")
picM2S1.Image = Image.FromFile("c:\programming\M2S\" &
    vTrials(vRandNumber(vCounter), 1) & ".bmp")
picM2S2.Image = Image.FromFile("c:\programming\M2S\" &
    vTrials(vRandNumber(vCounter), 2) & ".bmp")
picM2S3.Image = Image.FromFile("c:\programming\M2S\" &
    vTrials(vRandNumber(vCounter), 3) & ".bmp")
vTrack = 1
Case 2
picM2S0.Image = Image.FromFile("c:\programming\M2S\" &
    vTrials(vRandNumber(vCounter), 0) & ".bmp")
picM2S1.Image = Image.FromFile("c:\programming\M2S\" &
    vTrials(vRandNumber(vCounter), 2) & ".bmp")
picM2S2.Image = Image.FromFile("c:\programming\M2S\" &
    vTrials(vRandNumber(vCounter), 1) & ".bmp")
picM2S3.Image = Image.FromFile("c:\programming\M2S\" &
    vTrials(vRandNumber(vCounter), 3) & ".bmp")
vTrack = 2
Case 3
picM2S0.Image = Image.FromFile("c:\programming\M2S\" &
    vTrials(vRandNumber(vCounter), 0) & ".bmp")
picM2S1.Image = Image.FromFile("c:\programming\M2S\" &
    vTrials(vRandNumber(vCounter), 3) & ".bmp")
picM2S2.Image = Image.FromFile("c:\programming\M2S\" &
    vTrials(vRandNumber(vCounter), 2) & ".bmp")
picM2S3.Image = Image.FromFile("c:\programming\M2S\" &
    vTrials(vRandNumber(vCounter), 1) & ".bmp")
vTrack = 3
Case 4
picM2S0.Image = Image.FromFile("c:\programming\M2S\" &
    vTrials(vRandNumber(vCounter), 0) & ".bmp")
picM2S1.Image = Image.FromFile("c:\programming\M2S\" &
    vTrials(vRandNumber(vCounter), 1) & ".bmp")
picM2S2.Image = Image.FromFile("c:\programming\M2S\" &
    vTrials(vRandNumber(vCounter), 3) & ".bmp")
picM2S3.Image = Image.FromFile("c:\programming\M2S\" &
    vTrials(vRandNumber(vCounter), 2) & ".bmp")
vTrack = 1
```

```
Case 5
picM2S0.Image = Image.FromFile("c:\programming\M2S\" &
    vTrials(vRandNumber(vCounter), 0) & ".bmp")
picM2S1.Image = Image.FromFile("c:\programming\M2S\" &
    vTrials(vRandNumber(vCounter), 2) & ".bmp")
picM2S2.Image = Image.FromFile("c:\programming\M2S\" &
    vTrials(vRandNumber(vCounter), 3) & ".bmp")
picM2S3.Image = Image.FromFile("c:\programming\M2S\" &
    vTrials(vRandNumber(vCounter), 1) & ".bmp")
vTrack = 3
Case 6
picM2S0.Image = Image.FromFile("c:\programming\M2S\" &
    vTrials(vRandNumber(vCounter), 0) & ".bmp")
picM2S1.Image = Image.FromFile("c:\programming\M2S\" &
    vTrials(vRandNumber(vCounter), 3) & ".bmp")
picM2S2.Image = Image.FromFile("c:\programming\M2S\" &
    vTrials(vRandNumber(vCounter), 1) & ".bmp")
picM2S3.Image = Image.FromFile("c:\programming\M2S\" &
    vTrials(vRandNumber(vCounter), 2) & ".bmp")
vTrack = 2
End Select
'picM2S0.Image.FromFile("c:\programming\M2S\" & vStimuli(0)
    & ".bmp")
End Sub

Sub Load_Random_Trials()
Dim i, r, x, y
'FileOpen(1, "C:\programming\M2S\M2S.txt", OpenMode.Input)
'For i = 1 To 3
'Input(1, x)
'Input(1, y)
'Next i
For i = 1 To 18
Input(1, x)
Input(1, vTrials(i, 0))
Input(1, vTrials(i, 1))
Input(1, vTrials(i, 2))
Input(1, vTrials(i, 3))
Next i
Randomize()
For i = 1 To 18
r = Int(18 * Rnd() + 1)
If vRandNumber(r) < 1 Then
```

```
vRandNumber(r) = i
Else
i = i - 1
End If
Next i
End Sub

Sub Show_Rand_Stim()
vCounter = vCounter + 1
End Sub
```

All should run just fine, except for when you finish trial 18. We deleted our code that closes frmM2S and shows frmIns2. Add the following code at the beginning of the Randomize_Stimuli_Position() subroutine (above the Select Case) to correct the problem:

```
If vCounter > 18 Then
Dim x As New frmIns2()
Me.Hide()
x.Show()
Else
```

Delete the automatically added *End If* that was inserted after *Else* and add the line:

```
End If
```

at the bottom of the subroutine (after "End Select" and before "End Sub").

4. Mastery Criterion

You may recall that requirement 4 of the outline stated that a criterion must be met by the participant before the program should advance to the next phase (A-C training). Specifically 16 out of 18 trials of A-B training must be correct. We can add a great degree of flexibility to the program if we allow a line in the text file to enable the user to change this criterion across participants or experiments. Open your M2S.txt file using Notepad or another text editor and just before the line beginning TRIAL1, and just below the INCORRECT, insert a new line and add:

```
CRITERION, 16
```

Also, retype your instructions in the first line.

Save the changes and close the text file. Declare a new variable to store the criterion value: something like vCriterion As Integer, as well as add code to read in the criterion just below the second input statement under the Form_Load() subroutine. Therefore, in the declarations of your frmM2S, add:

```
Dim vCriterion As Integer
```

And under the Sub Form Load() after the line Input(1, vNeg) add the following:

```
Input (1, vHeader)
Input (1, vCriterion)
```

Now that the criterion is stored in the computer, the computer needs a way to check and see if the criterion is met. For this we will have to create another variable that holds the number of correct responses made for each trial. Let's name it *vCorrect*. At the end of the trial, the program compares the value in vCriterion with vCorrect. And if vCriterion is greater than vCorrect (If vCriterion > vCorrect then) then it will go on to the next phase, otherwise it will repeat the phase.

Therefore add to the general declaration the following code:

```
Dim vCorrect As Integer
```

We will have to add a line of code within the existing subroutine that plays the positive .wav file so it also makes increments of vCorrect increase by 1. We can also monitor the number of correct responses during programming by writing the value of vCorrect to the Text of frmM2S. Therefore add the following code under the wp1.url = vPos, wp1.Play() portion and above the Show_Rand_Stim() portion of Private Sub picM2S0_Click:

```
vCorrect = vCorrect + 1
me.Text = vCorrect
```

Now we need to add code into the Randomize_Stimuli_Position subroutine to either repeat the previous phase or advance to the next one.
Edit the first section of the subroutine so that it appears like:

```
If vCounter > 18 Then
If vCriterion < vCorrect Then 'ADDED NOW
Dim x As New frmIns2()
Me.Hide()
x.Show()
Else 'ADDED NOW
Start_Over_Again()'ADDED NOW
End If 'ADDED NOW
Else
Randomize()
```

The modifications are placed in the subroutine that is already checking to see if the phase is over (*If vCounter > 18 Then*). Thus if the condition is met (i.e. vCounter is greater than 18) the program checks to see if the performance criterion has been met using a "Nested IF/ELSE statement." If the criterion is less than the number of correct responses then the computer proceeds. In this case it displays frmIns2 which thanks the participant. However, if the criterion is NOT met, the participant has to start the phase over again.

Starting over again is not too difficult. We already have several subroutines in place that we can recycle. We will just have to reinitialize (set back to zero) some of our variables. Let's begin by writing a new subroutine called Start_Over_Again. So, type, Sub Start_Over_Again() on the last line in the editor before *End Class*. Then type the following code within that subroutine:

```
Dim i, r
For i = 1 To 18
vRandNumber(i) = 0
Next i
vCounter = 0
vCorrect = 0
For i = 1 To 18
r = Int(18 * Rnd + 1)
If vRandNumber(r) < 1 Then
vRandNumber(r) = i
Else
i = i - 1
End If
Next i
```

Delete any automatically entered code including extra "End If" or "Next".

Run the program and try to click on all of the correct comparison stimuli. The caption bar should count up to 18 and the program will show the final instruction form. Now run the program again and miss 1 of the comparisons. The frmM2S text should count up to 17 and then show the final instruction form. So far we have met criterion. Let's run the program and miss two correct responses.

After running the program you may decide that it would be nice to have a Button on frmIns2 that closes the program. Add a Button named *butEnd*, change the Text to *End*, and type the following under the Private Sub butEnd_Click() subroutine:

```
Close
End
```

The *Close* command will close any existing file, and the *End* command will terminate the program. Also you may have noticed that the Text with the variable information only refreshes when a correct response is made. Go to the picM2S0_Click subroutine, delete the line: me.Text=vCorrect. Then add the following line directly above the line *End Sub* (of this subroutine):

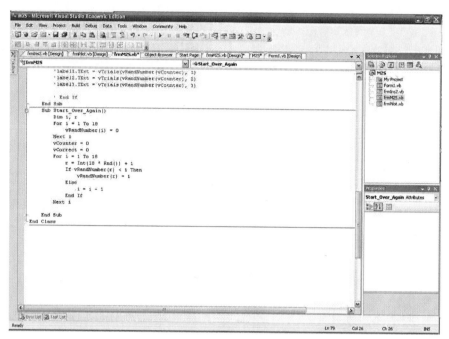

Figure 7.10 shows the newly added Start_Over_Again subroutine.

```
me.Text = "Criterion = " & vCriterion & " Correct      =
    " & vCorrect & " Trial# = " & vCounter
```

Now we can get new trial information even when we make an incorrect response. Of course you would remark out this line of code so the participants are not able to monitor their progress when the program is finalized.

Now run the program and ensure the changes worked. We have now finished meeting Requirement #4. Although the requirement is met, let's add something useful here. Let's have VB 2005 open a new text file and write the number criterion, number correct and the current phase. Start by going to the code level of frmIns1. Add the following code to open a text file in the Append mode and write a header with the current date and time to that file at the bottom of the frmIns1_Load() subroutine:

```
FileOpen(2, "C:\programming\M2S\M2S_OUT.txt",
    OpenMode.Append)
WriteLine(2, "**************************")
WriteLine(2, Date.Now)
WriteLine(2, "**************************")
```

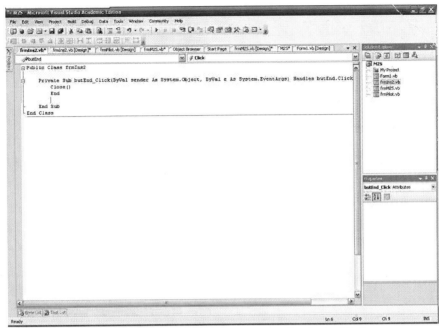

Figure 7.11 shows the code to end the program when frmIns2 is shown.

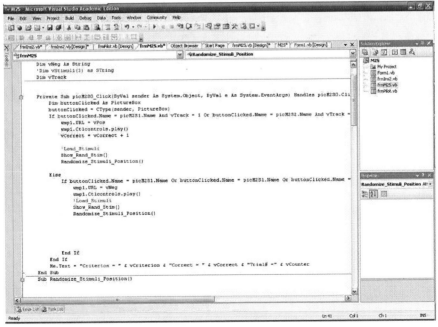

Figure 7.12 shows the code for the newly edited picM2S0_Click subroutine.

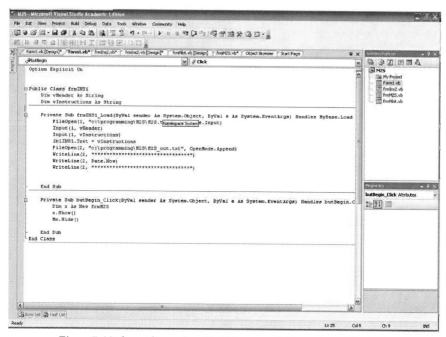

Figure 7.13 shows the newly added file output information of frmIns1.

Next, we will want to write the phase number to this data output file too. To do this we need to initially build the code in frmM2S, and then add it to the data file output information. We can add a line to our input text file using NotePad just below the INSTRUCTIONS command and just above the CORRECT command:

```
PHASE, 1
```

Save and close the text file. Finally, we can declare a new variable called vPhase on the frmM2S form by adding the following line of code under the Public Class statement:

```
Dim vPhase As Integer
```

The phase information we are storing is located before the other input information in the text file, therefore add the following line of code to read in this information above all the other input statements in the frmM2S_Load() subroutine:

```
Input (1, vHeader)
Input (1, vPhase)
```

Run the program, check the data output file M2S_OUT.txt and make sure the date and time are written correctly.

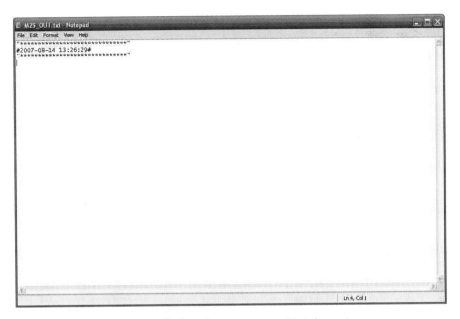

Figure 7.14 displays the correct output file information.

Streamlining Your Code

As you might be thinking, this subroutine, even this entire program in general is getting rather busy. We can streamline the code by reorganizing it into a series of independent subroutines. Let's create a subroutine for the input information called Input_Trial_Information by typing Sub Input_Trial_Information on the last line of the editor (before *End Class*), and then moving the input information there by cutting and pasting the code from frmM2S_Load(). The new Input_Trial_Information subroutine should look like this:

```
Sub Input_Trial_Information()
Input(1, vHeader)
Input(1, vPhase)
Input(1, vHeader)
Input(1, vPos)
Input(1, vHeader)
Input(1, vNeg)
Input(1, vHeader)
Input(1, vCriterion)
End Sub
```

Now add the necessary code to trigger the new subroutine when the form loads. Type the following at the top of frmM2S_Load():

```
Input_Trial_Information
```

The entire frmM2S_Load subroutine should now look like this:

```
Private Sub frmM2S_Load()
Input_Trial_Information()
Load_Random_Trials()
Show_Rand_Stim()
Randomize_Stimuli_Position()
End Sub
```

Run the program to ensure no changes were made that disrupt the working of the program. After this test, you should finish up creating the output file. A good place to write phase information is where the program checks to see if criterion has been met. In our program, this point is during the Randomize Stimuli_Position() subroutine. Edit the subroutine to look like this:

```
Sub Randomize_Stimuli_Position()
If vCounter > 18 Then
If vCriterion < vCorrect Then
Dim x As New frmIns2()
Me.Hide()
x.Show()
Else
WriteLine(2, "Phase =" & vPhase, "Criterion = " &
    vCriterion, "Correct = " & vCorrect)
Start_Over_Again()
End If
Else
Randomize()
Dim r
r = Int(6 * Rnd() + 1)

Select Case r
Case 1
picM2S0.Image = Image.FromFile("c:\programming\M2S\" &
    vTrials(vRandNumber(vCounter), 0) & ".bmp")
picM2S1.Image = Image.FromFile("c:\programming\M2S\" &
    vTrials(vRandNumber(vCounter), 1) & ".bmp")
picM2S2.Image = Image.FromFile("c:\programming\M2S\" &
    vTrials(vRandNumber(vCounter), 2) & ".bmp")
picM2S3.Image = Image.FromFile("c:\programming\M2S\" &
    vTrials(vRandNumber(vCounter), 3) & ".bmp")
vTrack = 1
```

```
Case 2
picM2S0.Image = Image.FromFile("c:\programming\M2S\" &
   vTrials(vRandNumber(vCounter), 0) & ".bmp")
picM2S1.Image = Image.FromFile("c:\programming\M2S\" &
   vTrials(vRandNumber(vCounter), 2) & ".bmp")
picM2S2.Image = Image.FromFile("c:\programming\M2S\" &
   vTrials(vRandNumber(vCounter), 1) & ".bmp")
picM2S3.Image = Image.FromFile("c:\programming\M2S\" &
   vTrials(vRandNumber(vCounter), 3) & ".bmp")
vTrack = 2
Case 3
picM2S0.Image = Image.FromFile("c:\programming\M2S\" &
   vTrials(vRandNumber(vCounter), 0) & ".bmp")
picM2S1.Image = Image.FromFile("c:\programming\M2S\" &
   vTrials(vRandNumber(vCounter), 3) & ".bmp")
picM2S2.Image = Image.FromFile("c:\programming\M2S\" &
   vTrials(vRandNumber(vCounter), 2) & ".bmp")
picM2S3.Image = Image.FromFile("c:\programming\M2S\" &
   vTrials(vRandNumber(vCounter), 1) & ".bmp")
vTrack = 3
Case 4
picM2S0.Image = Image.FromFile("c:\programming\M2S\" &
   vTrials(vRandNumber(vCounter), 0) & ".bmp")
picM2S1.Image = Image.FromFile("c:\programming\M2S\" &
   vTrials(vRandNumber(vCounter), 1) & ".bmp")
picM2S2.Image = Image.FromFile("c:\programming\M2S\" &
   vTrials(vRandNumber(vCounter), 3) & ".bmp")
picM2S3.Image = Image.FromFile("c:\programming\M2S\" &
   vTrials(vRandNumber(vCounter), 2) & ".bmp")
vTrack = 1
Case 5
picM2S0.Image = Image.FromFile("c:\programming\M2S\" &
   vTrials(vRandNumber(vCounter), 0) & ".bmp")
picM2S1.Image = Image.FromFile("c:\programming\M2S\" &
   vTrials(vRandNumber(vCounter), 2) & ".bmp")
picM2S2.Image = Image.FromFile("c:\programming\M2S\" &
   vTrials(vRandNumber(vCounter), 3) & ".bmp")
picM2S3.Image = Image.FromFile("c:\programming\M2S\" &
   vTrials(vRandNumber(vCounter), 1) & ".bmp")
vTrack = 3
Case 6
picM2S0.Image = Image.FromFile("c:\programming\M2S\" &
   vTrials(vRandNumber(vCounter), 0) & ".bmp")
```

```
picM2S1.Image = Image.FromFile("c:\programming\M2S\" &
    vTrials(vRandNumber(vCounter), 3) & ".bmp")
picM2S2.Image = Image.FromFile("c:\programming\M2S\" &
    vTrials(vRandNumber(vCounter), 1) & ".bmp")
picM2S3.Image = Image.FromFile("c:\programming\M2S\" &
    vTrials(vRandNumber(vCounter), 2) & ".bmp")
vTrack = 2
End Select
End If
```

While you don't want to go overboard on writing subroutines, subroutines make your code easier to follow in part due to the descriptive nature of the subroutine names.

Let's see if the output file works. Run the program and make some incorrect responses before you meet criterion. Close the program and look for the output file in the C:\programming\M2S directory. You should see a header with the time and date, plus the trial information. From observation of your data output file you will discover that your newly added phase and criterion information is only written for blocks of trials where you did not meet criterion. Look at the code in Figure 7.15 to figure out why this occurred. The WriteLine(2, "Phase =" & vPhase, "Criterion = " & vCriterion, "Correct = " & vCorrect) code only is read if vCriterion is not met. To have these data write to the output file regardless of vCriterion, add the identical line of code above Dim x as New frmIns2. Rerun the program, make at least 3 errors during the first 18 trials, and then make only 1 error on the next 18 trials. Check the output file. It should look like Figure 7.16.

You may have noticed a "bug" or flaw in the program. Is everything being presented correctly? Is everything being recorded correctly? If you can't find it don't worry we will point it out and fix it later.

5. A-C Training

Requirement #5 is for A-C training similar to the A-B training, however if the participant fails to meet criterion, A-B should not be repeated.

The first order of business is to open M2S.txt (our input file) and modify it to include A-C trials. We can copy and paste the PHASE, CORRECT, INCORRECT, AND CRITERION information and paste this at the end of the input file (remember to change the phase number information from 1 to 2). As with the A-B trials, type in the first three lines, (TRIAL1, A1, C1, C2, C3; TRIAL2, A2, C2, C1, C3; TRIAL3, A3, C3, C1, C2) then copy and paste. Then change the TRIAL information to increment by 1. Remove the END,,,, command from the bottom of Phase1 and move it to the bottom of Phase2. Save the changes and the input file should be complete. Your new text file should look like this:

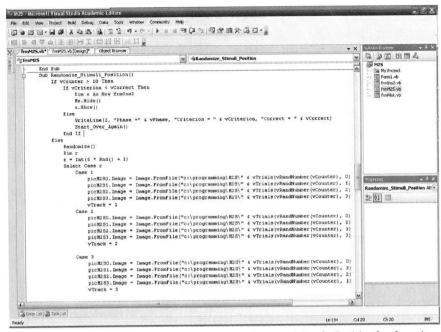

*Figure 7.15 displays the edited section of the Randomize_Stimuli_Position() subroutine
after it has been reorganized.*

*Figure 7.16 displays the M2S_OUT.txt file after correcting
the WriteLine statement placement.*

```
INSTRUCTIONS, This is where the instructions will go.
PHASE, 1
CORRECT, "c:\windows\media\chimes.wav"
INCORRECT, "c:\windows\media\chord.wav"
CRITERION, 16
TRIAL1,A1,B1,B2,B3
TRIAL2,A2,B2,B1,B3
TRIAL3,A3,B3,B1,B2
TRIAL4,A1,B1,B2,B3
TRIAL5,A2,B2,B1,B3
TRIAL6,A3,B3,B1,B2
TRIAL7,A1,B1,B2,B3
TRIAL8,A2,B2,B1,B3
TRIAL9,A3,B3,B1,B2
TRIAL10,A1,B1,B2,B3
TRIAL11,A2,B2,B1,B3
TRIAL12,A3,B3,B1,B2
TRIAL13,A1,B1,B2,B3
TRIAL14,A2,B2,B1,B3
TRIAL15,A3,B3,B1,B2
TRIAL16,A1,B1,B2,B3
TRIAL17,A2,B2,B1,B3
TRIAL18,A3,B3,B1,B2
PHASE, 2
CORRECT, "c:\windows\media\chimes.wav"
INCORRECT, "c:\windows\media\chord.wav"
CRITERION, 16
TRIAL1,A1,C1,C2,C3
TRIAL2,A2,C2,C1,C3
TRIAL3,A3,C3,C1,C2
TRIAL4,A1,C1,C2,C3
TRIAL5,A2,C2,C1,C3
TRIAL6,A3,C3,C1,C2
TRIAL7,A1,C1,C2,C3
TRIAL8,A2,C2,C1,C3
TRIAL9,A3,C3,C1,C2
TRIAL10,A1,C1,C2,C3
TRIAL11,A2,C2,C1,C3
TRIAL12,A3,C3,C1,C2
TRIAL13,A1,C1,C2,C3
TRIAL14,A2,C2,C1,C3
TRIAL15,A3,C3,C1,C2
TRIAL16,A1,C1,C2,C3
```

```
TRIAL17,A2,C2,C1,C3
TRIAL18,A3,C3,C1,C2
END,A1,A1,A1,A1
```

Rather than showing frmIns2 when criterion is met for Phase 1, we want to present the trials for Phase 2. Modify the code at that point in the Randomize_Stimuli_Position() subroutine. Right now this code shows frmIns2 once vCriterion < vCorrect. This works fine for an experiment with one phase, but not for the current experiment with multiple phases. A simple edit of this code will allow you to present subsequent phases without needing to use multiple forms. While multiple forms are possible here, they can become rather cumbersome with many different experimental conditions. The choice is yours. We will show you how to use just frmM2S for all training and testing conditions because it is the cleanest way to write the program.

Begin by declaring a new variable that will be used to hold information found in our "END, A1, A1, A1, A1" line from the text input file. Specifically, add the following line of code to the rest of the Dim statements found on frmM2S under the Public Class:

```
Dim vCheckEnd as Integer
```

Open your M2S.txt data input file in Notepad and change that useless "A1, A1, A1, A1" portion of the code to something we can use to determine if the program is completed or not. Rewrite the last line of your M2S.txt to read:

```
END, 0
```

Next, cut and paste this newly written line of text between the CRITERION line of A-B training and the first line of the trials (i.e. TRIAL1, A1, B1, B2, B3). Do the same for the A-C training phase except this time change the 0 to a 1 as shown below.

```
END, 1
```

Now the data file contains specific information, either a 0 or 1, which can be used to signal to VB 2005 if there are more phases of trials that are to be presented to the participant or if the program should terminate. The resulting M2S.txt file should look identical to Figure 7.17. Close your M2S.txt file and return to Visual Basic.

Add the following lines of code at the bottom of your Input_Trial_Information() subroutine to acquire the newly added END statements and their associated values:

```
Input(1, vHeader)
Input(1, vCheckEnd)
```

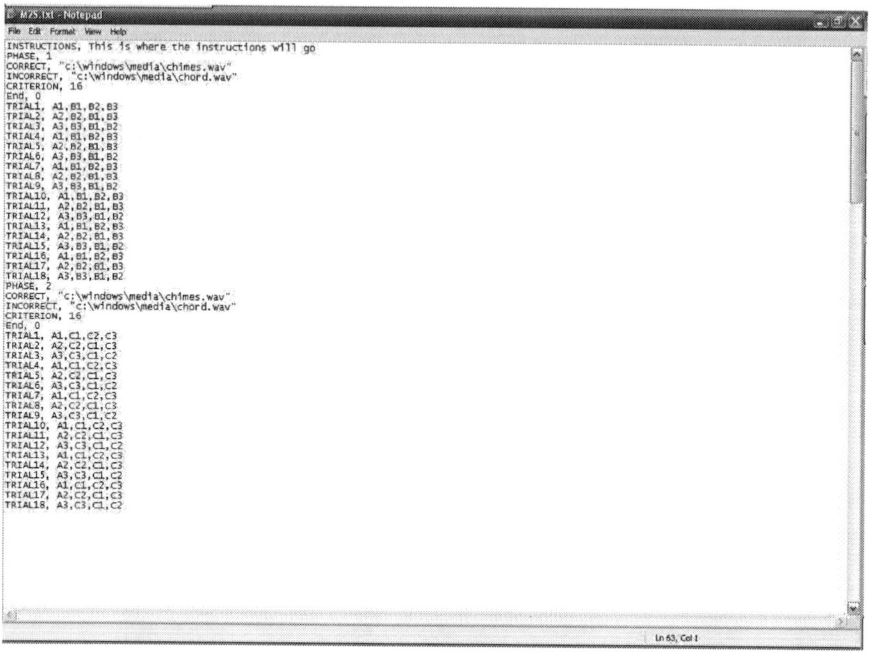

Figure 7.17 displays the correctly edited M2S.txt data input file.

The reason why we shifted that crazy END statement to the beginning of each phase instead of the end, is because all the other Input information preceded the randomization and presentation of that phase's trials. Shifting END right after the CRITERION line streamlines when VB 2005 accesses the text file for variable values.

The final step here to incorporate the A-C trials is to edit the Randomize_Stimuli_Position subroutine section that pertains to vCriterion. Edit this portion of the subroutine to read as follows (the Select Case statements are not shown here because no changes are made to them):

```
If vCounter > 18 Then
If vCriterion < vCorrect Then
WriteLine(2, "Phase =" & vPhase, "Criterion = " & vCriterion, "Correct = " &
    vCorrect)
If vCheckEnd = 1 Then
Dim x As New frmIns2()
Me.Hide()
x.Show()
End If
If vCheckEnd = 0 Then
Dim x As New frmM2S()
```

```
x.Show()
Me.Hide()
End If
Else
WriteLine(2, "Phase =" & vPhase, "Criterion = " & vCriterion, "Correct = " &
    vCorrect)
Start_Over_Again()
End If
Else
Randomize()
Dim r
r = Int(6 * Rnd() + 1)
```

Essentially what this code does is check to see if 18 trials have elapsed. If they have, it next checks if the criterion has been met. If it has, 1) data are written to the output file, 2) it checks to see if vCheckEnd is equal to 1. This would signify the end of the experiment. If vCheckEnd is equal to 1, then frmIns2 is shown. Yet, if vCheckEnd is equal to 0, more trials need to be presented. VB 2005 should move on down the data input file, and bring in the new trials and their related information. Essentially, the program should start again, only now with the next phase of trials. Instead of showing the frmIns2 form, we simply reshow, or reload, the same frmM2S form. The whole process starts again, but now with the next set of trials! Run the program; meet the criterion in A-B, than A-C training should start. At this point fail the A-C criterion initially, than pass it. The program should run without a hitch, and eventually display frmIns2. Check your M2S_OUT.txt file to check out your performance. This should take care of requirement #5.

6. Mixed Training

Requirement #6 requests that 36 mixed trials of A-B and B-C be randomly presented. This is just like requirement #5 except that there is two times the number of trials. Our arrays are set for 18 and the FOR/NEXT statements are set for 18 as well. As they stand, only phases with 18 trials or less will work correctly in the program. To customize this feature to allow for more than 18 trials per phase, you will need to make a few code and input file adjustments. Start off by opening M2S.txt and under the PHASE command for phase 1 and 2 add the following new command:

```
NUMBEROFTRIALS, 18
```

The NUMBEROFTRIALS, 18 will change to 36 for the mixed trials in phase 3. But don't do the mixed trials just yet, because we need to make sure the changes work with what we just did to the input file. Save your changes to the text file and return to frmM2S. Declare a new variable on this form as follows:

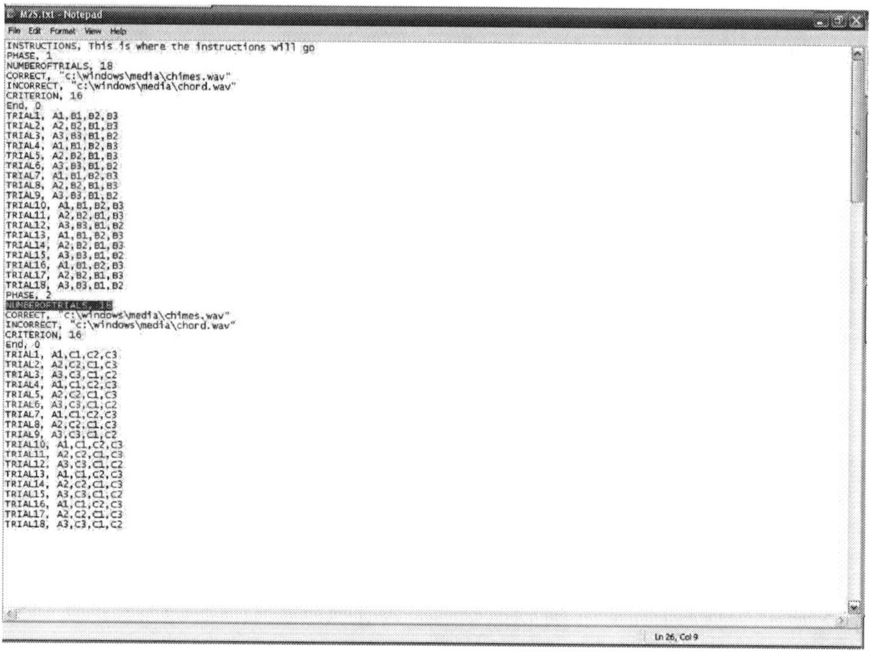

Figure 7.18 shows the M2S text file after adding the new command:
NUMBEROFTRIALS.

```
Dim vNumberTrials as Integer
```

Add the following input lines under the Input_Trial_Information() subroutine right under the vPhase line:

```
Input(1, vHeader)
Input(1, vNumberTrials)
```

The Input_Trial_Information() subroutine should now look like this:

```
Sub Input_Trial_Information()
Input(1, vHeader)
Input(1, vPhase)
Input(1, vHeader)
Input(1, vNumberTrials)
Input(1, vHeader)
Input(1, vPos)
Input(1, vHeader)
Input(1, vNeg)
Input(1, vHeader)
```

```
Input(1,vCriterion)
Input(1, vHeader)
Input(1,vCheckEnd)
End Sub
```

We can't easily change the size of variable arrays during run time, but we can adjust them to the largest size we anticipate using. Remember this point if you designed larger sets of training or testing pahses in your own research. Therefore change:

```
Dim vTrials((18),(3))
Dim vRandNumber(18) As Integer
```

to read:

```
Dim vTrials((36),(3))
Dim vRandNumber(36) As Integer
```

We also need to change the following code in the Randomize_Stimuli_Presentation() subroutine:

```
If vCounter > 18 Then
```
to
```
If vCounter > vNumberTrials Then
```

Now if the number of trials is greater than 18 the program won't check the criterion early. Similarly change all four of the FOR/NEXT statements throughout the form that read:

```
For i = 1 To 18
```

to read

```
For i = 1 To vNumberTrials
```

Also change the two random functions that read:

```
r = Int(18 * Rnd + 1)
```

to read

```
r = Int(vNumberTrials * Rnd + 1).
```

Run the program a few times making different criterion for the two phases and see if the changes worked.

Now we can add the mixed trials for requirement #6. Open the input file. Select rows 2 to 7 and copy and paste them at the end of the file. Change the PHASE to 3, NUMBEROFTRIALS to 36. We will use the same .wav files and set the criterion at 32 (twice the previous criterion). We must change the END command in phase 3, to a 1 and to a 0 in Phase 2. Now copy the A-B trials and paste them at the bottom of the input file. Do the same with the A-C trials. Renumber to change the trial headers to read 1-36. Save the input file. Run the program.

7. Test Trials

Requirement #7a indicates that the trials for testing should provide no feedback. Open the input file and copy the lines from *Phase 3* to *End,1* and paste it at the bottom of the input file and make the following changes:

```
PHASE, 4
NUMBEROFTRIALS, 27
CORRECT, "c:\windows\media\nothing.wav"
INCORRECT, "c:\windows\media\nothing.wav"
CRITERION, -1
END, 1
```

Notice that there are new .wav files specified for this text phase called *nothing.wav*. To remove the auditory feedback you need to "trick" VB 2005 into playing a soundless .wav file. Go to the *Accessories* Program Group on your computer's operating system, select *Entertainment* and then select *Sound Recorder*. Make your soundless *nothing* .wav file by pressing the *Record* Button once, and then quickly pressing the *Stop* Button. Save the file as *nothing.wav* in the c:\windows\media directory, then close the Sound Recorder.

Also notice that criterion is set to –1. This is because there is no criterion. Because of the way we wrote the code, the number correct has to be greater than the criterion. If for some reason the participant does not make a correct choice, then the number correct would not be greater than the criterion. So –1 it is. Change the END command in phase 3 to END, 0 so the program will continue to run. Now add the trials for phase 4 – Reflexivity. A1-A1, A2-A2, etc. The first nine trials should look like this:

```
TRIAL1,  A1,A1,A2,A3
TRIAL2,  A2,A2,A1,A3
TRIAL3,  A3,A3,A1,A2
TRIAL4,  B1,B1,B2,B3
TRIAL5,  B2,B2,B1,B3
TRIAL6,  B3,B3,B1,B2
TRIAL7,  C1,C1,C2,C3
```

Figure 7.19 shows the M2S text file with the Mixed training section.

```
TRIAL8,  C2,C2,C1,C3
TRIAL9,  C3,C3,C1,C2
```

Now copy and paste in two more sections to make 27 trials. Remember to change the TRIAL headers. Run the program. You can see that as the number of trials grows, the more effort it is to test and trouble shoot your program. If the program runs and there is no feedback during the testing trials, requirement #7a should be met.

Requirement #7b is a test for Symmetry. This will involve the B-A and C-A relations each presented six times. There will be 18 trials, no feedback, and again no criterion. Therefore, copy and paste the command header and make the necessary changes in the input file as before. The header and the first six trials of our symmetry test should look like this:

```
PHASE, 5
NUMBEROFTRIALS, 18
CORRECT, "c:\windows\media\nothing.wav"
INCORRECT, "c:\windows\media\nothing.wav"
CRITERION, -1
END, 1
TRIAL1, B1,A1,A2,A3
```

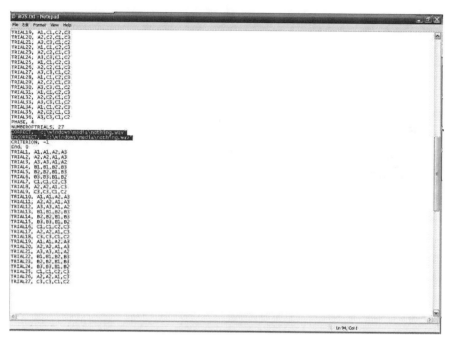

Figure 7.20 shows the M2S text file with the Reflexivity Phase added.

```
TRIAL2,  B2,A2,A1,A3
TRIAL3,  B3,A3,A1,A2
TRIAL4,  C1,A1,A2,A3
TRIAL5,  C2,A2,A1,A3
TRIAL6,  C3,A3,A1,A2
```

Make sure to change the End statement of Phase 4 from 1 to 0. Save your changes then run the program.

Requirement #7c is a test for Transitivity involving B-C relations. There will be 18 trials with each relation tested 6 times, no feedback, and no criterion. The first few lines of the input file should look like this:

```
PHASE,  6
NUMBEROFTRIALS,  18
CORRECT,  "c:\windows\media\nothing.wav"
INCORRECT,  "c:\windows\media\nothing.wav"
CRITERION,  -1
END,  1
TRIAL1,  B1,C1,C2,C3
TRIAL2,  B2,C2,C1,C3
TRIAL3,  B3,C3,C1,C2
```

```
M2S.txt - Notepad
File  Edit  Format  View  Help
TRIAL7,  C1,C1,C2,C3
TRIAL8,  A2,A2,A1,C3
TRIAL9,  C3,C3,C1,C2
TRIAL10, A1,A1,A2,A3
TRIAL11, A2,A2,A1,A3
TRIAL12, A3,A3,A1,A2
TRIAL13, B1,B1,B2,B3
TRIAL14, B2,B2,B1,B3
TRIAL15, B3,B3,B1,B2
TRIAL16, C1,C1,C2,C3
TRIAL17, A2,A2,A1,C3
TRIAL18, C3,C3,C1,C2
TRIAL19, A1,A1,A2,A3
TRIAL20, A2,A2,A1,A3
TRIAL21, A3,A3,A1,A2
TRIAL22, B1,B1,B2,B3
TRIAL23, B2,B2,B1,B3
TRIAL24, B3,B3,B1,B2
TRIAL25, C1,C1,C2,C3
TRIAL26, A2,A2,A1,C3
TRIAL27, C3,C3,C1,C2
PHASE,  5
NUMBEROFTRIALS, 18
CORRECT,  "c:\windows\media\nothing.wav"
INCORRECT, "c:\windows\media\nothing.wav"
CRITERION, -1
End, 0
TRIAL1,  B1,A1,A2,A3
TRIAL2,  B2,A2,A1,A3
TRIAL3,  B3,A3,A1,A2
TRIAL4,  C2,A2,A1,A3
TRIAL5,  C2,A2,A1,A3
TRIAL6,  C3,A3,A1,A2
TRIAL7,  B1,A1,A2,A3
TRIAL8,  B2,A2,A1,A3
TRIAL9,  B3,A3,A1,A2
TRIAL10, C2,A2,A1,A3
TRIAL11, C2,A2,A1,A3
TRIAL12, C3,A3,A1,A2
TRIAL13, B1,A1,A2,A3
TRIAL14, B2,A2,A1,A3
TRIAL15, B3,A3,A1,A2
TRIAL16, C2,A2,A1,A3
TRIAL17, C2,A2,A1,A3
TRIAL18, C3,A3,A1,A2
```
                                                              Ln 159, Col 1

Figure 7.21 shows the M2S text file with the Symmetry Test trials.

Make sure to change END, 1 in the previous phase to END, 0. Save your changes then run the program.

Requirement #7d is a test for Equivalence. Here the C-B relations will be presented. There will be 18 trials with each relation tested 6 times, no feedback, and no criterion. The header and the first three lines of the trials should look like this:

```
PHASE, 7
NUMBEROFTRIALS, 18
CORRECT, "c:\windows\media\nothing.wav"
INCORRECT, "c:\windows\media\nothing.wav"
CRITERION, -1
END, 1
TRIAL1, C1,B1,B2,B3
TRIAL2, C2,B2,B1,B3
TRIAL3, C3,B3,B1,B2
```

Make sure to change END, 1 in the previous phase to END, 0. Save your changes then run the program. This should conclude all of the requirements for #7. All of the testing is complete.

Figure 7.22 displays the Transitivity test in the M2S text file.

Figure 7.23 displays the Equivalence test in the M2S text file.

8. Data Output

Requirement #8 regards writing data to an output file. We have already created code that writes summary data after each phase, however more reporting detail is usually desired. Requirement #8 specifically requests:

For each trial indicate the sample stimulus and the comparison stimulus chosen.
For each trial indicate the response latency (the time the sample stimulus was displayed and the time a comparison stimulus was chosen).
And total number of trials correct (we have already done this).

One way to satisfy this requirement is to capitalize on the information already being written into the Text bar of frmM2S. By adding a few more pieces of information to this existing code we can have a comprehensive data record which updates every trial.

One piece of information that currently is lacking in the me.Text is if a specific response is correct or wrong. Right now, we have values of vCorrect, but those values could be displayed more usefully. Therefore, add a new variable to the form by typing:

```
Dim vAnswer as String
```

Using this new variable we can produce a textual note that signals if the response made by the participant was correct or incorrect on every trial. We shall come back to vAnswer shortly. For now though edit the existing me.Text= code so that it reads as follows:

```
Me.Text = "Phase= " & vPhase & "Criterion= " & vCriterion
    & "Correct= " & vCorrect & "Trial# = " & vCounter &
    vTrials(vRandNumber(vCounter), 0) &
    vTrials(vRandNumber(vCounter), 1) & vAnswer & Date.Now
```

This is all one big long line of code, but it provides a really nice small amount of information in the Text bar. It now includes the newly created vAnswer variable, the stimulus presented as the sample, the stimulus that is the correct comparison, the phase in effect, and the time and date.

Cut this newly written line from its' current position and paste it into two different places under picM2S0_Click. The reason why we are shifting the code here is because we want the information to update immediately after the participant makes a response. This is especially true for the Date.Now function. Paste the above code as follows into the picM2S0_Click subroutine() and add the two new lines of code pertaining to generating a string for vAnswer. The new subroutine should now look like:

```
Dim buttonClicked As PictureBox
buttonClicked = CType(sender, PictureBox)
If buttonClicked.Name = picM2S1.Name() And vTrack = 1 Or
    buttonClicked.Name = picM2S2.Name() And vTrack = 2 Or
    buttonClicked.Name = picM2S3.Name And vTrack = 3 Then
wmp1.url = vPos
wmp1.Ctlcontrols.Play()
'Load_Stimuli()
vCorrect = vCorrect + 1
vAnswer = "Correct"
Me.Text = "Phase= " & vPhase & "Criterion= " & vCriterion
    & "Correct= " & vCorrect & "Trial# = " & vCounter &
    vTrials(vRandNumber(vCounter), 0) &
    vTrials(vRandNumber(vCounter), 1) & vAnswer & Date.Now

Show_Rand_Stim()
Randomize_Stimuli_Position()
Else
If buttonClicked.Name = picM2S2.Name() Or buttonClicked.Name
    = picM2S1.Name() Or buttonClicked.Name = picM2S3.Name
    Then
wmp1.url = vNeg
wmp1.Ctlcontrols.Play()
'Load_Stimuli()
vAnswer = "Wrong"
Me.Text = "Phase= " & vPhase & "Criterion= " & vCriterion
    & "Correct= " & vCorrect & "Trial# = " & vCounter &
    vTrials(vRandNumber(vCounter), 0) &
    vTrials(vRandNumber(vCounter), 1) & vAnswer & Date.Now
Show_Rand_Stim()
Randomize_Stimuli_Position()
End If
End If
```

Run the program and see your changes appear in the Text bar of frmM2S. There is a lot of information here, but you can sort out what is useful to you when running your own experiments.

Now that me.Text is displaying the data you wish to record, the next step is to place this information into M2S_OUT.txt. Add the following line under BOTH locations you just placed the me.Text = ... code:

```
WriteLine(2, "Phase= " & vPhase, "Criterion= " & vCriterion,
    "Correct= " & vCorrect, "Trial# = " & vCounter,
```

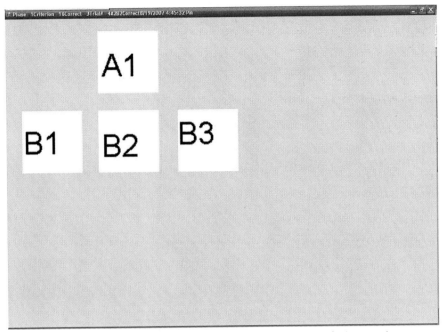

Figure 7.24 displays the revisions to me.Text as they appear during run time.

```
vTrials(vRandNumber(vCounter), 0),
vTrials(vRandNumber(vCounter), 1), vAnswer, Date.Now)
```

Run the program and check your data output file. It should look similar to a section displayed in Figure 7.25.

You might notice a little bit of a problem here with your data output file as well as that displayed in Figure 7.25. Examine the line of data written after the first 18 trials. There are errors in it including the trial number's value is zero. Now look 18 trials down the data file and note that there were 19 responses made in a block of trials that should have been 18. Yep, the programming bug has raised its ugly head.

Debugging

Solving the Problems in Your Program One Step at a Time

We had told you earlier that there was a bug in the program and would deal with it later. The problem was that trial 18 was being recorded twice. This was not preventing the program from running, but it does present a problem now that we are trying to write the data to file. Computer programming bugs can sometimes take hours, days, or weeks to find and solve. Do not become discouraged when attempting to identify and fix problems that arise in your program. They will occur and they will take some time to "debug." The bug that is currently in the M2S project

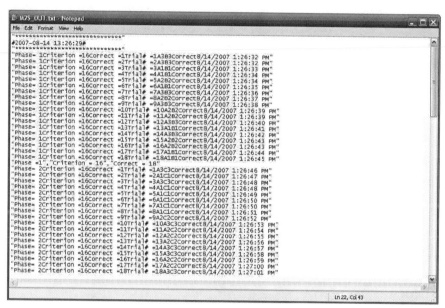

Figure 7.25 displays an example of the data output file.

took us over 30 hours to fix when we designed this program initially. It will take you 3 seconds to fix it. The dissimilarity in time illustrates the difference between being a contingency shaped versus a rule-governed programmer. Spend some time attempting to figure out where the bug is before reading on.

The best way to potentially identify bugs in your program is to track the values of your variables step by step as your program goes through the code. This may appear hard to do in Visual Basic 2005 because the graphical interface covers up your code when running and everything happens so fast. A complete running through of all your code might take the computer less than a millisecond. There are others way though to track your variable values. We have been using one all along in this chapter. It is via the me.Text display at the top of your screen. Although we did not place all our variables within this display, you easily could do so when encountering bugs in your program. Another way to track the values of your variables is to create a series of TextBoxes on the side of your form that you write the variable values into each time the values are loaded. When you run the program you can watch the values within these TextBoxes change correctly or incorrectly at the moment they are generated. After finding the bug(s), simply delete the TextBoxes from the form or make them Visible = False.

Now back to our current bug. The problem that we are experiencing here only appears to happen when a given criterion is not met and the participant is "recycled" through the same phase of the experiment again. This should be your first clue. Something is wrong with the code that reinitiates the same phase again. The relevant code begins when the participant clicks on picM2S(1-3) which is found in the picM2S0_Click subroutine. Look now at the code which becomes read by VB 2005 if the responses are correct or incorrect. We know that the .wav files are playing correctly so this is not the problem. However, there are directions here to start the Randomize_Stimuli_Presentation subroutine which will then check to see if the criterion is met or not. Here is where the problem begins. When the criterion is not met, there are directions to go to the Start_Over_Again subroutine. This subroutine is only accessed when a criterion is not achieved, and our error is only occurring when a criterion is not achieved. The problem must lay here.

Take a good look at this subroutine. What does it actually do?

```
Sub Start_Over_Again()
Dim i, r
For i = 1 To vNumberTrials
vRandNumber(i) = 0
Next i
vCounter = 0
vCorrect = 0
For i = 1 To vNumberTrials
r = Int(vNumberTrials * Rnd() + 1)
If vRandNumber(r) < 1 Then
vRandNumber(r) = i
Else
i = i - 1
End If
Next i
End Sub
```

First it declares the letters i and r to be used as variables only within this subroutine. Next it clears out the previous values of i and r that were used to hold the random trial and position information from our two dimensional array. When starting the phase of trials over again we wanted to clear out the values from the "used" trials that had already been presented to the participant. We also reset some variables back to 0; specifically vCounter and vCorrect. Think about what each of these variables do. vCorrect tracks the frequency of correct responses made during a given. Shifting this value back to 0 appears to be logically correct. Now look at vCounter. This variable tracks the trial number the participant is on. Shifting this value back to 0 means that the next trial presented to the participant will be trial 0, when in fact it should really be trial 1. Here is the bug. The value of vCounter should be reset to 1 and not 0. Change the code accordingly and run the program. The bug should be fixed. Edit this subroutine so that:

```
vCounter = 0
```

is changed to:

```
vCounter = 1
```

Summary

There are many ways to build upon this working matching to sample program. You can put any stimuli you create into the program. Simply delete the images you currently have, and replace them with your new images (keeping the same file names of course). If you want to add more stimuli than the 9 we used here, all you need to do is change the names in the data input file and the size of some of the variables. If you want to add more trials or longer phases you just need to change the array sizes and the variable ranges. You can add entirely different sets of stimuli by adding another frmM2S with different stimuli and having this form show instead of the debriefing instructions. You could change the background colors during certain phases. You could add a point counter to track obtained reinforcers. You could use video clips as reinforcing or punishing stimuli. The possibilities are endless.

We took you on a pretty windy road to get to the end of this chapter's program. There were many detours and even some dead ends. It was done purposely to illustrate a programmer's real travel route from start to finish. In case you missed any of the subtle changes that we made throughout the chapter, here is the frmM2S code in its entirety:

```
Option Explicit On
Public Class frmM2S
Inherits System.Windows.Forms.Form
Dim vTrack
Dim vHeader As String
Dim vPos As String
Dim vNeg As String
'Dim vStimuli(3) As String
Dim vTrials((36), (3))
Dim vRandNumber(36) As Integer
Dim vCounter As Integer
Dim vCriterion As Integer
Dim vCorrect As Integer
Dim vPhase As Integer
Dim vCheckEnd As Integer
Dim vNumberTrials As Integer
Dim vAnswer As String


Private Sub picM2SO_Click(ByVal sender As System.Object,
    ByVal e As System.EventArgs) Handles picM2S1.Click,
    picM2S2.Click, picM2S3.Click
```

```
Dim buttonClicked As PictureBox
buttonClicked = CType(sender, PictureBox)
If buttonClicked.Name = picM2S1.Name() And vTrack = 1 Or
    buttonClicked.Name = picM2S2.Name() And vTrack = 2 Or
    buttonClicked.Name = picM2S3.Name And vTrack = 3 Then
wmp1.url = vPos
wmp1.Ctrcontrols.Play()
'Load_Stimuli()
vCorrect = vCorrect + 1
vAnswer = "Correct"
Me.Text = "Phase= " & vPhase & "Criterion= " & vCriterion
    & "Correct= " & vCorrect & "Trial# = " & vCounter &
    vTrials(vRandNumber(vCounter), 0) &
    vTrials(vRandNumber(vCounter), 1) & vAnswer & Date.Now
WriteLine(2, "Phase= " & vPhase, "Criterion= " & vCriterion,
    "Correct= " & vCorrect, "Trial# = " & vCounter,
    vTrials(vRandNumber(vCounter), 0),
    vTrials(vRandNumber(vCounter), 1), vAnswer, Date.Now)
Show_Rand_Stim()
Randomize_Stimuli_Position()
Else
If buttonClicked.Name = picM2S2.Name() Or buttonClicked.Name
    = picM2S1.Name() Or buttonClicked.Name = picM2S3.Name
    Then
wmp1.url = vNeg
wmp1.Ctlcontrols.Play()
'Load_Stimuli()
vAnswer = "Wrong"
Me.Text = "Phase= " & vPhase & "Criterion= " & vCriterion
    & "Correct= " & vCorrect & "Trial# = " & vCounter &
    vTrials(vRandNumber(vCounter), 0) &
    vTrials(vRandNumber(vCounter), 1) & vAnswer & Date.Now
WriteLine(2, "Phase= " & vPhase, "Criterion= " & vCriterion,
    "Correct= " & vCorrect, "Trial# = " & vCounter,
    vTrials(vRandNumber(vCounter), 0),
    vTrials(vRandNumber(vCounter), 1), vAnswer, Date.Now)
Show_Rand_Stim()
Randomize_Stimuli_Position()
End If
End If
End Sub
```

```
Private Sub frmM2S_Load(ByVal sender As System.Object,
    ByVal e As System.EventArgs) Handles MyBase.Load
Input_Trial_Information()
Load_Random_Trials()
Show_Rand_Stim()
Randomize_Stimuli_Position()
End Sub

Sub Randomize_Stimuli_Position()

If vCounter > vNumberTrials Then
If vCriterion < vCorrect Then
WriteLine(2, "Phase =" & vPhase, "Criterion = " &
    vCriterion, "Correct = " & vCorrect)
If vCheckEnd = 1 Then
Dim x As New frmIns2()
Me.Hide()
x.Show()
End If
If vCheckEnd = 0 Then
Dim x As New frmM2S()
x.Show()
Me.Hide()
End If
Else
WriteLine(2, "Phase =" & vPhase, "Criterion = " &
    vCriterion, "Correct = " & vCorrect)
Start_Over_Again()
End If
Else
Randomize()
Dim r
r = Int(6 * Rnd() + 1)

Select Case r
Case 1
picM2S0.Image = Image.FromFile("c:\programming\M2S\" &
    vTrials(vRandNumber(vCounter), 0) & ".bmp")
picM2S1.Image = Image.FromFile("c:\programming\M2S\" &
    vTrials(vRandNumber(vCounter), 1) & ".bmp")
picM2S2.Image = Image.FromFile("c:\programming\M2S\" &
    vTrials(vRandNumber(vCounter), 2) & ".bmp")
```

```
picM2S3.Image = Image.FromFile("c:\programming\M2S\" &
   vTrials(vRandNumber(vCounter), 3) & ".bmp")
vTrack = 1
Case 2
picM2S0.Image = Image.FromFile("c:\programming\M2S\" &
   vTrials(vRandNumber(vCounter), 0) & ".bmp")
picM2S1.Image = Image.FromFile("c:\programming\M2S\" &
      vTrials(vRandNumber(vCounter), 2) & ".bmp")
picM2S2.Image = Image.FromFile("c:\programming\M2S\" &
   vTrials(vRandNumber(vCounter), 1) & ".bmp")
picM2S3.Image = Image.FromFile("c:\programming\M2S\" &
   vTrials(vRandNumber(vCounter), 3) & ".bmp")
vTrack = 2
Case 3
picM2S0.Image = Image.FromFile("c:\programming\M2S\" &
   vTrials(vRandNumber(vCounter), 0) & ".bmp")
picM2S1.Image = Image.FromFile("c:\programming\M2S\" &
   vTrials(vRandNumber(vCounter), 3) & ".bmp")
picM2S2.Image = Image.FromFile("c:\programming\M2S\" &
   vTrials(vRandNumber(vCounter), 2) & ".bmp")
picM2S3.Image = Image.FromFile("c:\programming\M2S\" &
   vTrials(vRandNumber(vCounter), 1) & ".bmp")
vTrack = 3
Case 4
picM2S0.Image = Image.FromFile("c:\programming\M2S\" &
   vTrials(vRandNumber(vCounter), 0) & ".bmp")
picM2S1.Image = Image.FromFile("c:\programming\M2S\" &
   vTrials(vRandNumber(vCounter), 1) & ".bmp")
picM2S2.Image = Image.FromFile("c:\programming\M2S\" &
   vTrials(vRandNumber(vCounter), 3) & ".bmp")
picM2S3.Image = Image.FromFile("c:\programming\M2S\" &
   vTrials(vRandNumber(vCounter), 2) & ".bmp")
vTrack = 1
Case 5
picM2S0.Image = Image.FromFile("c:\programming\M2S\" &
   vTrials(vRandNumber(vCounter), 0) & ".bmp")
picM2S1.Image = Image.FromFile("c:\programming\M2S\" &
   vTrials(vRandNumber(vCounter), 2) & ".bmp")
picM2S2.Image = Image.FromFile("c:\programming\M2S\" &
   vTrials(vRandNumber(vCounter), 3) & ".bmp")
picM2S3.Image = Image.FromFile("c:\programming\M2S\" &
   vTrials(vRandNumber(vCounter), 1) & ".bmp")
vTrack = 3
```

```
Case 6
picM2S0.Image = Image.FromFile("c:\programming\M2S\" &
    vTrials(vRandNumber(vCounter), 0) & ".bmp")
picM2S1.Image = Image.FromFile("c:\programming\M2S\" &
    vTrials(vRandNumber(vCounter), 3) & ".bmp")
picM2S2.Image = Image.FromFile("c:\programming\M2S\" &
    vTrials(vRandNumber(vCounter), 1) & ".bmp")
picM2S3.Image = Image.FromFile("c:\programming\M2S\" &
    vTrials(vRandNumber(vCounter), 2) & ".bmp")
vTrack = 2
End Select

End If

End Sub
Sub Load_Random_Trials()
Dim i, r, x, y

For i = 1 To vNumberTrials
Input(1, x)
Input(1, vTrials(i, 0))
Input(1, vTrials(i, 1))
Input(1, vTrials(i, 2))
Input(1, vTrials(i, 3))
Next i
Randomize()
For i = 1 To vNumberTrials
r = Int(vNumberTrials * Rnd() + 1)
If vRandNumber(r) < 1 Then
vRandNumber(r) = i
Else
i = i - 1
End If
Next i
End Sub

Sub Show_Rand_Stim()
vCounter = vCounter + 1
End Sub

Sub Start_Over_Again()
Dim i, r
For i = 1 To vNumberTrials
```

```
vRandNumber(i) = 0
Next i
vCounter = 1
vCorrect = 0
For i = 1 To vNumberTrials
r = Int(vNumberTrials * Rnd() + 1)
If vRandNumber(r) < 1 Then
vRandNumber(r) = i
Else
i = i - 1
End If
Next i

End Sub
Sub Input_Trial_Information()
Input(1, vHeader)
Input(1, vPhase)
Input(1, vHeader)
Input(1, vNumberTrials)
Input(1, vHeader)
Input(1, vPos)
Input(1, vHeader)
Input(1, vNeg)
Input(1, vHeader)
Input(1, vCriterion)
Input(1, vHeader)
Input(1, vCheckEnd)

End Sub
```

References

Green, G., & Saunders, R. R. (1998). Stimulus equivalence. In K. A. Lattal & M. Perone (Eds.), *Handbook of research methods in human operant behavior*. Plenum Press: New York.

Chapter 8: Complex Schedules and Data Exportation

Beyond the Simple Schedule

Many of the contemporary research questions being asked by human operant researchers can not be answered using just simple schedules of reinforcement. Such questions involve response allocations on concurrently available schedules, sensitivity (or insensitivity) to programmed contingencies on mixed or multiple schedules, and the effects of negative reinforcement or punishment conditions on behavior. For example, you may wish to examine behavior when a subject is exposed to a differential reinforcement of low rate schedule and then compare it to when he/she is exposed to a negative reinforcement schedule for high rates. This could be done using a multiple or mixed schedule with a different Visual Basic.NET Windows Form being utilized for each schedule component. You might also wish to examine whether a subject allocates his responses proportional to the relative rates of reinforcement obtained across two response options in a concurrent choice paradigm. Here one Windows Form could house both response options, and using two different Buttons, you could link the two different schedules together. There are many ways to build upon the simple schedules of reinforcement that we presented in Chapter 3. In this chapter we will show you a couple of ways you can do so. At the same time, we will teach you the important process of transferring your output data into a spreadsheet of analysis.

Data analysis is often a labor intensive process. It often can take just as long to analyze the data as it can to acquire it. By taking some preventative measures at the beginning of your program, you can design data output files that can be easily read into spreadsheets or databases for analysis. By haphazardly writing your data output code while programming, you will spend hours reworking or reentering your data into an acceptable format for the spreadsheet or other program to read. In Chapters 5, 6, and 7 we integrated data output files into our programs. We checked the workability of the output files by popping open Notepad or Word. Some programs you design may produce data that are sufficiently analyzed using a word processor. Others will require more in-depth analysis and graphing. We will construct examples of these latter types of programs in this chapter as we design a few complex schedules of reinforcement.

Building a Multiple Schedule of Negative Reinforcement

Creating the Interface

Multiple schedules are nothing more than two or more simple schedules of reinforcement that are alternated in presentation to the participant following the elapsing of a given amount of time or a given number of reinforcers contacted. Each schedule has a discriminative stimulus associated with it which allows for responding to come under discriminative control. In a sense the two (or more) schedules and their associated discriminative stimuli actually flip-flop in presentation. For example, after 10 minutes of responding to a VR schedule with an orange colored screen background, the participant may be presented with a VI schedule with a red colored screen background in which to respond. After another 10 minutes, the VR schedule returns. This process repeats over and over again until a steady state of responding has occurred, or a pre-determined amount of schedule presentations have been made.

Let us begin creating a multiple schedule of reinforcement which contains one component that is a Fixed-Ratio (FR) schedule and another component that is a Differential Reinforcement of Low Rate (DRL). We discussed the Fixed-Ratio schedule contingencies in Chapter 3, but have not mentioned what a DRL schedule consists of yet. As the name "low rate" suggests, this schedule provides reinforcement for responding at a low rate, or at a slow pace. In the working example, we will use pre-set values for these schedules as we did in Chapter 3. Specifically we will use a FR-3 and a DRL-1. Here however, as opposed to previous chapters, the schedules will be negative reinforcement schedules, whereby the participant will *avoid* point loss by emitting behavior consistent with the parameters of the schedule component in place at a given time. Programmers who wish to construct a more customizable version of a multiple schedule could explore including a parameters or options form at that start of the program similar to what will be described in Chapter 9.

Start by opening Visual Basic 2005 and creating a new Windows Application Project entitled *Multiple*. Change the name of the form to frmFR and the text to FR. This form will serve as the Fixed Ratio form. Now click on *Project* from the main menu, and select the option *Add Windows Form*, change the name to frmDRL, and click *Add*.

The text of the newly added form will appear as *frmDRL* automatically, therefore alter the text property so that it reads *DRL* instead. Visual Basic 2005 will automatically change the Text property of the form to match its Name property when it is added to the Project. This new form will serve as the DRL form. As noted above, each schedule component in a multiple schedule has a distinctive discriminative stimulus associated with it. This stimulus might consist of a PictureBox with different pictures, a Label object with various textual characters, or a variation in screen BackColor. Here we will alter the forms' background colors to serve as the discriminative stimuli. Select frmFR from the Solution Explorer window by double-clicking on it, and change the BackColor property of this form to a shade of green. Now select *frmDRL* from the Solution Explorer window and change the BackColor property of this form to a shade of red. The colors are arbitrary and can be altered to suit your own color preferences if you wish.

At this time we may wish to alter some additional properties of both forms to make them suitable for actual participants. First, change the WindowState properties to *Maximized*. Second, change the MinimizeBox properties to *False*. This will

*Figure 8.1 displays the dialog box used for inserting a second form
into the Multiple Project.*

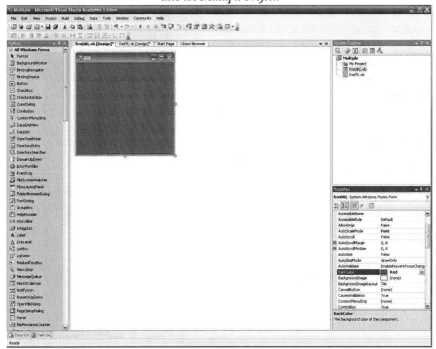

Figure 8.2 displays the altered BackColor properties of frmDRL.

keep the participant from being able to minimize the forms when the program is running. Third, change the MaximizeBox properties to *False*. This will have a similar effect whereby the participant can not alter form size and then re-maximize the form during program running. Change the StartUp object to the frmFR form and run the program to check your progress.

You might have discovered that while a participant can not minimize or maximize the form, they can still "close" the form while it is running using the small box in the top right hand corner. We can remove this box too, by changing the ControlBox property of our forms to *False*. Yet, if we do, we too will have trouble terminating the program while it is being constructed. Save this last safeguard for later, once the program is up and running and ready for real participants.

The next step will be to add a response operanda for the participant. Select a Button object and place it onto your FR form. Position the Button in the middle of the form, change its name to *butResponse*, and its Text to blank. You may also wish to alter the BackColor property of this Button to suit your tastes. Make a similar Button on your DRL form, change its name also, to *butResponse*, and its Text to *blank*. You may be curious how you were able to change both of these Button objects to the same Name (butResponse) without Visual Basic 2005 delivering you an Error message. The reason why is because while the objects do in fact have the same name, they reside on different forms. As a result, there is no problem. If the FR form is running, then the Button on frmFR is accessed and if the DRL form is running, then the Button on frmDRL is accessed. Even if both forms are running simultaneously, Visual Basic 2005 can keep track of which Button refers to which form and access them accordingly.

Now add a TextBox to each form that will be used to display points to the participant. Change the name of these TextBoxes to *txtPoints* and the text property to *blank*. Also add a Label above the TextBoxes, change the name to *lblPoints* and the text to *Points*.

Code for the FR Schedule Component

The backbone of this form needs to be a Timer object which will occasionally check to see if the FR has been meet within a given amount of time. This schedule might more accurately be conceptualized as Differential Reinforcement of High Rates (DRH). However, it does lack a specific interresponse interval contingency. Therefore, for ease of discrimination while programming it will be simply referred to as a FR. The function of this "given amount of time" is to generate relatively high rates of responding, and compare and contrast these rates to the hopefully lower rates of responding that are inherent in a DRO schedule. Also, because we are using a negative reinforcement contingency with this schedule component, we need to specify an allotted amount of time we allow the participant to respond before we take away or subtract points from their point total.

For ease of illustration, we will use a 3 second time period in which we want to see three responses made by the participant. In other words, we want a rate of about

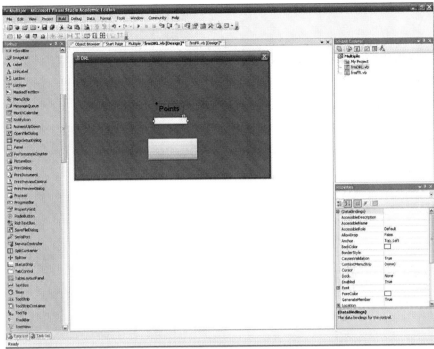

Figure 8.3 displays the DRL form with the addition of Button, TextBox, and Label objects.

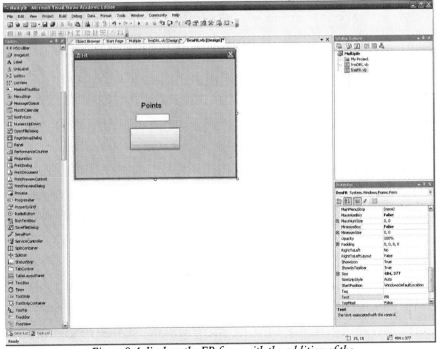

Figure 8.4 displays the FR form with the addition of the Button, TextBox, and Label objects.

1/sec. To develop code for this contingency, we need to do a couple of things. First, we need a variable that will keep track of each participant response on the Button object. Second we need the Timer to kick in every three seconds and see if the responses are at least 3. Your specific programming needs may differ from the parameters we will use as an example here, but customization will only require you to change the values from 3 seconds to X seconds and from 3 responses to X responses. Plus you may consider looking ahead to Chapter 9 and the descriptions of how to include a parameters screen and combine that with some of the controls and skills described in Chapter 4 to allow further modifications.

Add a Timer object to frmFR and rename it *tmrCheck*. Change the Enabled property to *True* and change the Interval property to 3000. Now when the form loads, the Timer will automatically begin ticking away and upon the elapsing of 3000 milliseconds (3 seconds), any code we place under the Timer will activate. Double-click on tmrCheck and enter the edit mode. Place the following code under Private Sub tmrCheck_Tick():

```
If vClicks < 3 Then 'FR 3 THEN AVOID POINT LOSS
vPoints = vPoints - 1
txtPoints.Text = vPoints
End If
vClicks = 0
```

What we have created here is a little If-Then statement which states that if a variable named vClicks (we still need to declare this variable), is less than 3, take away a value of 1 from a variable named vPoints. If the value of vClicks is greater than 3, Visual Basic 2005 skips this If-Then statement and jumps down to the next line of code which resets vClicks to 0. Now as the next 3 second interval begins, the value of vClicks has been reset to allow for rechecking of the above If-Then statement upon the completion of the next interval.

Let us now declare vClicks under the Public Class frmFR line of code by typing:

```
Dim vClicks As Integer
```

Declaring vPoints on the other hand is a little bit more tricky. Pretend we declare it as we did for vPoints. What will happen when this component of the multiple schedule terminates and the DRO component starts? How will the value of vPoints transfer across the forms? As you may recall, using multiple forms in a project requires you to create a new instance of the form each time it is presented on the computer screen. If you create this new instance, the value of vPoints which is located in the txtPoints object on frmFR will be blank when frmDRO appears! The way around this problem is to use a Module to hold the value of vPoints. This Module is just another object that sits within your Multiple project and stores values of variables that are to be recognized over and above the single form level. Because we want our points to remain constant across the two components of the multiple schedule, we can declare the variable of vPoints here on the Module instead of on the individual forms.

Begin by adding a Module to your project by selecting the text "Multiple" in your Solution Explorer window and right clicking on this text. A popup menu will appear. Select the option "Add" and then the sub-option "Module." You can change the name of the Module if you like or leave it as Module1. More complicating programming may require multiple modules, but you will probably never need to use more than one.

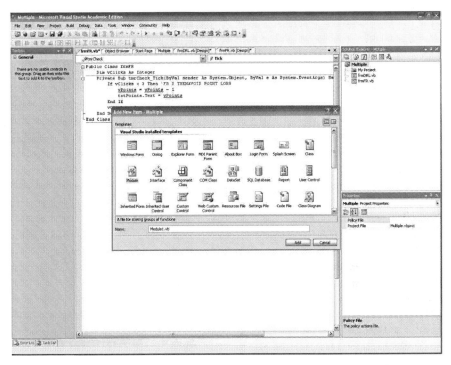

Figure 8.5 displays the popup dialog box for adding a Module to the Multiple Project.

Declaring the vPoints variable on the new Module is rather simple. First double-click on the new Module which has been added to your Solution Explorer window. You will automatically enter the edit mode for the Module, because the Module has no visible components which appear during run time. Rather the Module is nothing more than a virtual container that holds information. Under the text Module Module1, type the following declaration:

```
Public vPoints
```

That is it: very simple. Remember during our discussion of variables in Chapter 5, that a variable spanning beyond a single form should be declared using the "Public" declaration rather than the "Dim" declaration.

Return to frmFR and double-click on the butResponse object to enter the edit mode. Here we need to add the necessary code to increase values of vClicks each time the Button is clicked upon. Therefore, add the following code under Private Sub butResponse_Click

```
vClicks = vClicks + 1
```

Run the program and test your progress. The FR form should open, and if you don't click fast enough on the Button, negative points will start accumulating in the txtPoints TextBox.

One small issue at this time is that the points in txtPoints start off at 0, actually they are displayed as a blank box, when the program loads. This may or may not be desirable. If it is not, you can start the program with a different value of vPoints than the default 0 when the form loads. The easy thing to do is to make vPoints = 100 or some other value. Yet, a problem arises when you begin the alternations of the FR and DRL forms in the multiple schedule. If each time you load the form, the value of vPoints resets to 100, participants will be extremely confused. Here is how to get around this problem. Begin by typing the following text under the Private Sub frmFR_Load()

```
If vSwitch = 0 Then vPoints = 100 'TO SET THE INITIAL POINT
    VALUE
txtPoints.Text = vPoints
```

The first line of code contains an If – Then statement which states if a variable called vSwitch = 0 (we still need to declare this variable) then make the value of vPoints = 100. The second line of code states to display the value of vPoints in the txtPoints TextBox. The new variable vSwitch can be used to count successive presentations of the multiple schedule's components. So once the FR component is completed, vSwitch will go from 0 to 1. If vSwitch is sitting at 0 right now, and it will be when the program is first started, turn vPoints to 100. Afterwards, vSwitch will never be 0 again, and VB.NET passes this If – Then statement and just moves down to the next one and places the value of the Public variable, vPoints, into txtPoints.

Declare vSwitch on your Module1 not on your FR or DRL forms because we will use this variable across forms to track the number of presentations of each component of the schedule. To declare vSwitch type:

```
Public vSwitch
```

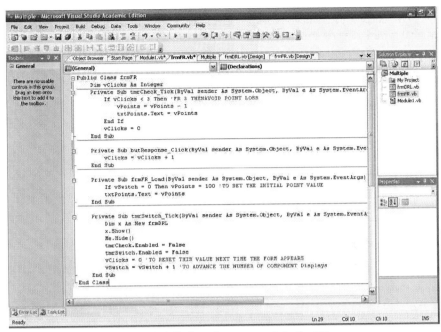

Figure 8.6 displays the correct code for frmFR.

All that is left to do on this form now is to add another Timer that will close this schedule component (and this FR form) and open the DRL form and initiate those contingencies. Begin by adding a Timer object and renaming it tmrSwitch. Also change the enabled property to True and the Interval property to 30000 (or 30 seconds). The 30000 millisecond interval will be used for the desired length of exposure to this component of the multiple schedule. You can change the interval to meet your own needs later. Finally add the following code under tmrSwitch:

```
Dim x As New frmDRL()
x.Show()
Me.Hide()
tmrCheck.Enabled = False
tmrSwitch.Enabled = False
vClicks = 0 'TO RESET THIS VALUE NEXT TIME THE FORM
    APPEARS
vSwitch = vSwitch + 1 'TO ADVANCE THE NUMBER OF
    COMPONENT DISPLAYS
```

This code generates a new instance of form frmDRL and shows the form while hiding the existing FR form (called *me*). Next both Timers are shut down so they do not continue to run while the DRL form is in action. The variable vClicks is also reset to 0 so that the next time frmFR is loaded it is not containing old values of vClicks, and a value of one is added to variable vSwitch. We can use this increasing value of vSwitch to eventually terminate the entire program with an If – Then vSwitch type statement. Run the program and check your progress. If done correctly, after 30 seconds of responding on frmFR, frmDRL should appear. Not much happens after this, but adding some code will fix it.

Code for the DRL Schedule Component

Much of the code used in the FR form can be recycled on the DRL form. Begin with the Private Sub frmDRL_Load subroutine and type (or copy and paste from frmFR) the following:

```
txtPoints.Text = vPoints
```

You will not need to add the other line of code found in the Private Sub frmFR_Load subroutine that set the initial value of vPoints to 100 because by now, vPoints will have a participant specific value after their exposure to the first component of the schedule.

The code under butResponse is the same for this form as it was on frmFR. Therefore copy and paste the following code from butResponse on frmFR to butResponse on frmDRL under the Private butResponse_Click subroutine:

```
vClicks = vClicks + 1
```

Also declare this variable under the Public Class frmDRL line in the code editor by typing:

```
Dim vClicks As Integer
```

As with the FR form, we will again need two Timers on the DRL form. The first Timer will check the rate of responding to ensure it is within our DRL contingencies, and the second Timer will control the total amount of time the DRL component is presented. Add the first of the two Timers and change the name to tmrCheck, the enabled property to True, and the Interval property to 3000 (for 3 seconds). For demonstration purposes, we will program a DRL schedule where only 1 response must occur within a three second time interval in order to avoid point loss. Therefore, add the following code under the Private Sub tmrCheck_Tick subroutine:

```
If vClicks <> 1 Then
vPoints = vPoints - 1
txtPoints.Text = vPoints
End If
vClicks = 0
```

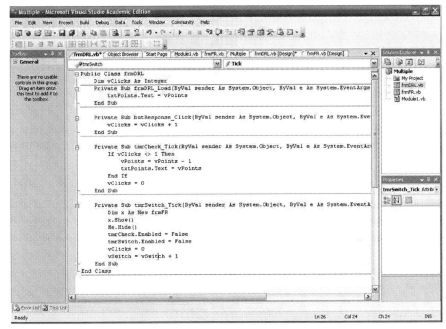

Figure 8.7 displays the correct code for frmDRL.

The first section of code, the If – Then statement, checks to see if the value of vClicks is not equal to 1. If the value is anything greater than 1 or less than 1, one point will be subtracted from vPoints and displayed in the txtPoints TextBox. After the elapsing of the 3 second interval, regardless of whether points were subtracted or not, vClicks are then reset back to 0 as the next interval begins.

Add the second Timer to frmDRL and rename it tmrSwitch as you did before on the second Timer you added to frmFR. Change the Enabled property to True and the Interval property to 30000 milliseconds. Double-click on tmrSwitch and enter the edit mode. Type the following code under Private Sub tmrSwitch_Click:

```
Dim x As New frmFR()
x.Show()
Me.Hide()
tmrCheck.Enabled = False
tmrSwitch.Enabled = False
vClicks = 0
vSwitch = vSwitch + 1
```

This code operates identically as its counterpart did on the FR form. Specifically, it generates a new instance of form frmFR and shows the form while hiding the existing DRL form (called *me*). The Timers are then shut down so they do not continue to run while the FR form is in action. The variable vClicks is also reset to 0 so that the next time frmFR is loaded it is not containing old values of vClicks, and the value of one is added to the variable vSwitch. Run the program and check your progress. If all goes well you will have a working multiple schedule of negative reinforcement with one component consisting of a FR (or DRH) schedule and another component consisting of a DRL schedule.

Enhancing the Multiple Schedule with Data Collection, Writing to an Output File, and Generating a Cumulative Record

There are a variety of different ways we could write to file the response data that are being collected with our multiple schedule. We could store values of vClick and write them to file at the end of the experiment. We could also write vClicks each time the butResponse is clicked for a molecular level analysis. We could create another Timer with an interval of x seconds specifically for writing data to file. Finally we could tie into the existing tmrCheck Timer and have it write to file upon completing its interval, which in this case is 3 seconds for both components. For illustration purposes, we shall do the last of these options and add data output code under the existing tmrCheck Timers. Begin with frmFR by double-clicking on tmrCheck and adding the following code above the line vClicks = 0 of the Private Sub tmrCheck_Tick subroutine:

```
WriteLine(1, vSwitch, vClicks, vPoints)
```

The new subroutine should look like:

```
If vClicks < 3 Then 'FR 3 THEN AVOID POINT LOSS
vPoints = vPoints - 1
txtPoints.Text = vPoints
End If
WriteLine(1, vSwitch, vClicks, vPoints)
vClicks = 0
```

This line of code writes the values of vSwitch and vClicks to a text file with an alias name called "1". It also writes the current point total to the same file. Add the exact code under the tmrCheck Timer on the DRL form, this time under vClicks=0.

We have not yet opened a file for the data to be written into, so we need to do so. The most logical place is right along with the code that sets the initial value of vPoints to 100 on frmFR. Therefore, add the following code under the existing If vSwitch = 0 Then vPoints = 100 code that is in the Private Sub frmFR_Load subroutine:

```
If vSwitch = 0 then FileOpen(1, "C:\data.txt",
   OpenMode.Append)
```

This code will open the file with a name of "data" in the c:\ directory and it will remain open until the program is terminated or additional code under an "Exit" Button or a Timer closes it. The data output raises another question: how long will the program run? You could design the program to terminate once a steady state of responding has been met. This could be assessed by creating an If – Then statement with code such that if no more than X number of points were subtracted from vPoints for a given number of vSwitch the program would end. You could also design the program to terminate regardless of responding patterns after x number of component presentations. In this example we will do the latter. The program will terminate after 10 presentations of both components of the multiple schedule. Therefore, add the following code under the Private Sub frmFR_Load subroutine:

```
If vSwitch > 10 then
FileClose(1)
End
```

Keep in mind that if you want the program to end after an odd number of vSwitch presentations (like 3, 9, 25), you will need to place the above code under the frmDRL Private Sub frmDRL_Load subroutine instead. Run the program, check your progress, and after 10 sequences the program should end. Afterwards, find your data file in the C:\ directory and check out your data using NotePad. It should look similar to Figure 8.8.

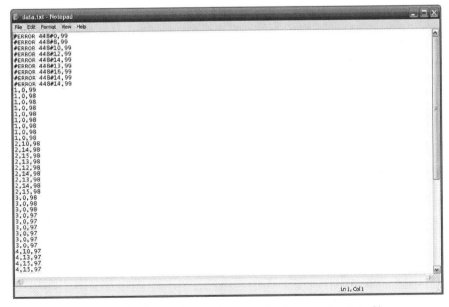

Figure 8.8 displays an illustrative example of the resulting data file.

From observation of the data file in Figure 8.8 you will notice that an error message (#Error 448#) was written in the vSwitch spot of the data file instead of the value 0. This will occur every time you have a variable with a value of 0 when you do not declare the variable as an Integer type. Remember in the discussion of variable types in Chapter 5 we discussed that Visual Basic 2005 by default defines variables as Variant type and that Visual Basic 2005 will later assign these variables to the proper type based on how they are used. Overall Visual Basic 2005 does a good job of this, however this example represents one instance where failing to fully define a variable can create an error. To avoid this error we could have declared our vSwitch variable as an Integer type variable when we declare it on Module 1. Before you save your data for analysis you might want to replace these error lines with the 0 value. Besides the error at the beginning of the file, all the desired data has been written. Researchers can now examine relative response rates on the multiple schedule. You could enhance this data file with more detail regarding which component is in effect when. Perhaps the values of vSwitch are not as important as naming the actual schedule component. If so, you could delete the vSwitch section of the data writing code and replace it with *FR* on frmFR and *DRL* on frmDRL. Another way to enhance the data file would be to generate values of a variable which continue to increase every time butResponse is clicked but not reset the way vResponse is. Doing so could allow for the creation of a cumulative record of responding. If we create such a cumulative variable it would need to be added to the Module rather than the form because it would span across forms the same way that vPoints does.

Add a variable to your Module entitled vCumm that will increase in value every time either butResponse Buttons are clicked upon. Let's also take into account the error we noted above in how values of 0 are written to our output file and make sure that we fully define the Variable Types on our Module. To do this add the following declaration code to Module1.

```
Public vCumm as Integer
```

Let's also go ahead and fix out problem from earlier by adding the Text "As Integer" to the declaration of both vPoints and vSwitch. Now add the following code under both butResponse Buttons directly below the existing code vClicks = vClicks + 1:

```
vCumm = vCumm + 1
```

Finally, alter the data file output code to include the vCumm values each time data are written to file. The new code under the tmrCheck Timers for both forms should now read:

```
WriteLine(1, vSwitch, vClicks, vCumm, vPoints)
```

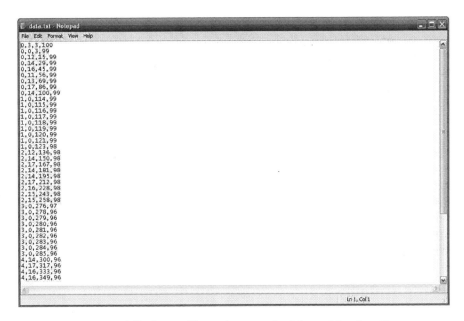

*Figure 8.9 displays an illustrative example of the resulting data file
with the addition of vCumm.*

Run the program and check your data file output to ensure it includes the new vCumm variable values. From observation of the data file you can see that it appears vCumm values are being recorded properly. Look a little closer though and examine the values of vClicks when the DRL schedule is operating. All the values are 0, regardless of how many clicks you actually made during that time period. Go back and examine your code on the DRL where vClicks is reset to 0. Do you see anything suspicious? Below is the existing subroutine:

```
Private Sub tmrCheck_Tick(ByVal sender As System.Object,
    ByVal e As System.EventArgs) Handles tmrCheck.Tick
If vClicks <> 1 Then
vPoints = vPoints - 1
txtPoints.Text = vPoints
End If
vClicks = 0
WriteLine(1, vSwitch, vClicks, vCumm, vPoints)
End Sub
```

From examination above, you might notice that we have made the value of vClicks = 0 before we write the values to file in the next WriteLine statement. That is our problem! To fix it, just reverse these two lines of code, and then all should

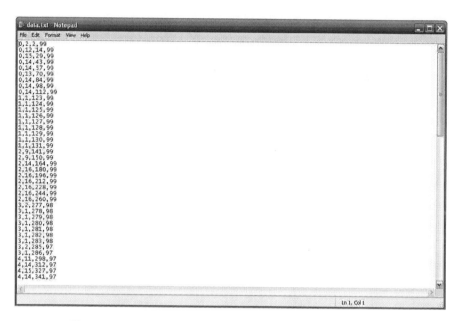

Figure 8.10 displays the data file output after correcting the code error that made all values of vClicks equal 0 on the DRL component.

work properly. Run the program and check the data file. Everything should now work properly including that crazy error in the data file that occurred when vSwitch is still at 0.

Transferring the Data File into Excel for Analysis

Locating the File

Until now we have viewed our data file in Notepad or another text editor. This is fine for some data collection applications, but other applications that may lead to complex graphs and data analyses are better examined and manipulated in spreadsheets like Microsoft Excel 2007. The process will be similar in other spreadsheets but we will provide you with an example using Excel because it is the most commonly used program. In addition the recent release of Office 2007 by Microsoft warrants a description of how to employ the latest version of Excel for your data analysis needs. Before getting your data into Excel, you will need to tell Excel what type of file it is and how you want it configured. This sounds more complicated than it really is. In fact, the process is very easy and can open up endless analysis possibilities for you. Before opening Excel, figure out what directory your data file is in. If you have been following along with this chapter's example, it should be in the C:\ directory.

The Transfer Process

Open Microsoft Excel 2007. A blank worksheet should appear similar to that shown in Figure 8.11. Click on the Microsoft Office icon in the upper left of the screen, select the *Open* option, and an open file dialog box will appear. Change the *Files of Types* option from *All Excel Files* to *All Files* using the downward arrow to the right of this option. Now browse through your directories until you find the *data.txt* file you created in the above example. Select the data.txt file and click on *Open*. Figure 8.12 displays the open file dialogue box.

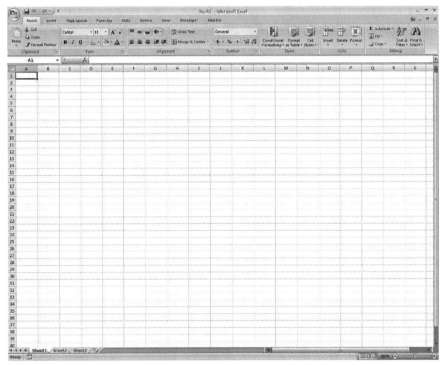

Figure 8.11 displays a blank worksheet in Microsoft Excel 2007.

The next screen which appears is probably less familiar than the previous ones. This new screen is dialogue box called the *Text Import Wizard*. An example of this dialogue box is displayed in Figure 8.13. The dialogue box contains a variety of information which is used to help Excel 2007 understand the type of file you are trying to place within it. The first section of the dialogue box asks you to tell Excel if your Data are *Delimited* or *Fixed Width*.

Data that are *delimited* means that different sections of the data are on each line of the file are separated by a *delimiter* or a textual character – in our case a comma. Data that are *fixed width* means that different sections of the data that are on each line of the file are separated by a set number of spaces. Our data file fits the first

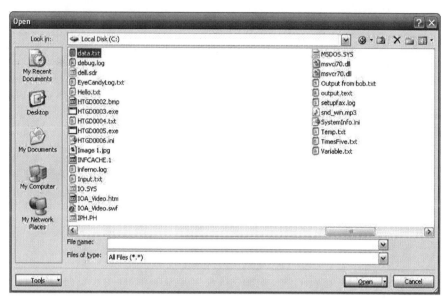

Figure 8.12 displays the open file dialogue box,
the change made to "Files of Type", and the selection of "data.txt".

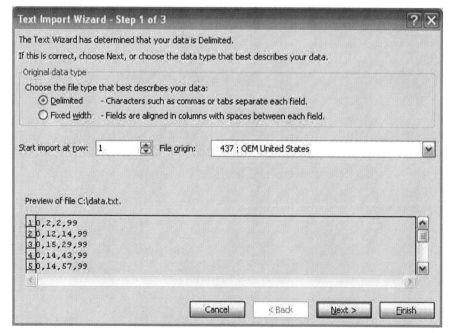

Figure 8.13 displays the first screen of the Text Import Wizard
used to open a text file in Excel 2007.

category, delimited, so select that option if it's not already. The next question that Excel wants you to answer is at what row should Excel start importing your data. This is an outstanding feature, because you might not want to start importing your data into Excel at row 1 of the data.txt file every time. This is especially the case when using an appended data file, as we have been using which keeps a running archive of all participants that we have run in the experiment. For now, let us assume you want to start importing the data at row 1, so leave this option as it is, and click the *Next* button. The second screen of the Text Import Wizard asks you to supply more information.

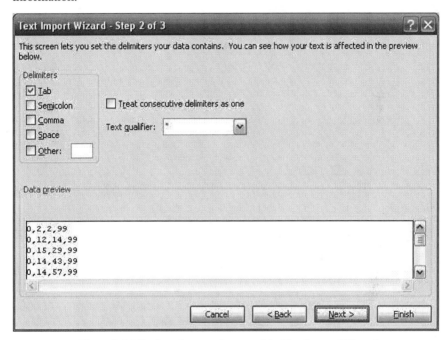

Figure 8.14 displays the second screen of the Text Import Wizard used to open a text file in Excel 2007.

Because you selected the *Delimited* option on the previous screen, Excel now wants to know what specific type of delimiter was used to separate the data fields. The default selection is a *Tab*. We used a *Comma* to separate our data, so change this option accordingly. As soon as you make this change, Excel draws vertical lines through your data columns as depicted in Figure 8.15.

At this point click on the *Next* button to advance to the final screen of the Text Import Wizard. This last screen asks you if you with to convert any of your data to dates, or dates to values, or text to other types of characters. Such alterations do not apply to our data file, so just click on the *Finish* button.

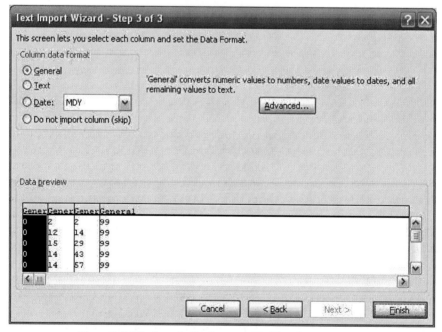

Figure 8.15 displays the second screen of the Text Import Wizard
following the selection of "Comma" delimiter.

Figure 8.16 displays the final screen of the Text Import Wizard
allowing you to transpose data from numbers to dates or dates to numbers.

Once you click on the *Finish* button, the Text Import Wizard goes away and you return to the main Excel 2007 program. Your data.txt data are magically entered into the Excel worksheet for endless data analysis as displayed in Figure 8.17.

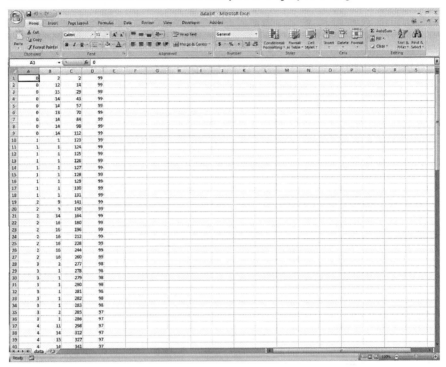

Figure 8.17 displays the Excel 2007 worksheet containing data.txt.

While the purpose of this book is not to teach you how to graph in Excel 2007, a quick illustration will be provided to show you how truly easy this feat is to accomplish. To create a cumulative record from our data.txt file, highlight the third column of data containing the values of vCumm as displayed in Figure 8.18.

With this column highlighted, select the *Insert* option from the main menu at the top of the screen. Five collections of icons for the types of objects that can be inserted into a worksheet should be displayed across the top of the screen. From the third group, *Charts*, we can select various types of graphs for our data. The most appropriate one for our data type is the *Line* chart. Click on this option and from the resulting sub options select the third sub option, *Line With Markers*, as displayed in Figure 8.19.

Once you click on the *Line With Markers* option your graphs should appear in your Excel 2007 worksheet as displayed in Figure 8.20. At this point we want to make several modifications to this basic graph. With your graph selected you will note three new options at the right end of the main menu at the top of the screen. Under

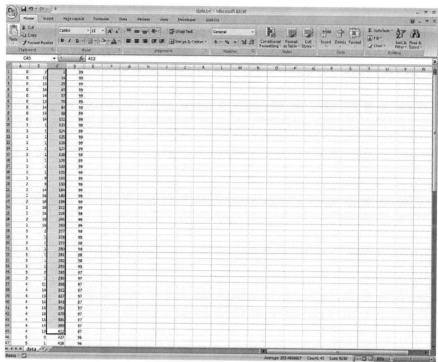

Figure 8.18 displays the correctly highlighted columns of the data.txt worksheet.

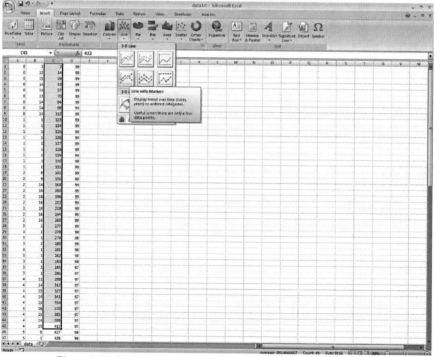

Figure 8.19 displays the selection of the "Line With Markers" graph
from the "Line" Chart Types.

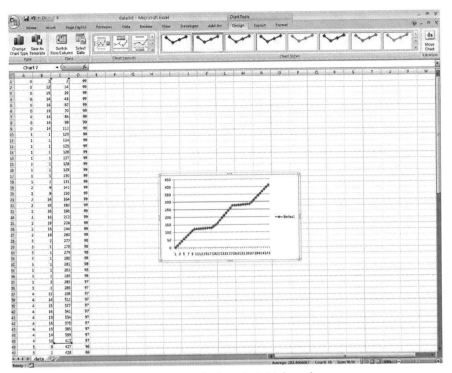

Figure 8.20 displays the initial graph.

a heading of *Chart Tools* you should see tabs for *Design, Layout,* and *Format.* The *Design* tab displays options for selecting the data associated with the chart, various chart layout styles, as well as some preselected chart color styles that may be applied to the graph. The *Format* tab presents some advance formatting options for shapes and text styles within a char, while the *Layout* tab gives formatting options for Chart Titles, Axes styles and titles, Gridline styles, as well as options for inserting pictures, shapes, and text into our graphs. These are the options we need at this time so go ahead and select the *Layout* tab.

The first addition we need to make to our graph is to insert a title. From the third group of option select the *Chart Title* option and from the resulting sub options select the *Above Chart* option as displayed in Figure 8.21. This should insert the text "Chart Title" at the top of your graph. Select this title by clicking on it with your mouse, highlight the current text, and type a title for your graph. To insert a title for the vertical axis click on the *Axis Titles* option at the top of the screen and from the resulting sub options select *Primary Vertical Axis Title* and *Rotated Title* as displayed in Figure 8.22. To edit the axis title, click on the default "Axis Title" text and replace the current text with an appropriate title such as "Cumulative Responses". To insert a title for the horizontal axis, once again click on the *Axis Titles* option, but this time select the *Primary Horizontal Axis Title* and *Title Below Axis* sub options as displayed in Figure 8.23. Follow the steps described above to edit the newly inserted axis title. To remove the legend on the left of the graph, click

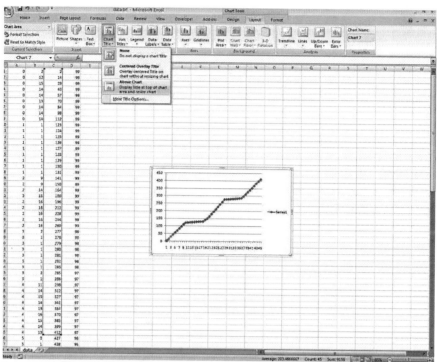

Figure 8.21 displays the selection of the "Above Chart" sub option
from the "Chart Title" options.

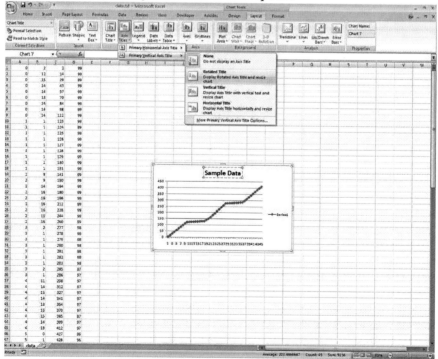

Figure 8.22 displays the selection of the "Rotated Title" sub option
from the "Primary Vertical Axis Title" option.

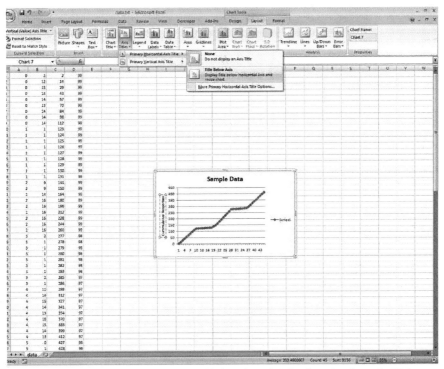

Figure 8.23 displays the selection of the "Title Below Axis" sub option from the "Primary Horizontal Axis Title" option

on the *Legend* option at the top of the screen then select the *None* sub option. Finally to remove the horizontal gridlines from the graph, click on the *Gridlines* option located in the *Axes* group box, then select the *Primary Horizontal Gridlines* and *None* sub options.

The last modification you may wish to make to your graph is the labeling of schedule component presentations. This can be done by drawing vertical lines between the data points that end one component and begin the next. For example, after nine 3 second intervals of the FR component, the DRL component goes into effect. As a result we would want to draw a line between the 9th and 10th data points and label the components accordingly. To do this, make sure that you are still within the *Layout* options of the *Chart Tools* header and click on the *Shapes* option within the *Insert* group box. From the second collection of shapes, the *Lines* collection, select the first line shape. Position the mouse cursor on your chart between data points 9 and 10 on the horizontal axis and draw a line vertically between them. Repeat this process for the other component changes displayed on your chart. The final step is to add labels above the components to identify FR (DRH) or DRL contingencies. Next to the *Shapes* option within the *Insert* group box is the *Text Box* option. Select this drawing option and place it on your chart in the desired location. Type the desired text. Repeat this process for the other components. The resulting chart should look similar to Figure 8.24.

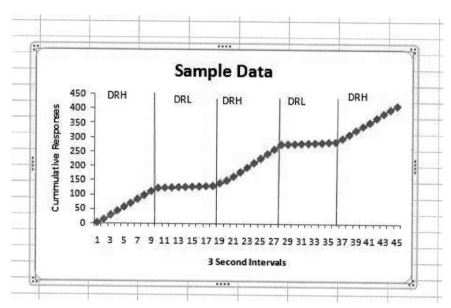

Figure 8.24 displays the final chart layout for the cumulative record of responses.

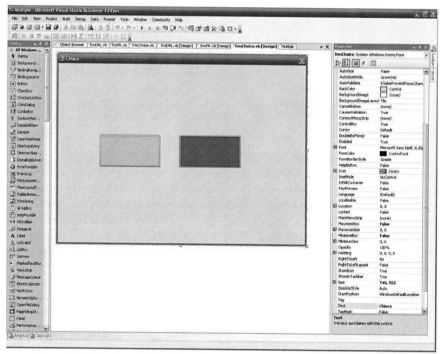

Figure 8.25 displays the final chart layout for the cumulative record of responses.

Building a Mixed Schedule of Reinforcement

A Simple Modification

If you wish to conduct research using a mixed schedule of reinforcement instead of a multiple schedule, only one simple modification is needed to the existing program. A mixed schedule is identical to a multiple schedule except that the mixed does not have a discriminative stimulus associated with each schedule component. In our working example, that discriminative stimulus is *BackColor*. Alter the BackColor properties of both forms so they are the same color. Now, you should have a working version of a mixed schedule.

Building a Concurrent Schedule of Reinforcement

Creating the Interface

Altering the multiple schedule to a mixed schedule was very simple. It is also quite easy to alter the multiple schedule to a concurrent schedule of reinforcement. In a concurrent schedule, both schedule components are presented simultaneously, and the participant selects which of the two components he/she wishes to respond to. Sometimes participants may have "forced choices" when only one component is available for selection, and other times when they may have "free choices" when both components are available. The forced or single choice trials are presented to ensure the participant has made contact with the programmed contingencies associated with each component, and therefore can make an "informed" choice when presented with a free or two choice trial.

We will need to add another form to our existing project to serve as the "choice" interface for our two schedule components. To do this, add a Windows form by clicking on the Project option in the main toolbar, and on the sub-option "Add Windows form". Name the form frmChoice and click *Add*. Change the Text property of this form to *Choice*, the WindowState to *Maximized*, and the MaximizeBox and MinimizeBox properties to *False*. Next add two Buttons to the form, to which we will link the components of the schedule. Change the names of these Buttons to butLeft and butRight and the Text property to *blank*. If we are going to use discriminative stimuli for each schedule component, as we did in the multiple schedule, place those stimuli on frmControl as well. In our example, we used screen BackColor. Our frmFR had a green BackColor and our frmDRL had a red BackColor. Change the BackColor of your butLeft to resemble the green BackColor of frmFR and the BackColor of butRight to resemble the red BackColor of frmDRL. We will not describe how to randomize the positions of these Buttons on frmChoice, but you may wish to have them randomized at each choice point control for a position bias. Randomization code examples are found throughout this book and can be incorporated into this situation as well if desired.

To link the butLeft and butRight Buttons to their respective forms, you need to place some code under each of them. Start with butLeft by double-clicking on it to enter the edit mode. Under Private Sub butLeft_Click type the following:

```
Dim x As New frmFR()
x.Show()
me.Hide()
```

Now place the following code under butRight:

```
Dim x As New frmDRL
x.Show ( )
me.Hide ( )
```

A few other alterations need to be made to our individual component forms as well. First, go to frmFR and change the line of code under tmrSwitch from:

```
Dim x As New frmDRL()
to
Dim x As New frmChoice()
```

Second, repeat the same steps on frmDRL by changing the code under tmrSwitch from:

```
Dim x As New frmFR()
to
Dim x As New frmChoice()
```

Third, change the location of the code that opens the data file and checks to see if vSwitch is greater than 10 from frmFR's Private Sub frmFR_Load to frmChoice's Private Sub frmChoice_Load. Specificially cut and paste the following code:

```
If vSwitch = 0 Then vPoints = 100 'TO SET THE INITIAL POINT
    VALUE
If vSwitch = 0 Then FileOpen(1, "C:\data.txt",
    OpenMode.Append)
If vSwitch > 10 Then
FileClose(1)
End
End If
```

Forth, move the following line of code to the beginning of the tmrSwitch_Tick subroutines on both frmFR and frmDRL:
```
vSwitch = vSwitch + 1
```

The resulting subroutine should look like this for frmFR:

```
vSwitch = vSwitch + 1
Dim x As New frmChoice()
x.Show()
me.Hide()
tmrCheck.Enabled = False
tmrSwitch.Enabled = False
vClicks = 0
```

and look like this for frmDRL:

```
vSwitch = vSwitch + 1
Dim x As New frmChoice()
x.Show()
Me.Hide()
tmrCheck.Enabled = False
tmrSwitch.Enabled = False
vClicks = 0
```

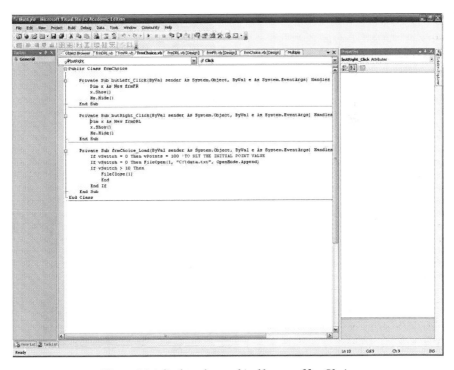

Figure 8.26 displays the graphical layout of frmChoice.

The movement of this line of code is critical. If you fail to do it an error will occur the second time you return to frmChoice because you load frmChoice prior to adding one to vSwitch. As a result, frmChoice attempts to re-open data.txt, a file that is already open, and Visual Basic 2005 shoots you an error.

Finally, change the startup object from frmFR to frmChoice. Run the program and check your progress. If all goes well you should have a working concurrent schedule of reinforcement. Enjoy.

Summary

In summary, this chapter has provided you with a series of new tools to create more complex schedules of reinforcement you can use for research purposes. In addition, this chapter has shown you the steps necessary to import your data files into spreadsheets such as Microsoft Excel and how to make simple charts from the data. Any researcher that takes the information found in this chapter along with the various additional control objects from Chapter 4 and the multimedia from Chapter 5 will be able to develop an endless array of research projects incorporating schedules of reinforcement.

Chapter 9: Relational Responding and Contextual Control

Beyond Matching to Sample

To date, most of the published literature which has examined derived relational responding has utilized matching to sample procedures such as those described in Chapter 7. Many successful advances have come from the use of this methodology, and many more will surely occur in the future. Yet, in an effort to ensure that our descriptions of behavior are not merely descriptions of a procedural artifact, an increasing number of behavior analysts are moving beyond the sole use of matching to sample procedures in their respective research programs. For example, Leader, Barnes and Smeets (1996), developed a respondent-type (ReT) training procedure whereby subjects simply observed pairs of stimuli on the computer screen and were later able to make derived relations in matching to sample test trials. Fields, Reeve, Varelas, Rosen, and Delanich (1997) also developed an alternative procedure whereby subjects viewed stimulus pairs on the computer screen and were required to respond on one of two keys (a yes or a no key) following the presentation. Many of Fields et al., (1997) subjects were subsequently able to derive relations following this type of training-type procedure. More recently, Cullinan, Barnes, and Smeets (1998) developed a procedure they termed the precursor to the relational evaluation procedure (pREP) which employed a form of go/ no-go procedure. A typical trial in this procedure consisted of the presentation of a single sample stimulus followed by either a positive or a negative comparison stimulus. Participants were required to respond to the presentation of positive comparison stimuli by pressing a key on the computer's keyboard within a set period of time and to respond to negative comparison stimuli by not pressing the response key during the allotted response interval. Cullinan, Barnes-Holmes, and Smeets (2001) later refined this procedure to include the presentation of two response options on the computer screen, one for positive sample-comparison stimulus pairs and one for negative sample-comparison stimulus pairs. These response options would consist of two buttons presented side by side on the computer screen following the presentation of both the sample and comparison stimuli and would remain on the screen until a participant emitted a response. The stimuli presented on these two response options could consist of images, abstract symbols, or various verbal labels such as the words *same* and *different* or *yes* and *no*. All told the respondent-type and pREP procedures offer Behavior Analysts alternatives for studying relational responding beyond match to sample procedures.

The pREP as an Illustrative Example of Building Flexibility into Applications

One purpose of this chapter is to outline how we can construct alternative training and testing procedures for the study of relational responding and contextual control that move beyond match to sample procedures discussed in Chapter 7. In this chapter we will outline how to construct an application to carry out both the Go/No-Go and 2 Response Options formats of the pREP procedures described in Cullinan et al., (1996) and Cullinan et al., (2001). While we have chosen the pREP as our illustrative example, the techniques and methods described in this chapter could rather easily be modified to allow one to craft versions of the respondent-type procedure described by Leader et al., (1996). Furthermore, even if your interests never involve the study of relational responding, this chapter will serve to demonstrate the logic and ease of building in experimenter choice and flexibility with the use of certain controls described previously in Chapter 4 of this book.

Program Requirements

Creating Support Files

Before we begin constructing the program, let's first consider some of the support files you will need for this application. In essence this program will be quite similar to the program constructed previously in Chapter 7 on match to sample procedures. This program will use audio *.wav* files as feedback for the accuracy of responses for training phases, the program will read trial input from a text file similar to the one constructed in Chapter 7, and stimuli will consist of image files. Also, as we did in Chapter 7, we will construct our pREP program to train relationships for three 3-member classes which means that you will need nine image files: A1, A2, A3, B1, B2, B3, C1, C2, and C3.

To start with let's create a directory structure where we will save our program and store all of the appropriate support files that go along with it. Open the *"C"* drive of your computer and if you do not already have it, create a folder and name it *"programming"*. Open the *"programming'* folder and create a new folder and name it *"pREP"*. Open the newly created *"pREP"* folder and create a new folder and name it *"Input Files"*. In this folder we will store our text files, images, and the sound files that we will use for this program.

Creating the Stimuli

If you have already completed Chapter 7 from this program you may find it more convenient to reuse the image files you created previously for the Match to Sample program for this program as well. If you have already created the images then simply locate the folder where you saved them previously then copy and paste them to the *"C:\programming\Input Files\"* folder we created above. If you do not have these images then we can create them using the Paint program provided with Microsoft Windows.

Locate the Paint program and open it on your computer. Once the Paint program is open, select *Image* then *Attributes* from the main menu. Change the width and height to 200 pixels. You can then use the text tool to type *A1* and save the image as "A1.bmp" in the *"C:\programming\Input Files\"* directory. Follow these directions to create the eight other images and save them to the same directory.

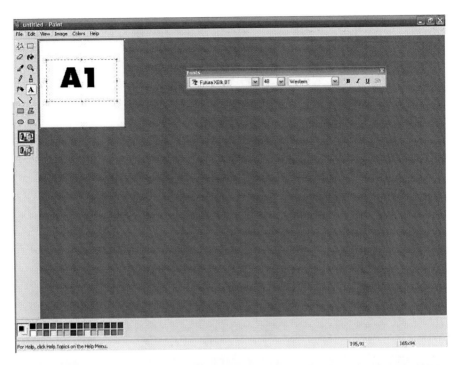

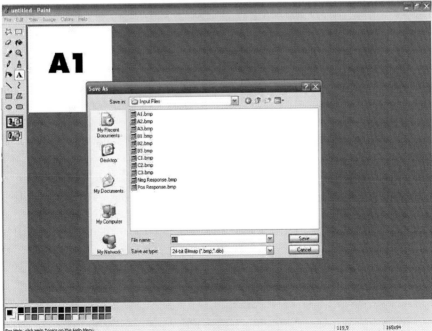

Figure 9.1 displays the A1 stimulus being created in Microsoft Paint

One element of functionality we want to include with this program is the ability to use either text or images as stimuli for the response options included in the Go/No-Go or 2 Response Options formats of the pREP. Let's create two more image files to use as stimuli for positive and negative response options. With Paint still open on your computer create a new image and select *Image* then *Attributes* from the main menu. Change the width to 200 pixels and height to 100 pixels. Use the *Ellipse* tool in the lower left of the toolbar to draw a circle or oval shape in the center of the image. Then click on the bucket tool, select a color from the bottom of the screen, and click on the center of your new shape to fill the shape with your chosen color. Save your image as *"Pos Response.bmp"* in the in the *"C:\programming\Input Files\"* directory. Now follow the same steps to create another image of the same size, but this time use the *Rectangle* tool to draw a square and use a different fill color. Save this image as *"Neg Response.bmp"* in the *"C:\programming\Input Files\"* directory. Close Microsoft Paint.

Training with Reinforcement

As we did with Chapter 7, we want to use auditory stimuli to signal accurate and inaccurate responses for our participants during training. To accomplish this we can have the program play a relatively positive sounding audio file when the participant makes a correct response and a relatively negative sounding audio file when the participant makes an incorrect response. These files could be anything of your choosing but should be relatively brief so the participant does not have to wait for them to finish playing for too long before moving on to the next trial. For the sake of illustration we will again use two of the basic system sound files from your computer, the "chimes.wav" and "chord.wav" files, as our auditory feedback. To locate these files open your "C" drive and then open the "Windows" folder. Locate and open the "Media" folder and then locate the "chord.wav" and "chimes.wav" files. Copy these files and place them in the "C:\programming\Input Files\" directory.

Configure the Forms

Now that we have most of our support files in place we can move on to starting the development of our actual program and get an idea of what this thing is going to look like. Open Microsoft Visual Studio 2005 and create a new Windows Application. Name the application "pREP" and click "OK". We can now consider the number of forms we will need to create within our project to accomplish all of our goals. One of the main purposes for this chapter is to demonstrate how we can build in experimenter choice and flexibility that allows us to choose between two types of pREP procedures and to customize features of the training format, so we need one form devoted to allowing us to set up our study format. Change the name property of *Form 1* to *frmSetup* in both the Properties and Solution Explorer windows, the text property to *pREP Setup*, the size property to *1024, 786*, and the WindowState to *Maximized*. We will discuss the details of all the controls we will need to include on this form in more detail later, now let's move on to the other forms we will need.

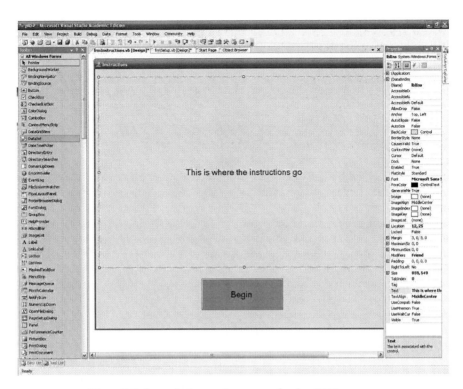

Figure 9.2 shows the instructions screen for the pREP program.

We will also need a form to deliver instructions to participants. Create a new Windows Form and name it *frmInstructions*. Change the text property to *Instructions*, the Size property to *1024, 786*, and the WindowState property to *Maximized*. We need a place to display the instructions, so add a Label object to the form. Change the name to *lblIns*, the Autosize property to *False*, the Text property to *"This is where the instructions go"*, and the TextAllign property to *MiddleCenter*. We also want the instructions to be easy to read so change the size of the Font property to *18*. We also need a button to advance to the main form once the participant has read the instructions, so add a Button object to the form below the instructions label, change its name to *butBegin*, the size of the Font property to 18, the BackColor to a green color, and the text property to *"Begin"*.

Creating Some Input

Before we can create any of the code to run our program we have to create an input file much like we did for the Match to Sample program in Chapter 7. Open a text editor such as NotePad, and create a new text file, call it *pREP Input.txt* and save it in the *"C:/programming/pREP/Input Files"* directory. On the first line of the document type the line:

```
GONOGOINSTRUCTIONS, This is where the go/no-go instructions
    go.
```

Note: type your instructions on the same line. Do **NOT** start a new line, press the ENTER button, or include any commas or quotation marks in the actual text of the instructions. If you do any of these things, Visual Studio will read these things as a line break and will stop its current reading step at that point.
Below that last line you typed, type the following line:

```
2RESPONSEINSTRUCTIONS,  This  is  where  the  2  response
    instructions go.
```

Now save and close the pREP Input.txt file. Before we move on to creating our main program, let's create the code that we'll need to open our text file and display the correct instructions to participants depending on the type of pREP format we want to use.

Return to the you program in Visual Studio and add a Module to the program by right clicking on *"pREP"* in the Solution Explorer. From the resulting options choose *Add* and then *Module*. You can leave the Module's name as *Module1* so go ahead and click on the "Add" button. We are including a module so that we can communicate important information such as the training format between our different forms. To communicate this information we will create a public variable to carry the pREP format. Under the text "Module Module1" type the following line:

```
Public Format as String
```

Now return to *frmInstructions*. Double click on the form, not the label or button, to open the code or edit level of the form, and type the following code in the Private Sub frmInstructions_Load subroutine:

```
Format = "Go/No-Go"
FileOpen(1,  "C:\programming\pREP\Input  Files\pREP
    Input.txt", OpenMode.Input)
Input(1, vHeader)
Input(1, vGONOGOIns)
Input(1, vHeader)
Input(1, v2RespIns)
Select case Format
Case "Go/No-Go"
lblIns.Text = vGONOGOIns
Case "2 Response"
lblIns.Text = v2RespIns
End Select
```

We also need to declare a few form level variables, vHeader, vGONOGOIns, and v2RsspIns. Under Public Class frmInstructions type:

```
Dim vHeader as String
Dim vGONOGOIns, v2RespIns as String
```

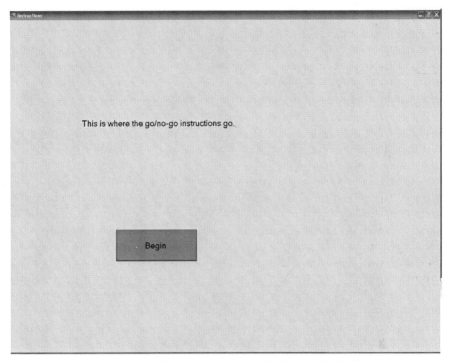

Figure 9.3 displays the instructions screen for the Go/No-Go Format

We can now test the program after we set the Startup Form to *frmInstructions*. Do so then run the program. When the form loads you should see the text for the Go/ No-Go format instructions. Now, stop the program and return to the edit level of *frmInstructions*. We want to make sure that the 2 Response Format instructions load correctly as well so change the line:

```
Format = "Go/No-Go"
```

To the following

```
Format = "2 Response"
```

Now run the program again and make sure the 2 Response Format instructions load properly.

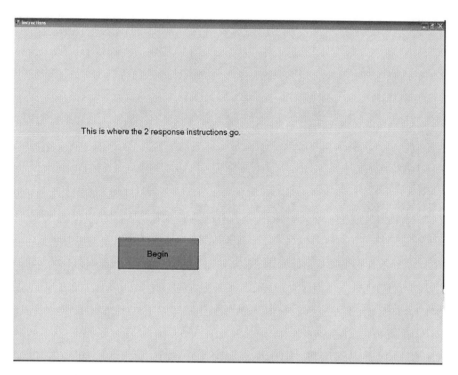

Figure 9.4 displays the instructions screen for the 2 Reponse Format

Creating the Main Form

We now need to create a form for the main program. Add a new Windows Form by right clicking on "pREP" in the Solution Explorer window and choosing *Add* and *Windows Form* from the resulting options. Name the new form *frmpREP*, set its Text property to blank, its Size property to *1024, 786*, and its WindowState property to *Maximized*. Since this form will open after the participant has read the instructions and clicked on the "Begin" button let's go back to *frmInstructions* and add that code. Return to the design level of *frmInstructions* then double click on *butBegin* to create the butBegin_Click subroutine. In this routine type:

```
Dim x as new frmpREP
x.Show()
me.Hide()
```

We can now return to the design level of frmpREP and consider all of the objects we will need to add to our main form. First and foremost we will need to use PictureBox controls to display the sample and comparison images for the program. Add a PictureBox to the form from the Toolbox. Change the PictureBox's name to *picSample*, set the Size to *200, 200*, the SizeMode property to *StretchImage*, and set the

Visible property to *False*. We will also need a PictureBox of the same dimensions to display the comparison stimulus so select *picSample*, and with your mouse, right click and copy the PictureBox. With your mouse, right click on the form and choose the *Paste* option. Position your new PictureBox below the first and change the Name property to *picComparison*.

We have now created the means for displaying our sample and comparison stimuli but we still need to include a way for participants to respond to them. For the 2 response format of the pREP, we can accomplish this by including two button controls, one that a participant can click when a positive comparison stimulus is displayed and another button control that the user can click when a negative comparison stimuli is displayed. For the Go/No-Go format of the pREP we will only need the positive response button, and we can use a timer object to mark the end of the response interval if a negative comparison stimulus is displayed. We will add the timer first

From the toolbox select a Timer control and add it to the form with your mouse. Change the name of the Timer to *tmrResponse* and make sure the Enabled property is set to *False*. In the original Cullinan et al., (1998) study the response interval was set to 5 seconds so set *tmrResponse*'s Interval property to 5000. Let's now add the two response buttons to the form as well. Select a Button object from the Toolbox and

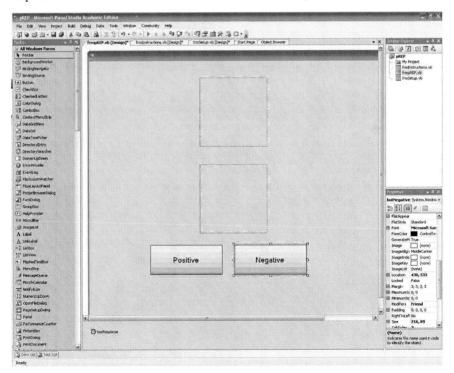

Figure 9.5 displays the screen layout with the PictureBoxes, Response Buttons, and Response Timer.

add it to the form. Change the button's name to *butPositive*, its size property to *200, 100*, it's Text property to *"Positive"*, and it's Visible property to *False*. We also want any text displayed on the response button to be clearly legible so increase the size of the Font property to 16. For the 2 response format of the pREP we will need another response button with the same properties as *butPositive*, so select it and with your mouse right click and copy the button. Paste the button on the form and change the name of the newly created button to *butNegative*, and its Text property to *"Negative"*.

Presentation of stimuli and response options in the pREP has historically been of a top to bottom nature in which a sample stimulus has been presented on the screen followed by a comparison stimulus below it, followed by response options below that. Keeping with this format, position the two response buttons side by side below *picComparison*. One thing we may also wish to consider is the possibility or randomizing the position of these two buttons during trials to prevent any positional bias for the two response buttons. With this in mind for later, we should take note of the exact locations of the two buttons. In the case of the screen displayed in Figure 9.5, the location of *butPositive* is set at *180, 533*, and the location of *butNegative* is set at *430, 533*. Either set the Location properties of your buttons to match these, or write down the locations of the buttons as you have them positioned on your

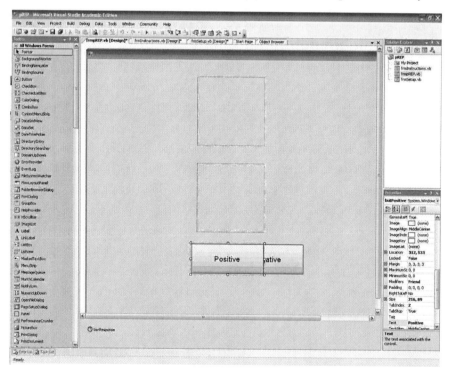

Figure 9.6 displays the Positive Response option positioned for the Go/No-Go Format.

screen for later use. We should also consider the location of where the positive response option, *butPositive*, would be during the go/ no-go format of the pREP. In this case we would want to position the button directly below the comparison stimulus image. Reposition *butPositive* so that it lies directly underneath *picComparison*, and take note of this location for later use. In the case of Figure 9.6 the location of the positive response button is at *328, 533*.

We've already discussed a bit of how stimuli and response options have been presented historically, but one thing we haven't discussed is how we might accomplish this in our program. In general, the sample image is displayed for a short period of time, then is removed and replaced by a blank screen for a short period of time, then the comparison image is presented for a period of time, and finally the comparison is removed and the response options are then revealed. One way that we could accomplish this type of presentation is with a single timer. Add another timer to the form and change its name to *tmrPresentation* and set its Enabled property to *False*. The interval of time during which stimuli and blackouts are generally displayed is rather short, normally 1-2 seconds so we'll set the Interval property of our presentation timer to 2000. We might want to also include another timer that we can use to administer a specified inter-trial interval between successive trials, so add a third timer to the form, set its name to *tmrITI*, its Enabled property to *False*, and for now we'll set its Interval property to 2000, or an ITI of 2 seconds.

Delivering Auditory and Visual Feedback

For the most part this is all of the controls we will need to present trials on the current form, but now we need to include some controls for delivering feedback to our participants on the accuracy of responses. Earlier we placed two audio files in our *Input Files* folder, one for accurate response and one for inaccurate responses. To play these files we can use a Windows Media Player object. Locate the Windows Media Player object in the toolbox and place it on the form. Change its name to *wmpCorrect*, and its Visible property to *False*. In previous chapters we showed you how to use code to set the Windows Media Player object to play specified files, but you can also set many of the properties or this control, such as the specific source file to be played and the volume and balance levels of the player, without adding any code. With your mouse right click on *wmpCorrect*, and choose *Properties* from the resulting options. From the resulting properties screen we can select the source file for the player to play. Under the *Source* heading click on the "Browse" button. Locate and select the "chimes.wav" file we saved in the *"C:/programming/pREP/Input Files"* directory, and click on the "Open" button. Also make sure that the *Auto start* checkbox under the *Playback options* header is deselected. If this box is left checked then the media player will automatically play the chosen file when the form first loads, which we don't want it to do. You may also want to set the Volume setting to *Max* to ensure that the sound played is salient. Now click on the "Apply" button to apply the current settings then click on the "OK" button to close the properties window.

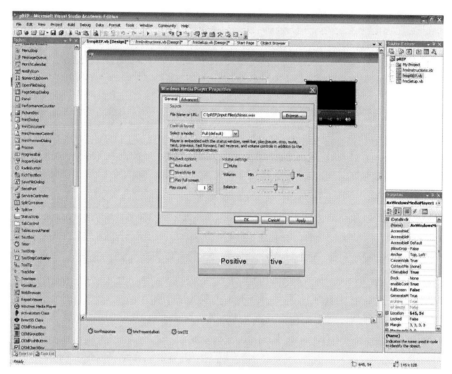

Figure 9.7 displays the properties selection for wmpCorrect.

We also want to include another hidden Windows Media Player Object to play the sound file for an inaccurate response. Copy and paste *wmpCorrect* to create another Windows Media Player object on the form. Change the name to *wmpIncorrect*, then right click on the player and select the *Properties* option. Like we did for the previous player click on the "Browse" button and locate and select the *"chord.wav"* file we saved previously in the *"C:\programming\pREP\Input Files"* directory. Then click on "Apply" then "OK" to close the properties window.

A final piece we want to include on the current form is a way of delivering visual feedback to participants. What we want to do is include a Panel object containing a Label that, when a participant responds during training, will cover up all other objects on the screen and display the text of "Correct" or "Wrong" depending on the accuracy of the response. From your Toolbox select a Panel object and with your mouse create a Panel that covers all of the form. You may have noticed something that doesn't seem right. Even though you sized the Panel so that it covered all of the objects on the screen, it seems that Panel is actually located behind all of the objects and is not covering them at all. This is something we discussed somewhat in Chapter 4, and you need to be cautious of when working with container controls such as panels. Because these controls are intended to house other controls, if you cover any other objects when you first place them on a form, they have a tendency to grab and encompass these other objects. You will see now that if you try to reposition the Panel, all other objects go with it because they are now housed on the panel itself instead of the form. To remedy this click on *Edit* on the main menu and then click on *Undo* or hit control + Z until the you undo the step where you created the panel. Now add another panel to the form, but this time just create a small panel in the upper left of the screen as you can see in figure 9.8. Now with your mouse click on the white box in the lower left of the new panel and drag the panel until it encompasses all of the objects on the screen. Note that this time the panel actually appears to be in front of all of the controls instead of behind them. Go ahead now and change the name of the Panel to *pnlFeedback* and set its Visible property to *False*.

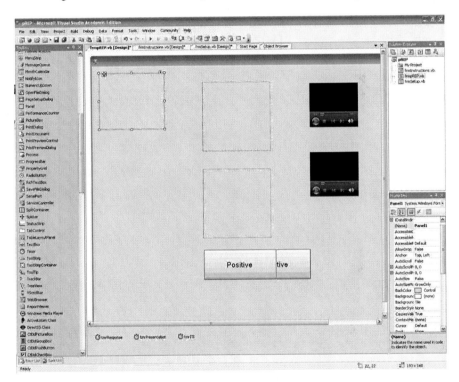

Figure 9.8 Displays the addition of pnlFeedback

We now need a way of displaying text on the panel, so add a Label object and position it so that it sits on the panel in the middle of the screen. Change the name of the Label to *lblFeedback*, set the AutoSize property to *False*, the size of the Font property to 36, the Text property to *"Feedback"*, set the TextAllign property to MiddleCenter, and set the Visible property to *False*. Now select *pnlFeedback* by clicking on it with your mouse. Let's look at the Size property for the panel in the Properties window. We now have all of the controls we will need on our main form.

In the case of my screen the size of the panel is currently *836, 692*. This is the size the panel needs to be to completely visually block all controls on the screen and deliver the text feedback on the label in its center. However, right now we need the panel out of the way so we can do anything we need to the controls that are sitting behind it. To get it out of the way you should write down the current size for use later, then change the size property to *100, 100*. This should make the panel into a small square up out of the way in the upper left of the screen. We'll increase the size back to its original dimensions later with code.

Creating the Trial Input

Now that we have the physical structure of the main program in place we can examine what our individual trials will consist of. In Chapter 7 for the Match to Sample program we created a text file which specified relevant variables for each phase of training and testing. The final version of this input file consisted of sections for each phase that might be carried out in a Match to Sample training and testing study, including A-B training, A-C training, Mixed A-B and A-C training, and un-reinforced tests of derived relations of reflexivity, symmetry, transitivity, and equivalence. Each phase in this input file consisted of a header section followed by a listing of individual trials. The header section for one phase is shown below.

```
PHASE, 1
NUMBEROFTRIALS, 18
CORRECT, "C:/windows/media/chimes.wav"
INCORRECT: "C:/windows/media/chord.wav"
CRITERION, 16
END, 0
```

This header section lists the name of the phase, the number of trials within the current phase, the source location of the sound files to be used for accurate and inaccurate responses, the criterion number of correct responses necessary to advance through the current phase, and a final variable to tell the program whether the program should end after the current phase or if it should continue and read in another phase from the input file.

The second section of the input for each phase in the input file we constructed in Chapter 7 consisted of the individual trials for the phase, an example of which you can see below.

```
TRIAL1, A1, B1, B2, B3
TRIAL2, A2, B2, B1, B3
TRIAL3, A3, B3, B1, B2
```

What the individual trials consist of is a trial number, the sample stimulus to be displayed followed by the 3 comparison stimuli to be displayed with the correct comparison being listed immediately after the sample stimulus. We're reviewing this file now, because the input for the pREP that we will construct now will be very similar, but will contain some key differences, which we will highlight below.

Let's begin by adding in the header information and the individual trials we will need to carry out A-B training. Open up the *pREP Input.txt* file we created previously in NotePad, and below the 2 response format instructions type the following:

```
PHASE, "A-B Training"
NUMBEROFTRIALS, 18
CRITERION, 16
END, 0
```

You'll note that this header is a couple of lines shorter than for the Match to Sample input files, due to the fact that we preset our Windows Media Player objects on the forms to play specific files, we can eliminate those two lines from the input. Now, below what you just typed, type the following:

```
TRIAL1,A1,B1,1,1
TRIAL2,A1,B2,2,1
TRIAL3,A1,B3,2,1
TRIAL4,A2,B2,1,1
TRIAL5,A2,B1,2,1
TRIAL6,A2,B3,2,1
TRIAL7,A3,B3,1,1
TRIAL8,A3,B1,2,1
TRIAL9,A3,B2,2,1
TRIAL10,A1,B1,1,1
TRIAL11,A1,B2,2,1
TRIAL12,A1,B3,2,1
TRIAL13,A2,B2,1,1
TRIAL14,A2,B1,2,1
TRIAL15,A2,B3,2,1
TRIAL16,A3,B3,1,1
TRIAL17,A3,B1,2,1
TRIAL18,A3,B2,2,1
```

You might note a couple of main differences between what you just typed and the format of the trials from the Match to Sample input file. As before you see text indicating the trial number followed by the sample and comparison images to be displayed. What are these final two numbers at the end of the line? The first number will be used to indicate whether the comparison image is a positive or negative comparison image, with a "1" indicating a positive comparison and a "2" indicating a negative comparison image. The final number we will use to tell the program whether feedback should be delivered on the given trial. In this case since all trials in the current phase are training trials in which we wish to deliver feedback, we use the number "1". In later testing phases where no feedback is given we will use the number "0". In Chapter 7 for the Match to Sample program you may remember that we accomplished this in the header section for a given phase by setting the sound files to be played for both accurate and inaccurate responses to a sound file that contained no sound. While this allowed us to streamline the code somewhat, it meant that the same feedback would be delivered throughout the entire phase. By employing the current method, we allow ourselves some flexibility by providing the option of intermixing trials in which feedback is delivered with trials in which no feedback is given if we should so desire.

While we still have our input file open let's go ahead and complete some more of the phases of training we might whish to include. At this point, we would also want to include a phase of A-C training and a round of mixed A-B and A-C training. Return to the *pREP Input.txt* file and with your mouse highlight and copy all of the text from "PHASE" on down. Paste this text below the A-B training. In the new text change the text for the phase to "A-C Training". Now move your cursor to the beginning of TRIAL1. To make things easier you can use the "Replace" functionality in NotePad to edit our new phase. On the main menu click on *Edit* then *Replace*. In the textbox to the right of the text "Find what" type the capital letter "B", and in the textbox to the right of "Replace with" type the capital letter "C". Also make sure that the "Match Case" checkbox below is checked. Click on the "Find Next" button. The cursor should stop on the first "B" in trial 1. Click on the "Replace" button. The program should replace the "B" in trial 1 with a "C" and jump to the "B" in trial 2. Click on the "Replace" button again and repeat this until all of the trials in the "A-C Training" phase have been edited. A popup box with the text "Cannot find "B" should appear when the end of the file is reached. Click the "Ok" button in the popup box and close the "Replace" dialog. Whatever you do, do not click on the "Replace All" button. Doing so will also replace all of the "B"'s in the "A-B Training" phase as well.

We can now add the mixed A-B and A-C training to our input file. Copy our current A-C training input and paste it at the bottom of the file. Delete trials 10 through 18. Now copy the first 9 trials of the A-B training and paste them below the A-C trials. Adjust the trial numbers on the newly pasted trials so that they become trials 10 through 18. Finally edit the phase text to read "Mixed A-B and A-C training. When you have completed these steps your input file should look like Figure 9.9. Save and close your input file.

Creating the Code for the pREP

Now that we have some input to work with, we can concentrate on creating the code necessary to carry out training. Return to the open instance of Visual Studio 2005 on your computer, and go to the design level of *frmpREP*. Double click on the form to open the edit level and the Private Sub frmpREP_Load subroutine. The first thing we will need the program to do is to read in the header information from the first training phase listed in our input file. We will create a new subroutine devoted

```
GONOGOINSTRUCTIONS, This is where the go/no-go instructions go.
2RESPONSEINSTRUCTIONS, This is where the 2 response instructions go.
PHASE, "A-B Training"
NUMBEROFTRIALS, 18
CRITERION, 16
END, 0
TRIAL1,A1,B1,1,1
TRIAL2,A1,B2,2,1
TRIAL3,A1,B3,2,1
TRIAL4,A2,B2,1,1
TRIAL5,A2,B1,2,1
TRIAL6,A2,B3,2,1
TRIAL7,A3,B3,1,1
TRIAL8,A3,B1,2,1
TRIAL9,A3,B2,2,1
TRIAL10,A1,B1,1,1
TRIAL11,A1,B2,2,1
TRIAL12,A1,B3,2,1
TRIAL13,A2,B2,1,1
TRIAL14,A2,B1,2,1
TRIAL15,A2,B3,2,1
TRIAL16,A3,B3,1,1
TRIAL17,A3,B1,2,1
TRIAL18,A3,B2,2,1
PHASE, "A-C Training"
NUMBEROFTRIALS, 18
CRITERION, 16
END, 0
TRIAL1,A1,C1,1,1
TRIAL2,A1,C2,2,1
TRIAL3,A1,C3,2,1
TRIAL4,A2,C2,1,1
TRIAL5,A2,C1,2,1
TRIAL6,A2,C3,2,1
TRIAL7,A3,C3,1,1
TRIAL8,A3,C1,2,1
TRIAL9,A3,C2,2,1
TRIAL10,A1,C1,1,1
TRIAL11,A1,C2,2,1
TRIAL12,A1,C3,2,1
TRIAL13,A2,C2,1,1
TRIAL14,A2,C1,2,1
TRIAL15,A2,C3,2,1
TRIAL16,A3,C3,1,1
TRIAL17,A3,C1,2,1
TRIAL18,A3,C2,2,1
PHASE, "Mixed A-B and A-C Training"
NUMBEROFTRIALS, 18
CRITERION, 16
END, 0
TRIAL1,A1,C1,1,1
TRIAL2,A1,C2,2,1
TRIAL3,A1,C3,2,1
TRIAL4,A2,C2,1,1
TRIAL5,A2,C1,2,1
TRIAL6,A2,C3,2,1
TRIAL7,A3,C3,1,1
TRIAL8,A3,C2,2,1
TRIAL9,A3,C2,2,1
TRIAL10,A1,B1,1,1
TRIAL11,A1,B2,2,1
TRIAL12,A1,B3,2,1
TRIAL13,A2,B2,1,1
TRIAL14,A2,B1,2,1
TRIAL15,A2,B3,2,1
TRIAL16,A3,B3,1,1
TRIAL17,A3,B1,2,1
TRIAL18,A3,B2,2,1
```

Figure 9.9 displays the input file through the Mixed A-B and A-C Training trials.

to this. Place your cursor at the end of the line "End Sub" and hit enter. On the new line type the following:

```
Sub Input_Trial_Information
Input(1, vHeader)
Input(1, vPhase)
Input(1, vHeader)
Input(1, vNumberofTrials)
Input(1, vHeader)
Input(1, vCriterion)
Input(1, vHeader)
Input(1, vCheckend)
End Sub
```

The preceding code reads each line of the header portion of the input file for the current phase and sets the information in those lines to the specified variables. Before we move on we need to declare these variables. Move your cursor below the text "Public Class frmpREP and type the following:

```
Dim vHeader as String
Dim vPhase as String
Dim vNumberofTrials as Integer
Dim vCriterion as Integer
Dim vCheckend as Integer
```

As we did in Chapter 7 we want to build in the functionality to read in each trial for the given phase at one time so that we can have the program randomize the presentation of all of the trials. In Chapter 7 we used a 2 dimensional array to hold this information and we will do the same thing here. First we need to declare the variable array to hold our trial information. Even though we currently are only including phases with 18 trials, we will go ahead and create an array that could handle as many as 100 trials. Underneath the variables you just declared type the following:

```
Dim vTrials((100), (3))
Dim vRandNumber(100) as Integer
Dim vCounter as Integer
Dim vFeedback as Integer
```

We can now create a subroutine to read in all of the trials for a given phase and randomize their order and a subroutine that will be called upon to advance each trial. Move your cursor to the right of the line "End Sub" in the Sub Input_Trial_Information subroutine and hit enter to create a new line. Type the following:

```
Sub Load_Random_Trials()
Dim i, r, x
For i = 1 to vNumberofTrials
Input(1, x)
Input(1, vTrials(i, 0))
Input(1, vTrials(i, 1))
Input(1, vTrials(i, 2))
Input(1, vTrials(i, 3))
Next i
Randomize()
For i = 1 to vNumberofTrials
r = Int(vNumberofTrials * Rnd() + 1)
If vRandNumber(r ) < 1 then
vRandNumber (r ) = i
Else
i = i -1
End if
```

```
Next i
End Sub

Sub Advance_Trial()
vCounter = vCounter + 1
End Sub
```

We can now create a subroutine that will take the information that was just read from the input file and place the correct stimuli on the screen. Under the text "End Sub" in the Sub Advance_Trial Subroutine type the following:

```
Sub Place_Stimuli()
picSample.Image = Image.FromFile("C:\programming\pREP\Input
    Files\" & vTrials(vRandNumber(vCounter), 0) & ".bmp")
picComparison.Image   =   Image.FromFile("C:\
    programming\pREP\Input  Files\"  &  vTrials
    (vRandNumber(vCounter), 1) & ".bmp")
vFeedback = vTrials(vRandNumber(vCounter), 3)
Button_Position()
vPresentation = 0
tmrPresentation.Enabled = True
End Sub
```

You may have noticed that the code you just typed created a couple of errors. The line "Button_Position" is calling to a subroutine that we have yet to create. Earlier we spent some time discussing where you would want to position the two response buttons depending on the format of the pREP being conducted as well as the possibility of randomizing the position of these two buttons in the 2 Response format of the pREP to prevent position bias. You were instructed to right down the exact locations previously. In the case of how the controls are arranged on my screen the intended location for the Positive response button for the Go/No-Go format was recorded to be at the location point 328, 533. For the 2 Response format the intended location for either button if placed in the left position was recorded to be at the location point 180, 533, and for either button if placed in the right position at 430, 533.

Before we can create a subroutine to accomplish the positioning of these buttons we need to declare a couple of variables. Eventually we will create a way for the experimenter to choose whether the position of the 2 response buttons will be randomized during trials or if they will rest in set locations. If the experimenter chooses not to have the position of the 2 buttons randomized, we also want to allow the experimenter to choose whether the positive response button will be placed on the left or the right of the negative response button. Let's create two public variables to carry this information. Double click on Module1 in the Solution Explorer to open our module. Create a new blank line beneath the line "Public Format as String" and type the following:

```
Public ResponsePosition as String
Public PositivePosition as String
```

Now return to edit level of frmpREP and scroll to the bottom of the code. We can now create a subroutine to set the position of the response buttons based on the variables just declared. Place your cursor to the right of the line "End Sub" in the Sub Place_Stimuli subroutine, hit enter to begin a new line and type the following.

```
Sub Button_Position()
Select Case Format
Case "Go/No-Go"
butPositive.Location = New System.Drawing.Point(328, 533)
Case "2 Response"
Select Case ResponsePosition
Case "Randomized"
Dim i as integer
Randomize()
I = Int(Rnd() * 2) + 1
PositivePosition = i
End Select
Select Case PositivePosition
Case 1
butPositive.Location = New System.Drawing.Point(180, 533)
butNegative.Location = New System.Drawing.Point(430, 533)
Case 2
butPositive.Location = New System.Drawing.Point(430, 533)
butNegative.Location = New System.Drawing.Point(180, 533)
End Select
End Select
End Sub
```

This code accomplishes a few things. If the experimenter chooses to use the Go/No-Go format of the pREP it will place the positive response button directly beneath the comparison image. If the experimenter chooses to use the 2 response format version of the pREP and to have the position of the response buttons randomized, the code will randomly choose the number 1 or 2. If the number 1 is chosen the positive response button will be placed to the left of the negative response button. If the number 2 is chosen it will be placed to the right of the negative response button. We'll discuss more of what happens if the experimenter chooses a set placement for the two response options when we build in the functionality for making that choice later.

You'll note that we still have an error in the Sub Place_Stimuli subroutine. There is a variable, vPresentation, that we have set to a value of 0, but we have not declared it as of yet. Return to the top of the code and under our last variable declaration type the following:

```
Dim vPresentation as Integer
```

Note that earlier we included a timer on our form that we intended to control the presentation of the stimuli and response options. We will use this new variable to advance through the presentation. Return to the design level of frmpREP. Locate and double click on the tmrPresentation object to create the Private Sub tmrPresentation_Tick subroutine. In this routine type the following:

```
tmrPresentation.Enabled = False
Select Case vPresentation
Case 0
picSample.Show()
vPresentation = 1
tmrPresentation.Enabled = True
Case 1
picSample.Hide()
vPresentation = 2
tmrPresentation.Enabled = True
Case 2
picComparison.Show()
vPresentation = 3
tmrPresentation.Enabled = True
Case 3
picComparison.Hide()
vPresentation = 4
tmrPresentation.Enabled = True
Case 4
Select Case Format
Case "Go/No-Go"
butPositive.Show()
tmrResponse.Enabled = True
Case "2 Response"
butPositive.Show()
butNegative.show()
End Select
End Select
```

Note by advancing the presentation variable each time the timer reaches the end of its interval and by using a select case statement we use the same timer to carry out sequential actions with a set interval of time between each action. Here is also a place where you could consider adding your own custom features. If you wished to display stimuli for longer periods of time while keeping the blackout periods between displays short, you could include code in each case above that reset the interval of the timer to whatever values you desired.

We should probably test our progress thus far, but before we do we need to add some more code. Move your cursor back to the Private Sub frmpREP_Load subroutine and type the following:

```
Input_Trial_Information()
Load_Random_Trials
Advance_Trial()
Place_Stimuli()
```

We also need to set values for some of the variables we declared regarding button positioning. Since we declared these variables as Public variables let's set them on the instructions form. Return to the edit level of frmInstructions. Create a new line underneath the text "Format = "2 Response" in the Private Sub frmInstructions_Load subroutine. On this line type the following:

```
ResponsePosition = "Randomized"
```

Now click on *Debug* then *Start Debugging* from the main menu. Our instructions for the 2 response format should appear. When you click on the begin button the program should advance to the main form. After 2 seconds you should see your sample image for 2 seconds, the screen should go blank for 2 seconds, you should then see the comparison image for 2 seconds, followed by a blank screen for 2 seconds, and then the 2 response options should appear. Whether either the positive or the negative buttons are on the left or right should be completely random so either could be true. If everything worked correctly let's go back now and see what would happen if we used a set order for the two response options in this format. Stop debugging and return to the edit level of frmInstructions. In the line "ResponsePosition = "Randomized"" change the text "Randomized" to "Set Order" then hit enter to create a new line. On this line type:

```
PositivePosition = 1
```

Now run the program again. Note that this time the Positive response option should definitely appear on the left side

Now let's see what happens when the PositivePosition variable is set to the value 2. Stop debugging and return to the edit level of frmInstructions. Change the value of the PositivePosition variable to equal 2 and run the program again. Note that this time the Positive response option is located to the right of the Negative response option.

Now let's see what happens when the response format is set to the Go/No-Go format. Stop Debugging and return to the edit level of from instructions. Change the line "Format = "2 Response"" to "Format = "Go/No-Go"". Be very careful when editing these string variables that you make no errors in spelling, capitalization and that you use quotation marks where indicated or you will run into errors when your program runs.

Run the program again. Note that now only the Positive response option appears and that it is located directly below the comparison image location. We've now tested a few different single trial examples, but in order to advance through trials we need to include the code for the responses. Stop the program and we will do so now.

Return to the design level of frmpREP and double click on *butPositive* to open the Private Sub butPositive_Click subroutine. Remember that with each trial in the input file we included a numerical variable to indicate whether the displayed comparison stimuli was a positive or a negative comparison. For this variable a value of 1 was used to indicate a positive comparison and a value of 2 was used to indicate a negative comparison. What we want to accomplish when the participant clicks on the positive response option is for a correct response to be recorded if this variable is set to the value of 1 and for an incorrect response to be recorded if this variable is set to 2. We also want the program to deliver auditory and visual feedback if the given trial is indicated as a training trial, and to advance to the inter-trial interval and the next trial after the response is made. We can accomplish this with a large If...Then statement. Also remember that earlier we had you take note of the size the Panel object included to deliver feedback would need to be to cover all items on the screen. You will use that information here to resize the panel with code. In the Private Sub butPositive_Click routine type the following:

```
If vTrials(vRandNumber(vCounter), 2) = 1 Then
vAnswer = "Correct"
lblFeedback.Text = vAnswer
vCorrect = vCorrect + 1
Select Case vFeedback
Case 0
lblFeedback.Hide
Case 1
wmpCorrect.Ctlcontrols.Play()
lblFeedback.Show
End Select
pnlFeedback.BringToFront()
pnlFeedback.Size = New System.Drawing.Point(836, 692)
pnlFeedback.Show()
tmrITI.Enabled = True
picSample.Hide()
PicComparison.Hide()
```

```
butPositive.Hide()
butNegative.Hide()
tmrResponse.Enabled = False
Else
vAnswer = "Wrong"
lblFeedback.Text = vAnswer
Select Case vFeedback
Case 0
lblFeedback.Hide()
Case 1
wmpIncorrect.CtlControls.Play()
lblFeedback.Show()
End Select
pnlFeedback.BringToFront()
pnlFeedback.Size = New System.Drawing.Point(836, 692)
pnlFeedback.Show()
tmrITI.Enabled = True
picSample.Hide()
PicComparison.Hide()
butPositive.Hide()
butNegative.Hide()
tmrResponse.Enabled = False
End If
```

Now return to the design level of frmpREP and double click on *butNegative* to create the Private Sub butNegative_Click subroutine. In all actuality the code for this button will be almost exactly the same as for the positive response option with one exception, so we can just reuse the code we typed previously. With your mouse select all of the code you typed in the Private Sub butPositive_Click subroutine and copy and paste it into the Private butNegative_Click subroutine. We only need to change one character in all of the code. Change the line:

```
If vTrials(vRandNumber(vCounter), 2) = 1 Then
```
to
```
If vTrials(vRandNumber(vCounter), 2) = 2 Then
```

You might have also noted that we have included two variables that we have yet to declare, vAnswer and vCorrect. Return to the top of the code and under the last variable you declared type the following:

```
Dim vAnswer as String
Dim vCorrect as Integer
```

This should take care of all of our current errors as well as both response options for the 2 response format of the pREP and the "Go" response for the Go/No-Go format. Now we need to take care of what happens when a negative comparison stimulus is displayed during the Go/No-Go format. Essentially the timer object we included to end the response interval during the Go/No-Go format, *tmrResponse*, will perform the same function as the Negative response button does for the 2 Response format, so we can reuse the code for this button in the code for the timer. Return to the design level of frmpREP and locate and double click on tmrResponse to create the Private Sub tmrResponse_Tick subroutine. Select all of the code we placed in the Private Sub butNegative_Click routine and copy and paste it into the Private Sub tmrResponse_Tick subroutine.

We have one final bit of code to address before we can test our program again. We need to include some code for the timer we included to control inter-trial intervals, tmrITI, in order to advance trials. Return to the design level of frmpREP and locate and double click on tmrITI to create the Private Sub tmrITI_Tick subroutine. In this subroutine type the following:

```
tmrITI.Enabled = False
Advance_Trial
Place_Stimuli
pnlFeedback.Hide()
```

We are now ready to test if everything is working or multiple trials. Let's first try a 2 Response format with randomized placement of the response buttons. Return to the edit level of frmInstructions. Make sure the Format variable is set to "2 Response" and that the ResponsePosition variable is set to equal "Randomized". Run the program and advance through a several trials, getting some wrong and some correct. Note that sometimes the Positive response option is on the left sometimes on the right, and that both the auditory and the visual feedback is delivered when you respond on the two buttons.

Now let's try some Go/No-Go trials. Stop the program and return to the edit level of frmInstructions. Change the Format variable so that it equals "Go/No-Go" and run the program again. Note that only the positive response button is displayed and, that if you do not click within the allotted response interval, that either positive or negative feedback is delivered by the response timer.

Go ahead and progress through the first 18 trials of our first training phase. You should run into a problem that crashes the program at the end of the 18 trials in the A-B training phase. Up to this point we have failed to include any code to check and see if the criterion number of correct responses have been made and if so to advance to the next phase and if not to start over again. Let's take care of that now.

Return to the edit level of frmpREP. What we need to do is have the program check to see if the criterion number of correct responses has been achieved once the number of trials for the given phase has occurred. We'll do this in the Place_Stimuli routine. Move your cursor to this routine and create a new line below the text "Sub Place_Stimuli()". Type the following:

```
If vCounter > vNumberofTrials then
If vCorrect >= vCriterion then
Select Case vCheckend
Case 0
Dim x as new frmpREP
x.Show()
Me.Close()
End Select
Else
Start_Over_Again
End If
Else
```

We also need to include a final "End If" statement at the bottom of this subroutine. Scroll down to the bottom of the subroutine and before the text "End Sub" type "End If". The text "Start_Over_Again" should have generated an error due to the fact that it calls to a subroutine that we haven't created yet. We need to create a subroutine that kicks in if a participant fails to reach criterion during a training phase and re-randomizes all of the trials for that phase. Create a new line between the text "End Sub" and the text "Sub Button_Position" and type the following:

```
Sub Start_Over_Again()
Dim i, r
For i = 1 to vNumberofTrials
vRandNumber(i) = 0
next i
vCounter = 1
vCorrect = 0
For i = 1 to vNumberofTrials
r = Int(vNumberofTrials * Rnd() + 1)
If vRandNumber(r) < 1 then
vRandNumber(r) = i
Else
i = i - 1
End If
Next i
Place_Stimuli()
End Sub
```

Now run the program again. Our settings should still be set for Go/No-Go trials, but note that now when you reach the end of A-B training, if you reached 16 correct responses the program advances to A-C training, and if you failed to reach 16 correct responses the program will start the A-B training over again. As the program advances through the different phases you will probably not be able to event note that it has advanced until you realize that different comparison stimuli are being displayed.

All should progress fine until you advance past the mixed A-B and A-C training. Remember that we only completed our input file for three phases, A-B Training, A-C Training, and Mixed A-B and A-C training. We still need to include phases for tests of derived relations, so let's do that now.

Test for Derived Relations

Stop the program and open the pREP Input.txt file we saved in the C:\programming\pREP\Input Files\ directory. In the test phases for the Match to Sample program in Chapter 7 we included separate tests for reflexivity and symmetry. However, for the sake of simplicity we will assume that participants should be able to derive relations of reflexivity and symmetry, and for now we will include one final test phase to examine the emergence of equivalence relations. Scroll to the bottom of the pREP Input.txt file and type the following:

```
PHASE, "Equivalence Test"
NUMBEROFTRIALS, 18
CRITERION, 16
END, 1
```

As we did previously we can use NotePad's *Replace* option to speed up the process of writing our individual trials. With your mouse highlight and copy the 18 trials in the "Mixed A-B and A-C Training" phase. Paste these trials below the text you just typed. Move your cursor down to the beginning of the first trial in the "Equivalence Test" phase. Click *Edit* from the main menu then *Replace*. If you followed the directions earlier in your chapter your fist 9 trials should consist of A-C trial and your final 9 trials should consist of A-B trials. All we really need to do if this is the case is replace all of the "A"s in the first 9 trials with "B"s and all of the "A"s in the last 9 trials with "C"s. In the replace dialog in the box next to the text "Find what" type "A" and in the box next to "Replace with" type "B". Make sure that "Match Case" checkbox is checked. Click on the "Find Next" button. Note that the cursor stops on the "A" in the word "Trial". We don't want to change this so click on "Find Next" again. Now the cursor should stop on the "A" in the first sample stimulus. Click on the "Replace" button. The cursor should now jump down to the "A" in the word "TRIAL" in the second trial. Click on "Find Next" and when it reaches the "A" in the next sample stimulus. Click on the "Replace" button. Repeat this for all of the first 9 trials. When the tenth trial is reached change the text in the

"Replace with" box to the letter "C" and repeat the above steps until you have changed the final 9 trials.

We need to change one final thing to these 18 trials to turn them from training trials into test trials. The final number at the end of each trial was included to indicate whether, for the given trial, feedback should be given. We used a "1" to indicate that the trial was a training trial and that feedback should be given, and we designated the number "0" to indicate test trials in which no feedback is to be delivered. For all 18 trials replace the "1" at the end of the trial with a "0" and save the file.

You may have noticed one other difference in the header for the equivalence test phase over what we included in the previous phase. The "END" variable in this case is set to "1" instead of "0". With the previous phases, we wanted them to advance to the next phase in the input file once they had been completed successfully. However, with this phase, once it is completed successfully we want the program to end. You may also remember from the Match to Sample program in Chapter 7, that we set the criterion number of correct responses to -1 so that no matter if the participant passed the test, the program would advance. However in most experiments, if a participant fails to pass tests for derived relations, we might want the program to retrain and test them again. As our program sits now, if the participant failed to reach the criterion of 16 correct responses set in this phase, the program would just keep repeating the test. What we need to do is to include some code so that if the participant fails to pass the equivalence test, the program will close the input file, reopen it, and read down past the instructions, and begin the training phases again. We will also include some code to end the program if the participant fails to pass the equivalence test in 3 attempts.

Close the pREP Input.txt file and return to the open instance of the program on your computer. Let's fist add another form to the program that we can use to debrief the participant at the end of the study. Right click on the text pREP in the Solution Explorer and choose the *Add* and *Windows Form* options. Name the new form *frmThankYou*, and click on "Add". Change the forms Size to *1024, 786*, its Text to *"End Study"*, and its WindowState property to *Maximized*. Add a Label object to the form, change its name to *lblThankYou*, its Autosize property to *False*, the size of its Font property to *36*, its Text property to *"Thank You for Your Participation"* and its TextAllign property to *MiddleCenter*. Also add a button object to the form, change its name to *butEnd*, the size of the Font property to *24*, and its Text Property to *"End Study"*. Let's also include a little code to end the program when the button is clicked. Double click on *butEnd* to create the Private Sub butBegin_Click subroutine. In this subroutine type the text "End".

Now return to the edit level of frmpREP and we'll write the code to send the participant to the final form if the equivalence test is passed. Scroll down to the Sub Place_Stimuli subroutine. Create a new line between the text "Me.Close()" and the text "End Select" and type the following:

```
Case 1
Dim x as New frmThankYou
x.Show()
Me.Close()
```

We now need to include some code that will return the participant to the first training phase if they fail to pass the equivalence test. Just below the code you just entered, replace the text "Start_Over_Again()" with the following:

```
Select Case vCheckend
Case 0
Start_Over_Again()
Case 1
FileClose(1)
RepeatTraining = RepeatTraining + 1
If RepeatTraining < 3 then
FileOpen(1, "C:\programming\Input Files\pREP Input.txt",
    OpenMode.Input)
Input(1, vHeader)
Input(1, vHeader)
Input(1, vHeader)
Input(1, vHeader)
Dim x as New frmpREP
x.Show()
Me.Close()
Else
Dim x as New frmThankYou
x.Show()
Me.Close()
End If
End Select
```

There's a variable in this code, "*RepeatTraining*", which we need to include to track the number of times the participant has repeated the training. Since the form reloads after trials we will need to declare this variable as a Public variable on Module1. Go to Module1 and under the last variable declared type:

```
Public RepeatTraining as Integer
```

Now take the time to test your program again. It should run through all 3 training phases and once you reach the equivalence test you should no longer receive feedback. You may wish to take the time to purposely fail the equivalence test and ensure that the program returns you to training. You may also want to try the program in both the 2 response and Go/No-Go formats. This may take a while but fully debugging these programs often requires you to run many scenarios to ensure that the program works in all possible permutations of responses from a participant. Ultimately this may require more time than the actual creation of the program, which is frustrating, but less so then a program that crashes after a participant is most of the way through it.

Building in Flexibility and Experimenter Choice

Besides the demonstration of how to create a program to carry out an alternative method of assessing relational responding we also intended to use this chapter to build in elements of flexibility and experimenter choice to a single program. So far we've demonstrated that our program, as is, can carry out both the Go/No-Go and 2 response option formats of the pREP. However, up till now we have had to change code whenever we have wanted or needed to switch between these two formats. Let's discuss now how we can build a choice screen that will allow us to control options such as the study format without requiring us to change actual code.

Earlier, we created a form that we named frmSetup. Let's return to the design level of this form and add the controls and code that will allow us to set options such as the study format. From the toolbox add a Panel object to frmSetup. Change the name of the panel to pnlFormat, and set its Size property to 300, 200. We also want to position it near the top left of the screen so set the Location to 12, 12. Now add a Label object to the panel we just added. Change the name of the Label to lblFormat, its AutoSize property to False, the size of the Font property to 16, the text to "Study Format", and the TextAllign property to MiddleCenter. Resize the label as you see fit and position it at the top of the panel.

To allow us to choose between the two formats of the pREP we will use a control called the RadioButton. The RadioButton control is similar to a checkbox in that it allows you to choose from an array of items. When you place a group of RadioButtons on a single container control, it allows you to select one option while deselecting all of the other options. Let's demonstrate this by adding two RadioButtons to pnlFormat. Locate the RadioButton control in the Toolbox and add 2 of them to the panel. Change the name of the first to rbGONOGO, its AutoSize property to False, its Checked property to True, the size of its Font property to 16, and its Text property to "GO/No-GO". Change the name of the second to rb2Resp, its AutoSize property to False, its Checked property to False, the size of its Font property to 16, and its Text property to "2 Response". Resize the two RadioButtons as you see fit and position them one above the other on the panel.

Now change the startup form to frmSetup and run the program. Note that when the form loads that the Go/No-Go option is already selected but when you select the 2 Response option the Go/No-Go option is deselected and vice versa. Now stop the program and return to the design level of frmSetup. Move the rb2Resp so that it is no longer located on the panel. Now run the program again. Note that now when you select one option, the other is not deselected, and it is possible to have them both selected at the same time. For RadioButtons to act as options in a single array they must be located on the same container control. Now stop the program and move rb2Resp back to pnlFormat. We will now add the code to actually set the format.

Return to the design level of frmSetup and double click on rbGONOGO to create the Private Sub rbGONOGO_CheckedChanged subroutine. This subroutine will be activated anytime the checked status of the RadioButton changes. Whenever the Go/No-Go RadioButton is selected/checked we want the program to set the Format variable so in this routine type the following:

```
If rbGONOGO.Checked = True Then
Format = rbGONOGO.Text
End If
```

Now return to the design level of frmSetup and double click on rb2Resp to create the Private Sub rb2Resp_CheckedChanged subroutine. In this subroutine type the following:

```
If rb2Resp.Checked = True Then
Format = rb2Resp.Text
End If
```

Now return to the design level of frmSetup and add a Button control to the form. Change the name of the button to butBegin, the size of the Font property to 16, and the Text to "Begin". Now double click on the button to create the Private Sub butBegin_Click subroutine. Let's include the code to advance to the instructions form, so in this subroutine type the following:

```
Dim x as New frmInstructions
x.Show()
Me.Hide()
```

We have one more thing to do before we test the program. Return to the edit level of frmInstructions. We need to delete the line of code that sets the study format. Depending on which format you last tested either delete the line "Format = "2 Response"" or "Format = "Go/No-Go"". Now run the program. Try both format options and make sure that the proper format is loaded for the option selected. If so we can move on to some other options.

One other option that we included earlier was the option to either randomize the position of the two response buttons in the 2 response format or to use a set order with the Positive response option either on the right or left. Return to the design level of frmSetup and add another Panel to the form. Change the name to pnl2Resp, set the Location to 12, 230, set the size to 650, 500, and change the Visible property to False. Now copy the Label and the 2 RadioButtons from pnlFormat and paste them on the new Panel. Change the name of the Label to lblButPos and change the

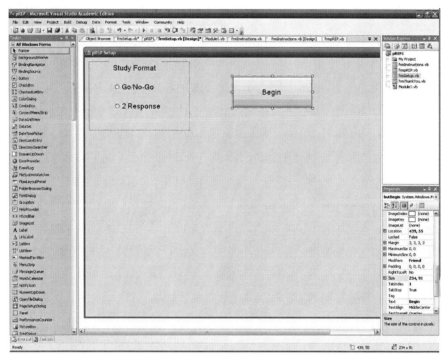

Figure 9.10 displays the setup form with the Study Format RadioButtons.

text to "Button Position". Change the name of one of the RadioButtons to rbRandomized and change the text to "Randomized". Change the name of the other RadioButton to rbSetOrder and change the text to "Set Order". Position lblButPos at the top of the Panel and position the two RadioButtons side by side beneath lblButPos. Now add another small panel within pnl2Resp. Change the name to pnlSetOrder, set the Size to 160, 50, and change the Visible property to False. Position the Panel directly below rbSetOrder and add 2 RadioButtons to pnlSetOrder. Name one RadioButton rbPosLeft, and change its Text to Positive Left. Name the other rbPosRight, and change its text to Positive Right.

We've now got this big panel for options for the 2 Response Format but we only need to see it when that format has been chosen. Double click on rb2Resp in the top panel to return to the Private Sub 2Resp_CheckedChanged subroutine. Beneath the text "Format = rb2Resp.text" add the line

```
pnl2Resp.Show()
```

Now move your cursor to the Private Sub rbGONOGO_CheckedChanged subroutine and beneath the text "Format = rbGONOGO.Text" add the line

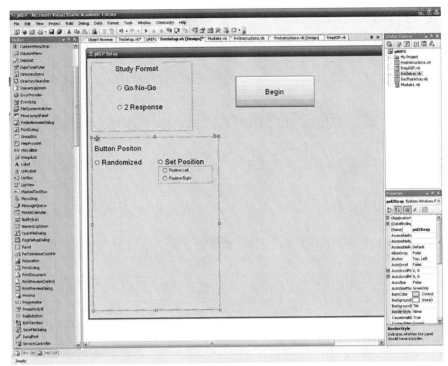

Figure 9.11 displays the setup form with the Button Position options for the 2 Response format.

```
Pnl2Resp.Hide()
```

Now return to the design level of the form. We need to include the code to set the variable for the positioning of the buttons to either a set order or randomized. We also need to include some code that, if the Set Order option is chosen, will reveal the panel with the two options for setting the position of the Positive response button to either the left or right position. Double click on the Randomized RadioButton to open the Private Sub rbRandomized_CheckedChanged subroutine. In this subroutine type the following:

```
If rbRandomized.Checked = True then
ResponsePosition = rbRandomized.Text
pnlSetOrder.Hide()
End If
```

Now return to the design level of frmSetup and double click on rbSetOrder to create the Private Sub rbSetOrder_CheckedChanged subroutine. In this subroutine type the following:

```
If rbSetOrder.Checked = True then
ResponsePosition = rbSetOrder.Text
pnlSetOrder.Show()
End If
```

Now return to the design level and double click on rbPosLeft to create the Private Sub rbPosLeft_CheckedChanged subroutine. In this subroutine type the following:

```
If rbPosLeft.Checked = True Then
PositivePosition = 1
End If
```

Return now to the design level of frmSetup and double click on rbPosRight. In the new subroutine type the following:

```
If rbPosRight.Checked = True Then
PositivePosition = 2
End If
```

We need to change one more thing before we test the program again. Return to the edit level of frmInstructions. Delete any lines in the Private Sub frmInstructions_Load subroutine that involve the ResponsePosition and PositivePosition variables. Now run the program and try out all of the different permutation of the two formats. If everything works properly we can move on to discussing some other options.

Response Option Stimuli

As things stand right now, our two response option buttons feature the text "Positive" and "Negative". In an actual study we might want to use different text on these two buttons, we might want to make them different colors, or we might want to use images instead. Currently, if we wished to change these we would need to directly edit the properties of these buttons on frmpREP. Let's now explore how we can add in the flexibility to set these options.

Return to the design level of frmSetup. Add another Panel to pnl2Resp and position it below the button position options. Change the name of the panel to pnlButFormat and set the size to 600, 350. With your mouse select and copy the Label at the top of pnl2Resp. Paste the copy the label onto pnlButFormat and position it at the top left of the panel. Change the name of the new Label to lblButFormat and change the text to "Button Format". Now add two RadioButtons to pnlButFormat and position them side by side to the right of lblButFormat. Name one RadioButton rb2RespImage, set the AutoSize property to False, change the size of the Font Property to 12, and change the Text property to "Image". Name the other RadioButton rb2RespText, set the AutoSize property to False, change the size of the Font property to 12, and change the Text property to "Text".

Now add 2 panels of equal size (275, 300) and position one below rb2RespImage and one below rb2RespText. Name the Panel below the Image option pnl2RespImage and set its Visible property to False. Name the Panel below the Text option pnl2RespText and set its visible property to False as well. Before we add any other controls lets add some code to make these panels visible and to set the format for the buttons. First of all we need to declare a variable to hold whether the button format should consist of images or text. Go to Module1 and add another declaration below the last variable by typing:

```
Public ButtonFormat as String
```

Now Return to the design level of frmSetup and double click on the Image option to create the Private Sub rb2RespImage_CheckedChanged subroutine. In this subroutine type the following:

```
If rb2RespImage.Checked = True Then
ButtonFormat = rb2RespImage.Text
pnl2RespImage.Show()
pnl2RespText.Hide()
End If
```

Return to the design level of the form and double click on the Text option to create the Private Sub rb2RespText_CheckedChanged subroutine. In this subroutine type the following:

```
If rb2RespText.Checked = True Then
ButtonFormat = rb2RespText.Text
pnl2RespImage.Hide()
pnl2RespText.Show()
End If
```

Let's return now to the design level of frmSetup. Add two PictureBoxes the size of our response buttons (200, 100) to pnl2RespImage. Name one PictureBox pic2RespPos and set its SizeMode property to StretchImage. Name the other pic2RespNeg and set its SizeMode property to StretchImage as well. What we want to happen is to include a way to open an OpenFile Dialog that would allow the experimenter to browse through the files on his or her computer and to choose an image for both the Positive response button and one for the Negative response button. Add two buttons to pnl2RespImage, and position one next to each PictureBox. Name one button but2RespPos and change its text to "Pos Image". Name the other button but2RespNeg and change its text to "Neg Image". Now double click on but2RespPos to create a new click subroutine for the button.

You may remember some of the code for the use of OpenFile dialogs from Chapter 4. In that chapter we actually added an OpenFile Dialog to the form. You can also create a dialog with code without actually adding an object to the form. We will use that here. In the Private Sub but2RespPos_Click subroutine type the following:

```
Dim ofd as OpenFileDialog = New OpenFileDialog
ofd.Filter = "Images|*.jpg;*.jpeg*;*.bmp;*tiff;*.png;*.gif"
If ofd.ShowDialog = Windows.Forms.DialogResult.OK then
Pic2RespPos.Image = Image.FromFile(ofd.FileName)
PosImage = ofd.FileName
End If
```

You may have noted an error generated for the variable PosImage. We need two variables to carry the names of the images for both the Positive and Negative response options, and we haven't declared them as of yet. Go to Module1 and under the last variable declared type the following:

```
Public PosImage, NegImage as String
```

Now return to the design level of frmSetup and double click on but2RespNeg to create a new click subroutine. In this subroutine type the following:

```
Dim ofd as OpenFileDialog = New OpenFileDialog
ofd.Filter = "Images|*.jpg;*.jpeg*;*.bmp;*tiff;*.png;*.gif"
If ofd.ShowDialog = Windows.Forms.DialogResult.OK then
Pic2RespNeg.Image = Image.FromFile(ofd.FileName)
NegImage = ofd.FileName
End If
```

Let's test our progress so far. Run the program and select the 2 Response Option. Now select the Image option for the Button Format. When you click on either the Pos Image or Neg Image buttons an OpenFile Dialog should open. Navigate to the "C:\programming\pREP\Input Files\" directory. Earlier we created two images for the response buttons, Pos Response.bmp and Neg Response.bmp. Try loading these images

Now let's create our options for the Text format for the buttons. Stop the program and return to the design level of frmSetup. Add a Label to pnl2RespText. Change its name to lbl2RespPos, its AutoSize property to False, its Font size to 16, its Size to 250, 40, its Text to "Positive Response Button", its TextAllign property to MiddleCenter and position it at the top of pnl2RespText. Now add a TextBox below this label. Change its name to txt2RespPos and its Font size to 16. Add a

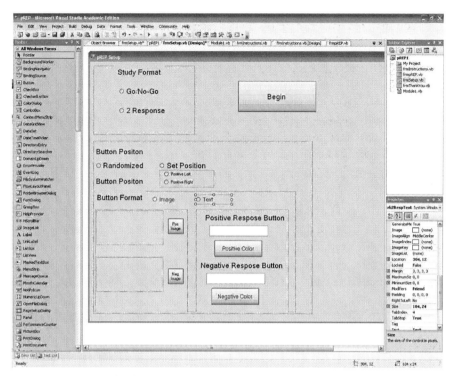

Figure 9.12 displays the Button Format options for the 2 Response format.

button below the TextBox, and change its name to but2RespPosColor, its Font size to 12, and its text to "Positive Color". Now copy the Label, the Textbox and the Button and paste them on the same panel just below the originals. Change the name of the newly pasted label to lbl2RespNeg and change its text to "Negative Response Button" Change the name of the newly pasted textbox to txt2RespNeg. Then change the name of the newly pasted button to but2RespNegColor and change its text to "Negative Color".

If we are going to set these options on this form we first need to declare a few more variables on Module1. Return to Module1 and add the following text:

```
Public PosText, NegText as String
Public PosColor, NegColor as Color
```

Now return to the design level of frmSetup. Double click on but2RespPosColor to create a new click subroutine. What we will do here is employ some code to open a ColorDialog that will allow the experimenter to choose a color for the Positive response option. In the new Private Sub but2RespPosColor_Click subroutine, type the following:

```
Dim cd as ColorDialog = New ColorDialog
If cd.ShowDialog = Windows.Forms.DialogResult.OK Then
but2RespPosColor.BackColor = cd.Color
PosColor = cd.Color
End if
```

Now return to the design level of the form and double click on but2RespNegColor
to open a new click subroutine. In the Private Sub but2RespNegColor_Click
subroutine, type the following:

```
Dim cd as ColorDialog = New ColorDialog
If cd.ShowDialog = Windows.Forms.DialogResult.OK Then
but2RespNegColor.BackColor = cd.Color
NegColor = cd.Color
End if
```

We now need some code to set the text variables for the Positive and Negative
response options. Scroll up to the Private Sub butBegin_Click subroutine. At the top
of this subroutine, before the text "Dim x as New frmInstructions", type the following

```
Select Case Format
Case "2 Response"
PosText = txt2RespPos.Text
NegText = txt2RespNeg.Text
End Select
```

Now we need some code on the main program to actually translate these settings
to the buttons on frmpREP. Return to the edit level of frmpREP and scroll to the
Private sub frmpREP_Load subroutine. At the top of the subroutine, before the text
"Input_Trial_Information", type the following text:

```
Select Case Format
Case "2 Response"
Select Case ButtonFormat
Case "Image"
butPositive.BackgroundImageLayout = ImageLayout.Stretch
butPositive.BackGroundImage = Image.FromFile(PosImage)
butPositive.Text = ""
butNegative.BackgroundImageLayout = ImageLayout.Stretch
butNegative.BackGroundImage = Image.FromFile(NegImage)
butNegative.Text = ""
Case "Text"
butPositive.BackColor = PosColor
butPositive.Text = PosText
```

```
butNegative.BackColor = NegColor
butNegative.Text = NegText
End Select
End Select
```

Now run the program. Select the 2 Response format and try various permutations of the button formats.

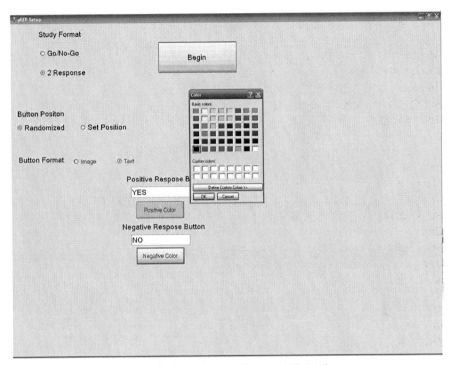

Figure 9.13 displays the use of the OpenFile Dialog to set the Positive Response Button Image.

Let's now move back to our options screen, frmSetup, and add some options for the Go/No-Go Format. The panel for all of our options for the 2 Response format, pnl2Resp, has gotten somewhat large, and may be taking up enough of the space of the form that adding anything else would be difficult. To work around that we can take note of the size the panel needs to be to display everything, which we set as 650, 500. Now we can make the panel smaller to get it out of the way, then add some code for the program to restore its size whenever the 2 Response format is chosen. Select pnl2Resp, then set its Size property to 100, 100. This should shrink the panel into a small box below the Study Format panel. While we can no longer see most of the objects on the panel, if we need to work on anything on the panel,

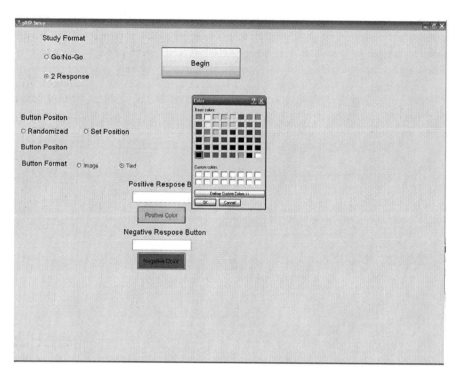

Figure 9.14 displays the use of the Color Dialog to set the Positive Response Button color.

we can just select the panel and reset its size to 650, 500. Return to the edit level of frmSetup and to the subroutine in which pnl2Resp is revealed, Private Sub rb2Resp_CheckedChanged. We'll add some code to reset the size and location of pnl2Resp. Create a line above the text pnl2Resp.Show() and type the following code:

```
pnl2Resp.Location = New System.Drawing.Point(12, 230)
pnl2Resp.Size = New System.Drawing.Size(650, 500)
```

Now let's add some options for the Go/No-Go Format. Return to the design level of frmSetup. Add a panel to the form, change its name to pnlGONOGO, set its Size property to 650, 500, and set its Visible property to False. Add a Label object to the Panel and position it at the top left of the panel. Change its name to lblGNGButFormat, set its AutoSize property to False, set its Font size to 16, set its Text to "Button Format", and change its TextAllign property to MiddleCenter. Now add two RadioButtons to pnlGONOGO and position then side by side to the left of lblGNGButFormat. Name the first RadioButton rbGNGImage, set its Font size to 16, and set its Text to "Image". Name the second RadioButton rbGNGText, set its Font size to 16, and set its Text to "Text".

Now add two Panels of equal size (275, 200) to pnlGONOGO and position them side by side beneath the two RadioButtons. Name the first panel pnlGNGImage and set its Visible property to False. Name the second panel pnlGNGText and set its Visible property to False.

Now add a PictureBox to pnlGNGImage, change its name to picGNGImage, set its Size to 200, 100, and set its SizeMode to StretchImage. Now add a Button to the panel and place it beneath the PictureBox. Change its Name to butGNGImage, and change its Text to "Load Image".

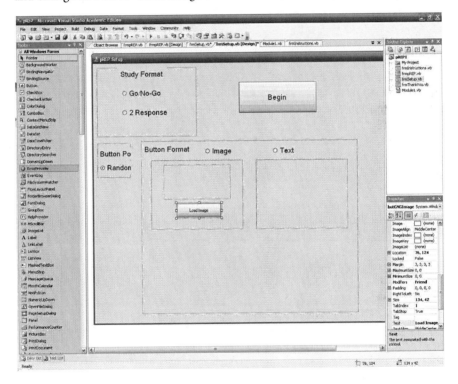

Figure 9.15 displays the addition of some of the Button Format options for the Go/No-Go format.

Now add a Label to pnlGNGText and position it at the top left of the panel. Change its Name to lblGNGText, set its Autosize property to False, its Font Size to 16, its Text to "Response Button Text", and set its TextAllign property to False. Add a Textbox beneath the Label, change its name to txtGNGText, and set its Font size to 16. Finally, add a Button beneath the Textbox, change its name to butGNGColor, and set its Text to "Response Button Color".

Now let's consider the code to set these options. First we need to include some code to reveal the Go/No-Go Options. Return to edit level of the form and scroll to the Private Sub rbGONOGO_CheckedChanged subroutine. Beneath the txt "pnl2Resp.Hide()" add the following:

```
pnlGONOGO.Location = New System.Drawing.Point(12, 230)
pnlGONOGO.Size = New System.Drawing.Size(650, 500)
pnlGONOGO.Show()
```

Now move your cursor to the Private Sub rb2Resp_CheckedChanged subroutine. Under the text "pnl2Resp.Show()" type the following:

```
pnlGONOGO.Hide()
```

Now return to the Design level of frmSetup and double click on the Image RadioButton to create the Private Sub rbGNGImage_CheckedChanged sub routine. In this subroutine type the following code:

```
If rbGNGImage.Checked = True Then
pnlGNGImage.Show()
pnlGNGText.Hide()
ButtonFormat = "Image"
End If
```

Now return to the design level of the form and double click on the Text RadioButton to create a new click subroutine. In the Private Sub rbGNGText_CheckedChanged subroutine, type the following code:

```
If rbGNGText.Checked = True Then
pnlGNGImage.Hide()
pnlGNGText.Show()
ButtonFormat = "Text"
End If
```

Now let's add some code to open up another OpenFile Dialog to allow the experimenter to set the response button image. Return to the design level of the form and double click on the Load Image Button, butGNGImage, to create a new click routine. In the Private Sub butGNGImage_Click subroutine, type the following:

```
Dim ofd as OpenFileDialog = New OpenFileDialog
ofd.Filter = "Images|*.jpg;*.jpeg*;*.bmp;*tiff;*.png;*.gif"
If ofd.ShowDialog = Windows.Forms.DialogResult.OK then
picGNGImage.Image = Image.FromFile(ofd.FileName)
PosImage = ofd.FileName
End If
```

Now let's add some code to allow the experimenter to select the color of the response button for the Go/No-Go Format. Return to the design level of frmSetup and double click on the Response Button Color Button. In the Private Sub butGNGColor_Click subroutine, type the following:

```
Dim cd as ColorDialog = New ColorDialog
If cd.ShowDialog = Windows.Forms.DialogResult.OK Then
butGNGColor.BackColor = cd.Color
PosColor = cd.Color
End if
```

Now let's test the program to make sure the code we've added works. Try selecting the Image Button Format for the Go/No-Go Format and load images for the response button. Also try the Text format and make sure you can choose a color for the response button. However, if you advance on to actually trying a few trials, you'll note that we haven't included any code to set these options to the actual program as of yet. Let's do that now.

Return to the edit level of frmSetup and locate the Private Sub butBegin_Click subroutine. Before the text "End Select" in the Select Case statement, add the following:

```
Case "Go/No-Go"
PosText = txtGNGText.Text
```

Now go to the edit level of frmpREP and locate the Private Sub frmpREP_Load subroutine. Create a new line in the Select Case statement before the text "Case "2 Response"" and type the following:

```
Case "Go/No-Go"
Select Case ButtonFormat
Case "Image"
butPositive.BackgroundImageLayout = ImageLayout.Stretch
butPositive.BackgroundImage = Image.FromFile(PosImage)
butPositive.Text = ""
Case "Text"
butPositive.BackColor = PosColor
butPositive.Text = PosText
End Select
```

Now test your program again. Try both formats and make sure that your images, text and colors all load when you run actual trials.

At this point we are almost done. There are four more options that we might want to include with the current program, one for the Go/No-Go Format and three more that would apply to both formats. Currently we have a timer to control the negative response for the Go/No-Go Format. We have it set at 5 seconds, because that was the value used in the original Cullinan et al., (1996) study, but we might want to include this as an option that can be set to different intervals. To do this we'll need to declare a public variable to hold the setting, some code on frmpREP to apply the setting to the timer, and a control on frmSetup to allow us to set the variable. To do this we'll use a NumericUpDown control.

Return to the design level of frmSetup. Add a Label to the Go/No-Go options panel, pnlGONOGO, beneath our Button Format options and panels. Change the label's name to lblResponse, its AutoSize Property to False, set its Font size to 16, change its Text to "Response Timer (sec)" and set its TextAllign property to MiddleCenter. Now locate the NumericUpDown control in the Toolbox, and add one to the form beneath lblResponse. Change its name to nudResponse, set its Font size to 16, and set its Minimum property to 1. Since our standard response interval is 5 seconds, we'll make that the default setting for this control, so set its Value property to 5.

Now let's add some code to set this option. Go to Module1. Let's add a Public variable to carry the response time. Under your last variable declaration add the following:

```
Public ResponseTime as Integer
```

Now return to the edit level of frmSetup. Locate the Private Sub butBegin_Click subroutine. Create a new line between the text "End Select" and "Dim x As New frmInstructions" and add the following line of code.

```
ResponseTime = nudResponse.Value
```

Now go to the edit level of frmpREP and locate the Private Sub frmpREP_Load subroutine. Create a line before the text "Input_Trial_Information()" and add the following:

```
tmrResponse.Interval = ResponseTime * 1000
```

Since we've added the functionality to modify the response interval timer, we might as well employ similar methods to allow the experimenter to modify the presentation timer and the ITI timer as well. Return to the design level of frmSetup. Add a Label and a NumericUpDown to the form and position them to the right of the "Study Format" panel. This may require you to move the "Begin" button to the left side of the form. Name the Label lblPresentation, set its Autosize property to False, its Font size to 16, set its Text property to "Presentation Timer (sec)", and set its TextAllign property to MiddleCenter. Name the NumericUpDown nudPresentation, set its Font size to 16, and set its Minimum property to 1. Since out default value for the presentation is 2 seconds, set the Value property to 2. Now copy both the newly added Label and NumericUpDown, paste them on the form, and position them to the right of lblPresentation and nudPresentation. Change the newly pasted Label's Name to lblITI and its Text to "ITI Length (sec)". Change the NumericUpDown's Name to nudITI, and set its Value to 1.

Now double click on the "Begin" button to go back to the Private Sub butBegin_Click subroutine. Beneath the text "ResponseTime=nudResponse.Value" add the following lines of code:

```
Presentation = nudPresentation.Value
ITI = nudITI.Value
```

We now need to declare the two variables to carry these values. Return to Module1 and add the following declaration:

```
Public ITI as Integer
Public Presentation as Integer
```

Finally let's add some code to the main program to set the timers to the values of these variables. Return to the edit level of frmpREP and locate the Private Sub frmpREP_Load subroutine. Under the text "tmrResponse.Interval=ResponseTime * 1000" add the following lines:

```
tmrITI.Interval = ITI * 1000
tmrPresentation.Interval = Presentation * 1000
```

Now run the program to test our new additions. Experiment with using different presentation intervals and ITI's with both formats. Experiment with different response intervals with the Go/No-Go format.

Our program is nearly complete. One thing you may have noticed previously is that up till now we have failed to include any code to write the results of the program to an output file. We've purposely left this out up until now to demonstrate how you can include some code to create a custom folder in which we can save the results of a session with a given participant. Let's add one final option to our setup form, frmSetup. Return to the design level of frmSetup. To the right of the Label and NumericUpDown for the ITI length add another Label and a Textbox. Name the Label lblParticipant, set its AutoSize property to False, its Font size to 16, its Text to "Participant Name/Number" and set its TextAllign property to MiddleCenter. Name the TextBox txtParticipant and set is Font size to 16.

Now let's declare a variable to carry our participant's name. Return to Module1, and under your last declaration enter the following:

```
Public Participant as String
```

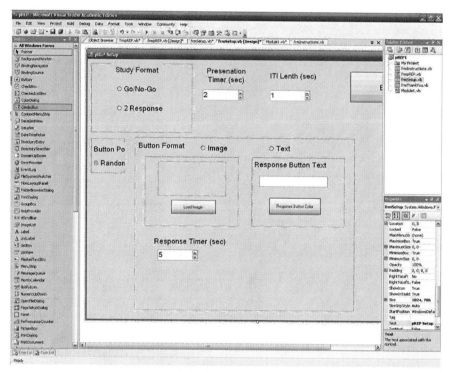

Figure 9.16 displays the addition of the various Timer Interval options.

Now return to the edit level of frmSetup and locate the Private Sub butBegin_Click subroutine. We'll now include the code to set the Participant variable, create an Output Files folder, create a folder for the current participant and open a file to write the output of the study to. Under the text "ITI = nudITI.Value" add the following.

```
Participant = txtParticipant.Text
My.Computer.FileSystem.CreateDirectory("C:\programming\pREP\Output
    Files\" & Participant)
FileOpen(2,  "C:\programming\pREP\Output  Files\"  &
    Participant & "\" & Participant & " pREP output.txt",
    OpenMode.Append)
WriteLine(2, "************************")
WriteLine(2, "Participant", Participant)
WriteLine(2, DateTime.Now)
WriteLine(2, "Format", Format)
WriteLine(2, "************************")
```

Now let's add some code to the main program to write to this output file. Return to the edit level of frmpREP. Let's add some lines to write the output of each individual trial to the output file. We will want this information to be recorded every time the participant makes a response by clicking on one of the response buttons, or when the participant does not respond in the Go/No-Go Format, so we will add code to both response buttons and to the response timer. Locate the Private Sub butPositive_Click subroutine. Between the text "End If" and the text "End Sub" add the following line:

```
WriteLine(2, "Phase= " & vPhase & " Criterion= " &
    vCriterion & " Correct = " & vCorrect & " Trial#= " &
    vCounter & " " & vTrials(vRandNumber(vCounter), 0) &
    vTrials(vRandNumber(vCounter), 1) & vAnswer &
    DateTime.Now)
```

Now copy the line you just typed and locate the Private Sub butNegative_Click subroutine. Paste the code in the same place (i.e. between the text "End If" and "End Sub"). Now copy the code again and locate the Private Sub tmrResponse_Tick subroutine. Paste the code in the same location in the subroutine as the previous two subroutines (i.e. between the text "End If" and "End Sub").

Now let's include a few more lines to write the results of the equivalence tests to the output file. Scroll up to the Sub Place_Stimuli subroutine. After the line of code "If RepeatTraining < 3 Then" add the following line:

```
WriteLine(2, "Failed to pass Equivalence Test. Training
    re-started.")
```

Now scroll down a bit and add the following line between the text "Else" and the text "Dim x As New frmThankYou".

```
WriteLine(2, "Failed to pass Equivalence in 3 tries. Study
    Ended")
```

Now that we have some code to record that the test for equivalence relations failed, let's add some code that will display the summary of each phase whether criterion is reached or not. Scroll up to the top of the Private Sub Place_Stimuli subroutine. Create a blank line after the text "If vCounter > vNumberofTrials Then". And on this line type the following:

```
WriteLine(2, "End of Phase" & " Criterion= " & vCriterion
    & " Correct= " & vCorrect)
```

We need to add one final line of code to close our output file when the participant completes all phases in the program. Return to our final form, frmThankYou. Double click on the "End Study" button to return to the edit level of the form. In the Private Sub butEnd_Click subroutine add the following code before the text "End"

```
FileClose(2)
```

Figure9.17 displays an output file from the program.

That should be it. Run the program again and try some different permutations of options. Check in the "C:\programming\pREP\" directory for a new "Output Files" folder. Within this folder you should find folders for any participant names or numbers you have used, and within these folders you should find a text output file. The output file should display the participant's name, the date and time the program was run, as well as the format and the results of each individual trial. Hopefully the current chapter has helped you to tie together some concepts from this book, and to see how thinking ahead to future changes in a research question or agenda can be included into a single application. Maintaining this type of foresight in the conceptualization and development of your programs, while initially more time intensive, will save you time, effort, and frustration down the road.

Chapter 10:
Software Packaging and Deployment

This chapter will provide you with the skills necessary to take any complicated program that you have developed in Visual Basic 2005 and package it for the running of actual experiments, installation on another computer, or distribution to other users. Up until now you have created Visual Basic 2005 Applications consisting of a project, forms, and perhaps a module or two. This collection of files is considered your application, and unfortunately if you were just to transfer these files to another computer, they could not be used unless the computer you were transferring them to also had Visual Basic 2005 installed. In addition you would have to copy and save all of these files independently. In addition you may have a number of support or system files such as images, text files that you are using for input, and dependent dynamic link library or .dll files that may also be needed to ensure that your program will run correctly. It is not our intention with this text to force you to either install Visual Basic 2005 on all computers you might wish to run your programs, nor is it to confine your work to the computer you have devoted to the development of your applications. Luckily there is an easy way to get around these problems. It is called Packaging and Deployment using something called a Setup Project.

Adding the Output to your Setup Project

The eventual goal of the Setup Project is to have a single file package that can be copied and shared across computers and users. This single file will consist of a Windows Installer or ".msi" file that will contain the output from the project you wish to install, as well as any support files you wish to include. Rather than use an existing project you created during the course of this book, open up a new instance of Visual Studio and create a very simple new application at this time called *Test*. To do this, click on the *Create Project* option under *Recent Projects*. From the *New Project* Dialog select *Windows Application*, name the new project *Test*, and click the *OK* button to begin. Now that you have created your new application, create a new folder named *Test* on the "C:\" drive of your computer and save your new application here.

Once you have saved your application rename the form *frmTest* and change the BackColor to Light Blue. Next add a Button and name it *butHello*, and change the text to *Hello*. Add a second Button named *butGoodbye* and change the text to *Goodbye*. Add a third Button named butExit and change the text to Exit. Now add a PictureBox, change the name to *picSalutation* and the SizeMode to *StretchImage*. (See Figure 10.1)

Now locate a couple of pictures you would like to use for greetings. One picture will appear in *picSalutation* when the user clicks the *Hello* button and one will appear when the user clicks the *Goodbye* button. In this example we will use two ".jpg" files which will be named *Hi.jpg* and *Bye.jpg* and will be saved in the "C:\Test\" folder we created previously.

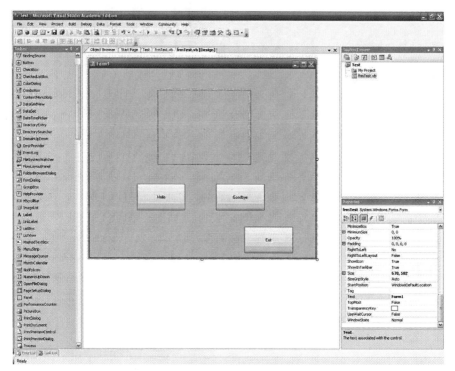

Figure 10.1 displays a possible configuration of the Test form layout.

Now double click on the *butHello* Button and enter the edit mode. Add the following code under the Private Sub butHello_Click() subroutine:

```
picSalutation.Image = Image.FromFile("C:\Test\Hi.jpg")
```

Under the Private Sub butGoodbye_Click() subroutine type:

```
picSalutation.Image = Image.FromFile("C:\Test\Bye.jpg")
```

Under the Private Sub butExit_Click() subroutine type:

```
End
```

Finally change the Startup form to frmTest, and run the program to make sure it works. The program should now result in your *Hello* picture appearing when you click on *butHello* and your *Goodbye* picture appearing when you click on *butGoodbye*. The program should also end when you click on *butExit*. Try clicking on the buttons a few times then click on *butExit* to end the program. Go ahead and save our new, but rather boring, Test project. Now we are ready to add a Setup Project to our application.

Initial Setup Using the Setup Wizard

Creating the Setup Project

With your mouse, click on *File* on the main menu at the top of your screen. From the resulting options locate the *Add* option and move your mouse over the black arrow to the right of *Add* to reveal the possible options. From these options select *New Project* as seen in Figure 10.2 to open the *Add New Project* dialog window. To date we have dealt exclusively with *Windows Applications*, but if you click on the + to the left of *Other Project Types* in the *Project Types* window, you will reveal a few new options. From these new options select *Setup and Deployment* by clicking on it with your mouse. You should now see several new options in the *Templates* window as displayed in Figure 10.3. From these options select *Setup Wizard*. Rename the project *InstallTest* and click on the *OK* button.

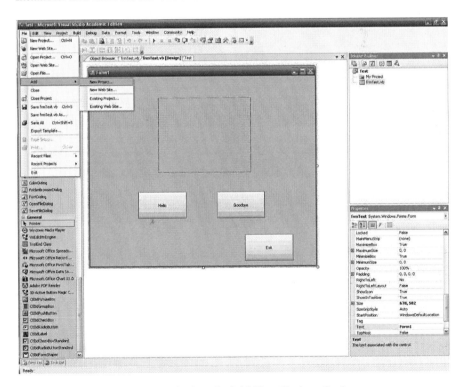

Figure 10.2 displays the Add New Project *Option.*

At this point a new window will appear in Visual Studio that states "Welcome to the Setup Project Wizard" as shown in Figure 10.4. This tool will provide you with a step-by-step guide to getting started creating your own professional looking install program. At this point, click on the *Next* button to continue the development process.

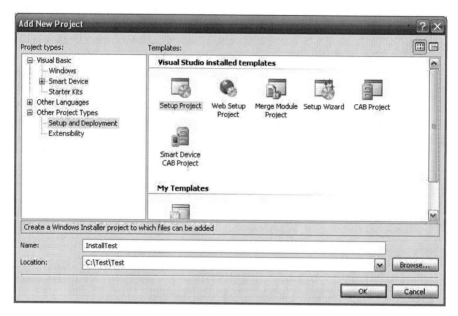

Figure 10.3 displays the appropriate "New Project" options found in the "Setup and Deployment" Project dialog.

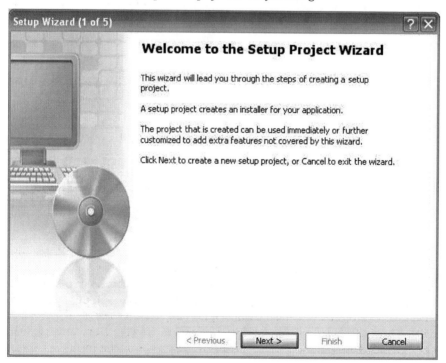

Figure 10.4 displays the first window of the Setup Wizard

The second window of the Setup Wizard asks you what type of project you wish to develop. You can choose between a Windows or Web Application. For the types of programs you have been developing in this book, you should select a *Windows Application*. Yet, a *Web Application* is just as easy to create and deploy when created in a similar fashion to what we have taught you. The second set of available option on this window asks if you wish to create a redistributable package. The CAB file is a type of compressed file that can easily be passed over the web or via email to other users, while the Merge Module, is a distributable package that can be customized in a variety of ways by the person whose computer will eventually hold the software. In most cases, neither of these options is needed so leave both unchecked and click on the *Next* button as shown on Figure 10.5.

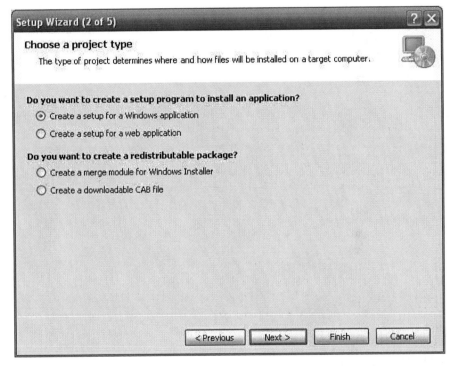

Figure 10.5 displays the second window of the Setup Wizard

The third window of the wizard asks which project output files that you wish to add to the Setup Project. The fourth option *Primary Output from Test* will often be enough for other users to run your program. By only including this option, the user will not be able to see what your code is, as the actual form will not be included in the Setup Project. Selecting only this option might be a really good idea if you do not want to "give away" your code to other users. However, if you wish to have your intended user(s) modify the code or alter your program (as might be the case

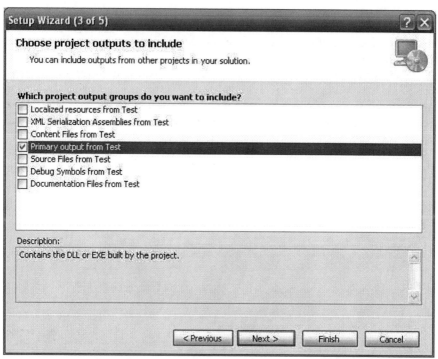

Figure 10.6 displays the third window of the Setup Wizard

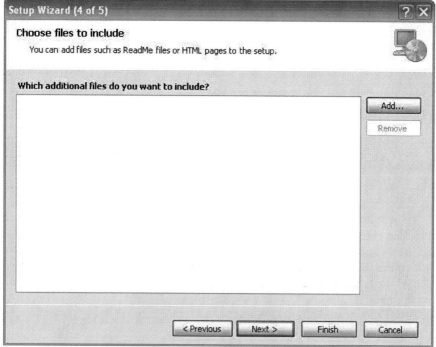

Figure 10.7 displays the fourth window of the Setup Wizard.

when two people are working on a program from remote locations) then check the remaining options. At this point, let's just select *Primary Output from Test* and click on next as shown in Figure 10.6.

The fourth window of the wizard asks which additional files you wish to package with your Setup Project. It is here where you would add all your individual support files such as individual stimuli image files, .wav files, media files, .txt files, etc. that should be included in the final computer program, but do not reside within Visual Basic 2005 when the program is run. Click the *Add* button and with the resulting Open File dialog locate and select the *Hi.jpg* and *Bye.jpg* files we saved in the C:\Test\ directory earlier, and click on the *Open* button. Now click on the *Next* button to move to the final window in the wizard.

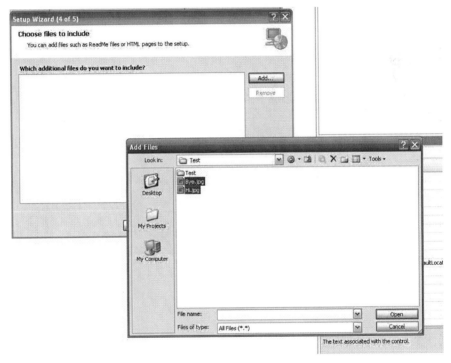

Figure 10.8 displays the addition of the "Hi.jpg" and "Bye.jpg" files to the Setup Wizard.

The last window of the wizard displays your previously selected choices and asks that you review them now, alter them if needed via clicking on the *Previous* button or accept them by clicking on *Finish.* Click on *Finish* as depicted in Figure 10.8. Visual Basic 2005 will now add some new options to our previously created *Test* application as can be seen if Figure 10.9.

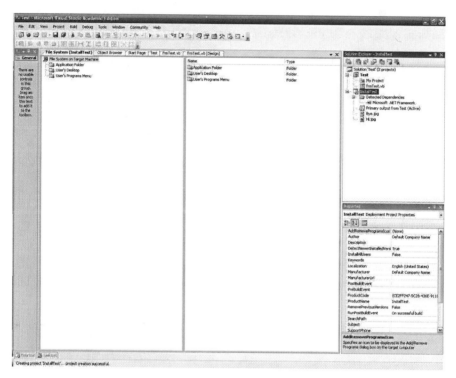

Figure 10.9 displays the layout window for customizing your Setup Project

In the center of your Object Browser you should see two separate panes. The pane on the left side depicts *File System on Target Machine* and the pane on the right depicts a variety of folders including *Application Folder, User's Desktop*, and *User's Programs Menu*. Plus the Solution Explorer now contains an entire second project titled *InstallTest*. We now have two projects sitting in one solution. One project is our test project and the other is our Setup Project.

Customizing the Setup Project

File Output Properties

A useful feature found in Visual Basic 2005 is the ability to specify the actual location you wish to install the program. In other words, once you create the Output, you can tell Visual Basic 2005 where it should install it when it is loaded on another computer. Users can change this if they want to, but your specification might be helpful to ensure proper installation of more complex programs that feature code to access files that should be stored in a specific location.

Click your mouse once on the *Application Folder* that is located in the left pane of the main project window to highlight it. Now right click on it with your mouse and select the *Properties Window* option. Your properties window on the right of the screen should change focus to the available properties for this folder as shown in Figure 10.10. Note that the *DefaultLocation* property currently is set to:

```
[ProgramFilesFolder][Manufacturer]\[ProductName]
```

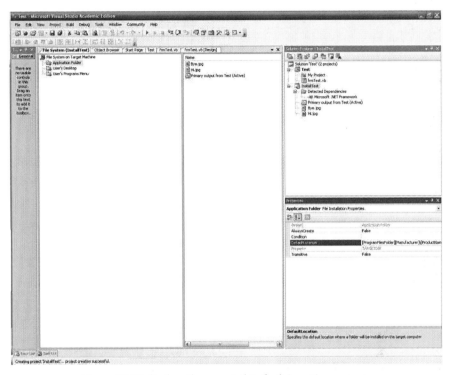

Figure 10.10 displays the suggested Default Location property.

What this means is that all of the Output from our Test project and any files included in the *Application Folder* will be installed in the Program Files Folder, in a subfolder with the name of the company you entered when you first installed Visual Basic 2005, and in a subdirectory with the name of our actual Output project. You can change this to better suit your needs. Perhaps, eliminate the middle folder so that the *DefaultLocation* property now reads:

```
[ProgramFilesFolder]\[ProductName]
```

A Cautionary Tale Regarding where Files are Installed

So we now have set the properties of the *Application Folder* to install everything located within it to a folder with the name of our Output project "Test", in the Program Files folder on the user's computer. But let's examine what all will be installed in this location. Click once on the *Application Folder* in the left pane. In the right pane you should see all of the files currently set to be included for installation at this location. Currently this should include the Primary output from our Test project, as well as the *Hi.jpg* and *Bye.jpg* images we want our program to display when the user clicks on the corresponding buttons. Remember the code we included in the click routines for *butHello* and *butGoodbye* referenced images located in the "C:\Test\" directory. With our current settings these images will not be installed to this location, so if a user uses the Install file we are creating then tries to run the program, the program will be unable to locate the images and will result in the program crashing.

This represents a flaw in using the Setup Wizard to choose any additional files you wish to include in a Setup Project. The wizard offers no method of specifying where those files should be installed. Thankfully we can quickly remedy this problem here. To accomplish this, with your mouse right click on the text *File System on Target Machine* located directly above the *Application Folder* in the left pane. This should reveal an *Add Special Folder* option with several options for the types of folders you might want to add. At the bottom of these available options select *Custom Folder*. This should add a new folder to the left pane named *Custom Folder #1*. Rename this folder *Test*, then with your mouse right click on it and select the *Properties Window* option. This should change the focus of the Properties Window on the right of the screen to our new *Test* folder. Now highlight the text in the *DefaultLocation* property and type the following:

```
C:\Test\
```

What this does is tell the install file we are creating to create a folder named *Test* on the "C:\" drive of the user's computer. Now we need to move the two image files from the *Application Folder* to our *Test* folder. With your mouse click on *Application Folder* in the left pane. You should now see the contents of this folder in the right pane. To move our *Hi.jpg* and *Bye.jpg* files to the *Test* folder simply hold down the *Ctrl* key on your keyboard and select both files with your mouse. Now simply drag them from the right pane to the *Test* folder in the left pane. Now click on the *Test* folder in the left pane and you should now see in the right pane, as seen in Figure 10.11, that the folder now contains the two images.

Changing Additional Output Properties

In addition to specifying the file folder for the project Output and the installation location for any additional needed files, you can also specify the image icon that will be placed on the desktop of the user, add additional support files, and create a shortcut on the Start Menu. These options may seem like overkill for a simple transfer from your office computer to your lab computer, but they may come in handy once you start selling your Visual Basic 2005 masterpieces.

To change the icon, click on the Application Folder in the left pane. You should now see the contents of this folder in the right pane, which should now consist of

*Figure 10.11 displays the addition of the "Test" folder to the
File System on Target Machine.*

the Output file for our Test project. Right click on this file and select the *Create
Shortcut to Primary output from Test (Active)*. What this will do is create a shortcut file
that can be placed on either the user's desktop, or in the user's Start menu to quickly
load the Test program. If you select this newly created Shortcut file by clicking on
it with your mouse you should see some of the properties that you can adjust in the
Properties window. Change the *Name* property to *Test*. Now when this file is
displayed on the user's desktop or in the user's start menu, it will have a simple and
short name to identify the program.

Right now there is no icon selected for your program as you will note by the *Icon*
property being currently set to {*None*}. You might want to associate an interesting
icon with this program. You may have some image editing software on your
computer that might allow you to make your own Icons, but if you don't you can
either use the "Search" tool on your computer to locate some available Icon (i.e. *.ico*)
files on your computer that you might use, or you can find many free icon libraries
on the internet.

Once you have located an icon file that you would like to associate with this
program you need to add it to the solution so that you can link it to your shortcut.
To add your chosen *.ico* file right click on the *Application Folder* in the left pane and

from the resulting options select *Add*, and from these options select *File* as shown in Figure 10-12. Use the resulting Open File dialog to locate and select your chosen icon on your computer and then click the *Open* button.

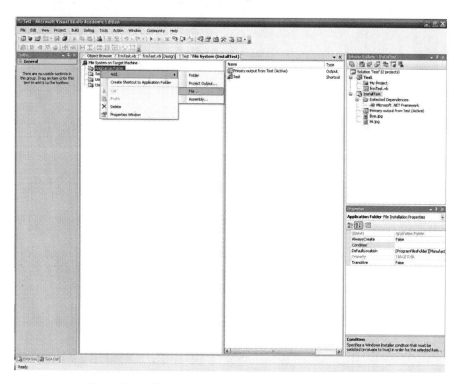

Figure 10.12 displays how to add a file to "Test" folder on the File System on Target Machine

Now that the icon is in our file structure, you can associate with our shortcut file. Click on the *Test* shortcut file in the right pane, and then locate the *Icon* property in the Properties window. The property is currently set to {*None*}, but if you click on this text a drop down arrow should appear to the right. If you click on this drop down arrow you should reveal a {*Browse...*} option. Click on this option to open the *Icon* browser as shown in Figure 10.13. If you click on the *Browse* button the dialog box will allow you to search the files we have currently added to the *File System on Target Machine*. Now double click on *Application Folder* and you should see the icon we added to the program in the steps above. Select this icon and click on the *OK* button. You will now be returned to the *Icon* browser and should see your chosen Icon in the center of the screen. Click on the *OK* button.

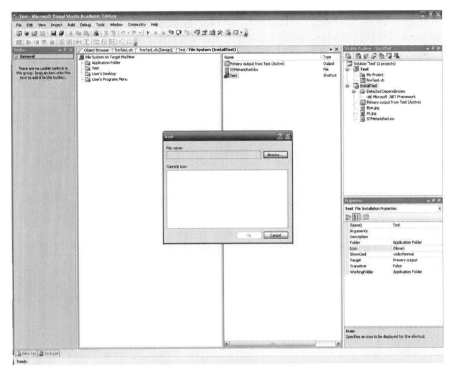

Figure 10.13 displays the Icon dialog.

Now that we have an Icon associated with the Test shortcut file we need to move it so that it will be installed on the User's desktop. To accomplish this simply drag the *Test* shortcut file from the right pane to the *User's Desktop* folder in the left pane. To also create a shortcut to the program in the Start menu of the user's computer we need to simply repeat some of the steps above. Return to the files located in the *Application Folder* by clicking on the folder in the left pane. Now select the *Primary output from Test (Active)* file in the right pane with your mouse, and right click and create a new shortcut file. Change the *Name* property of the new shortcut to *Test* and use the steps above to associate the Icon you saved in the *Application Folder* with this new shortcut file. Once you've se the Icon property simply move the new *Test* shortcut file to the *User's Programs Menu* folder in the left pane by dragging it from the right pane.

By the time you are ready to package your program up and transfer it over to your users, you will have hopefully corrected any programming errors that your program may have contained. Unless your user wishes to have the large and cumbersome Debugging features of Visual Basic 2005 installed on his/her computer for further error correction, you will need to change one last option from the *Build* option on the main menu toolbar. Click on *Build,* and select the last option, *Configuration*

Manager. A new dialog box will appear that shows a grid containing your Test project and your Output project *InstallTest.* Under the *Active solution configuration:* drop down box change the current setting from *Debug* to *Release* as shown if Figure 10.14. Finally, make sure that both Projects are checked in the *Build* row and click on the *Close* button.

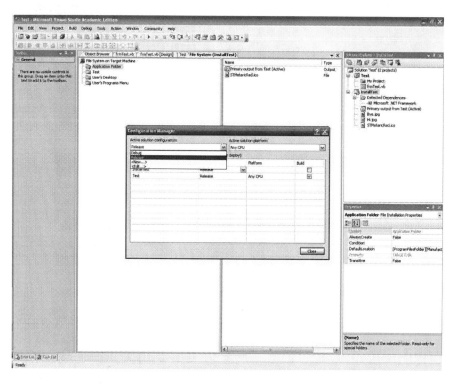

Figure 10.14 displays the Configuration Manager dialog box.

The Final Step: Building Your Install File

The final step in this build process is to generate the Output file. To do so, click on *Build* from the main menu at the top of the screen. From the resulting options, click on *Build InstallTest* as seen in Figure 10.15. Visual Basic 2005 will now begin the compiling process of packaging all your individual files into a single installation or *.msi* file to share your user's machine. You will see the progress of the build in the lower left the Visual Studio interface. As the file is building the text "Build started…" will be displayed and once the file has been created the text "Build succeeded" will be displayed.

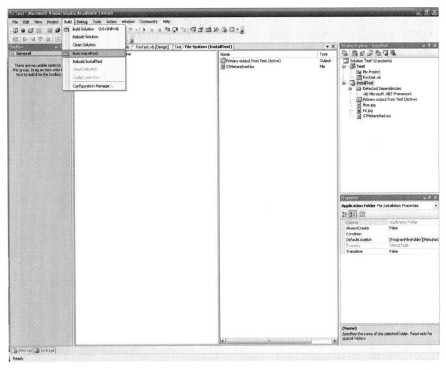

Figure 10.15 displays the Build options for the Setup Project.

To locate your newly created installation file, browse your file directories and find the "C:\Test\" folder we created earlier. Open the "Test" folder and you should see a directory with both a "Test" and an "InstallTest" folder. Open the "InstallTest" folder, and in the resulting directory locate and open the "Release" folder. You should see your installation file here. It is named *InstallTest.msi* and will have the file type of *Windows Installer Package*. Figure 10.16 displays the contents of your "InstallTest" folder's *Release* directory.

Deploying Your Setup Program

Running the Setup

Let us begin by attempting to install your newly created Install program right on the same computer you just created it on. We can copy the copy the *InstallTest.msi* install file and transfer it to another computer later. This step will ensure your packaging of all the necessary files was done correctly, prior to your transferring attempts. Go to the "C:\Test\Test\InstallTest\Release\" directory and double click on the *InstallTest.msi* file. After you do so, a dialog box similar to that found in Figure 10.17 will be displayed on your computer screen.

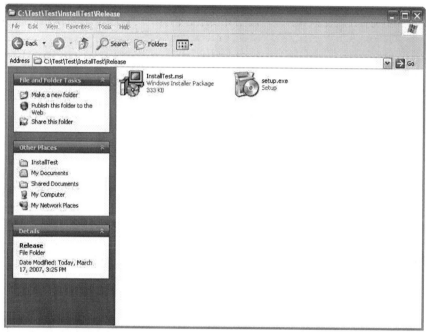

Figure 10.16 displays the contents of the Release directory.

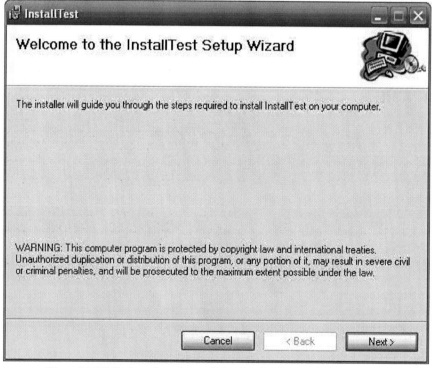

Figure 10.17 displays the welcome dialog box for the InstallTest program.

At this point, click on the *Next* option located in the bottom right hand corner of the screen, and view the subsequent dialog box requesting you to choose the directory you wish to place this program in (remember we created this option when we packaged our files earlier in the chapter!), and to determine if you wish to install this program for everyone who uses the computer or just yourself. Make your appropriate selections. Now notice the option entitled *Disk Cost*. Clicking here will display the system resources you have available and the "cost" or amount of space needed to install the program.

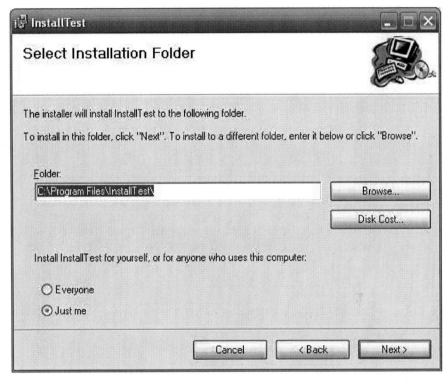

Figure 10.18 displays the Select Installation Folder dialog box for the InstallTest program.

Once satisfied with your selections, click on the *Next* option. You will be prompted one last time confirm you wish to have the *InstallTest* program installed on your computer. If you are sure you wish to do so, click on the *Next* option. Once done, your computer will begin to install the program as depicted in Figure 10.19.

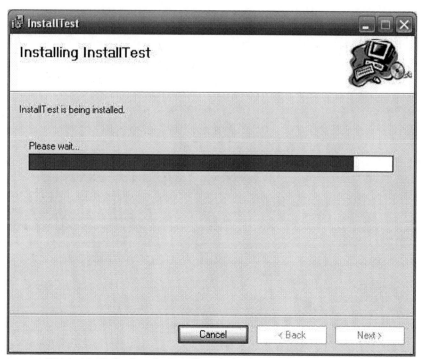

Figure 10.19 displays the Installing dialog box with progress indicator.

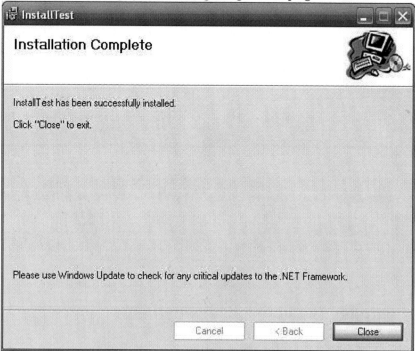

*Figure 10.20 displays the Install Complete dialog box that appears
following a successful installation.*

Running the Program

All that is left to do is check to see if your program runs. Remember, the program that we want to run is the exciting *Test* program that has a *Hello* and a *Goodbye* Button on it. The reason we did not call our installation program *Test* is that Visual Basic 2005 will not allow you to have the installation program and the Output named the same. You may wish to name all your installation programs after you own named followed by a suffix, like *DixonInstall1*. Just make it something useful and easy to remember. Locate your *Test* program by clicking on the *Start* image located on the bottom left of your computer screen. Next select *All Programs*. Browse through your existing programs and you will see a new shortcut listed named *Test* with the icon you chose when building the install file like that seen in Figure 10.21. This is it. Select this option and your *Test* program will magically begin to run on your computer. It does so, without ever opening Visual Basic 2005. It even has a little bit of a professional look to it. The reason your goofy little *Test* program looks professional is because you have become a computer programmer. Congratulations.

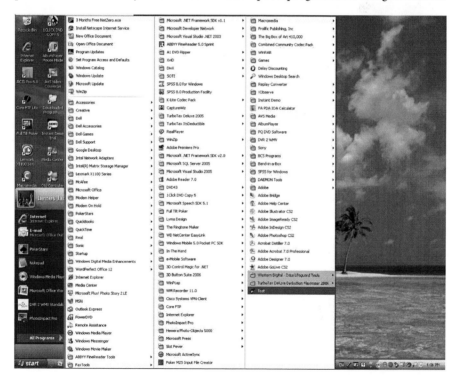

Figure 10.21 displays the appropriate selections to locate the "Test" program from the "Start" button.

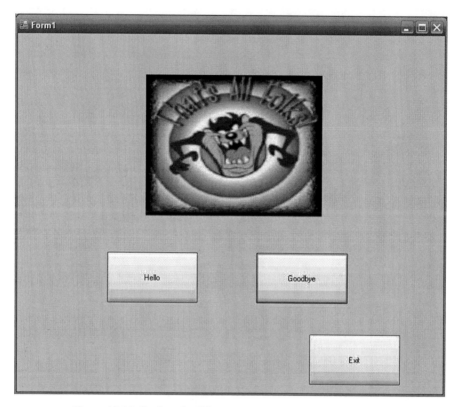

Figure 10.22 displays the "Test" program in action on the desktop.

Removing the Application You Have Installed

There are two ways in which you can remove the newly installed application from your computer. Both are relatively simple. One way to do so is to simply double-click on the *InstallTest.msi* file in your *Release* directory like you previously did to install the program. The resulting dialog box has different features this time though. The dialog box now asks you if you wish to either repair the program or remove it from your computer. Select *Remove* and click on the *Finish* option. That is it. The program will be removed.

Although the above removal process was about as simple as it gets, it may not work in every circumstance. For example you may have copied your *InstallTest* folder from your "C:\" drive to a CD-ROM so a different user could install this program on a different computer. If you did, and the user no longer has the CD-ROM this removal feature would not be available because the files were installed from a CD-ROM that is no longer available. Luckily, Microsoft Windows has a general program removal feature that you can use to accomplish this task.

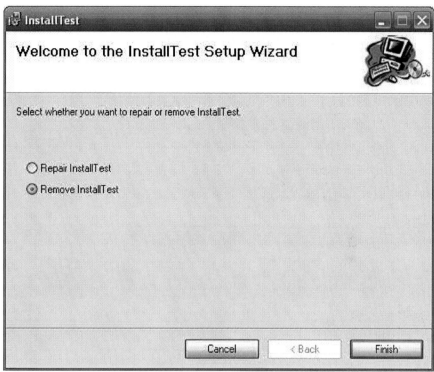

Figure 10.23 displays the dialog box allowing you to remove the InstallTest program from your computer.

To Take advantage of this process, you simply need to click on the *Start* icon on the bottom left corner of the computer screen, and, depending on whether your windows is currently set to classic or category view, click on either *Settings* or *Control Panel*. From the resulting window, locate the option within the Control Panel named *Add or Remove Programs* and double-click your mouse on it. Scroll down the various program selections until you find the *InstallTest* program. Uninstall the program by selecting it, and then clicking the mouse on the *Remove* option. Return to your programs from the Start options, and examine the available programs under the *All Programs* tab. The *Test* program should no longer be available.

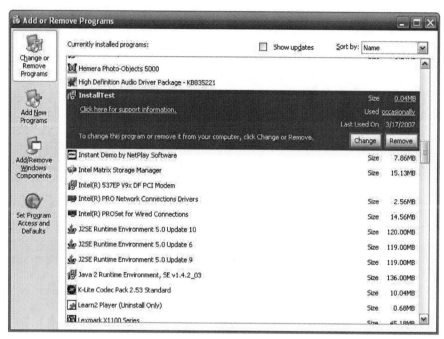

Figure 10.24 displays the Add/Remove Programs dialog box.

Chapter 11: User Controls

Overview

In previous chapters we discuss the need to create subroutines to encapsulate code that has become repetitive. For example, we may want the program to randomize a string of variables following three different events. Rather than writing the code three times, we can take the redundant code and reduce it to a single subroutine that each of the three different events can call on. Once you have begun writing research programs for yourself and others you will begin to realize that you repeatedly create similar graphical user interfaces. For example, if you are conducting research using match-to-sample, you may notice that every time you write a program you end up with four picture boxes in the same configuration. You might also notice that the code behind the boxes is very similar in that the subject is required to first click on the sample stimulus and then double click on the comparison stimuli to indicate a choice. In this case, not only do we use the same graphic interface, we use code that becomes redundant across programs, rather than events.

User Controls

Versions of VB 2005 beyond the standard edition allow us to create user controls which are custom reusable graphic interfaces. As with our match to sample example, the user controls combine existing VB 2005 controls into a single custom control that can be added to any new form just as easy as it is to add an existing control such as a button or a textbox. Not only can user controls be added easily, their properties can be updated or changed during the design phase or during run-time. Additionally, user controls can be exported and used by other programmers should you want to sell or share them with other programmers. Although the standard version of VB 2005 won't allow you to create user controls, the standard version will run the user controls you create.

TimeClock Control

Let's begin with a rather easy control that works like a clock counting the passage of time. Open a new project. Rather than select the Windows Application template, select the Windows Control Library template as seen in Figure 11.1. Change the name of the project to *TimeClock*. Click on the OK button. A new project will be created that looks very similar to the project we have already been working on as can be seen in Figure 11.2. Let's now tidy up the workspace by renaming the control from *UserControl1.vb to ctlTimeClock.vb* by right clicking on the user control in the Solution Explorer. Next add a label control and a timer control from the toolbox. Rename the label to *lblTimeClock*; change the text property to blank or empty; and the font size to 16. Rename the timer to *tmrTimeClock*; change the enabled property to true;

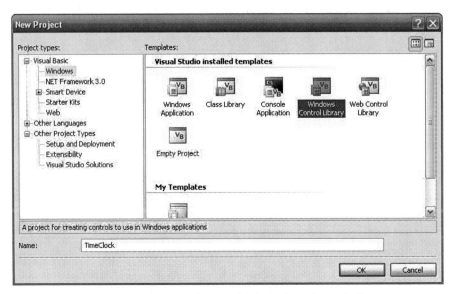

*Figure 11.1 displays the selection of the Windows Control Library
in the New Project Dialog.*

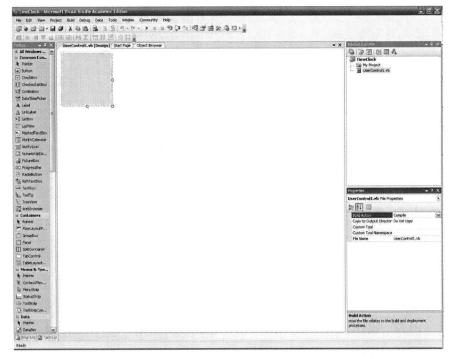

Figure 11.2 displays the main object browser for a Windows Control Library Project.

and change the interval property to 1000 so it fires every second. At this point our user control is not very impressive and won't do much until we add functionality by adding code.

Double click on the timer control to enter edit mode. Add the following code in the *tmrTimeClock_Tick()* subroutine VB 2005 created for you.

```
lblTimeClock.Text = Format(Now, "hh:mm:ss")
```

With this line of code, every second *tmrTimeClock* fires, the text in the label will be updated to the current time using the Now function. The Now function will also display the current date and indicate if it is AM or PM. We only want the time so we have formatted it to show hours, minutes, and seconds. To test the control, press the F5 key to run it. Something new will happen, a test container will appear showing the control and its properties as seen in Figure 11.3. The properties in the display are the user control properties we can change when we are using it in a new project. From here we could finish the user control to make it ready to be used in a new project. However, we might want to be able to have the option of changing some properties of the individual controls. Notice that we can't change the properties of the original controls for example, we can't change the display format such as text size. Nor can we change the timer properties so we can stop and start the clock.

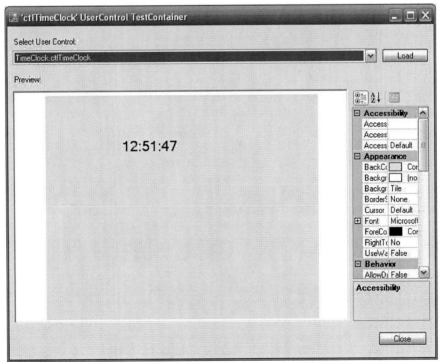

Figure 11.3 displays the ctlTimeClock test container.

Adding Control Properties

Let's design the control to allow the user to change the font of the clock. To do this we need to add the following code to *ctlTimeClock* by declaring a private variable to hold the new font value. Just below the existing line of code *Public Class ctlTimeClock* add:

```
Private vFont As Font
```

Next we define the new property by adding the following code. Notice that as soon and you begin to write the code, VB 2005 knows what you are up to and enters half of the code for you. You will simply have to fill in the lines that VB 2005 didn't. The entire code should look like this:

```
Property ClockFont() As Font
Get
Return vFont
End Get
Set(ByVal value As Font)
vFont = value
lblTimeClock.Font = vFont
End Set
End Property
```

We just told VB 2005 that we want a new Font Property called *ClockFont* to be added to the user control. We then instructed the computer to get the set value of *ClockFont* and store it in the variable *vFont*. We then used this new value to change the font property of the label. In order to see the changes, we need to run the project and scroll down to the bottom of the properties list to see our new property *ClockFont* as displayed in Figure 11.4

Let's add another property that allows us to stop and start the clock. To do this we need to alternate the enabled property of *tmrTimeClock* to true or false. As you might recall true and false are Boolean terms and use a Boolean variable. Declare a new private variable called *vOnOff* as Boolean under the *vFont* variable we recently created. Your code should look like this:

```
Public Class ctlTimeClock
Private vFont As Font
Private vOnOff As Boolean
Property ClockEnabled() As Boolean
Get
Return vOnOff
End Get
Set(ByVal value As Boolean)
```

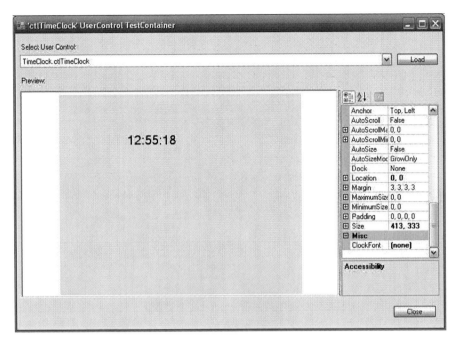

Figure 11.4 displays the new ClockFont property.

```
vOnOff = value
tmrTimeClock.Enabled = vOnOff
End Set
End Property
```

Run the program and see that our new property *ClockEnabled* has been added above the *ClockFont* property. You can change the value of these properties and see how they affect your user control.

Building the Control

The control does what we want it to do so now we have to get it ready to be used as a control in new projects. To do this we need to build the control by locating the build menu in the main menu and select *Build TimeClock*. Now from the File menu select Save All and make note where you are saving the control.

Adding the Control

Next open a new Windows Application project and name it *Clock*. Change the name of the form to *frmDisplay* and the text property to *Display*. Add a button to be used to turn the clock on and off. Rename it *btnClock* and change the text property to blank/empty. Next we want to add our user control, but where is it? And how do we get it in our form? Right click the toolbox and select choose items from the popup menu. A Choose Toolbox Items dialog box will appear. Select the *.NET Framework Components* tab, then click on the browse button on the lower right as displayed in Figure 11.5. Browse for the folder where the *TimeClock* project was saved to and double click it. Next double click the bin folder and then the debug folder to find the file *TimeClock.dll* which you need to select by double clicking. Our control is listed as *ctlTimeClock* and should have a checkmark to its left as seen in Figure 11.6. Close the dialog box by clicking on OK to now include the control in the toolbox as seen in Figure 11.7. Finally double click on the *ctlTimeClock* from the toolbox to add it to *frmDisplay*.

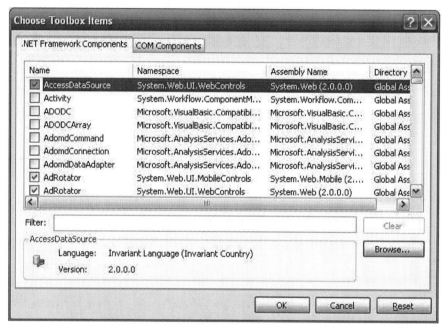

Figure 11.5 displays the Choose Toolbox Items dialog.

Using the Control

Notice that the control starts running as soon as we add it to the form. By changing it's *ClockEnabled* property to false we can turn it off. Now let's add some code that allows us to turn the clock on and off during run time. Change the name of the control to *ctlTimeClock* then double click *btnClock* to create the sub routine and to enter edit mode and enter the following:

```
If ctlTimeClock.ClockEnabled = False Then
btnClock.Text = "Turn Off"
ctlTimeClock.ClockEnabled = True
```

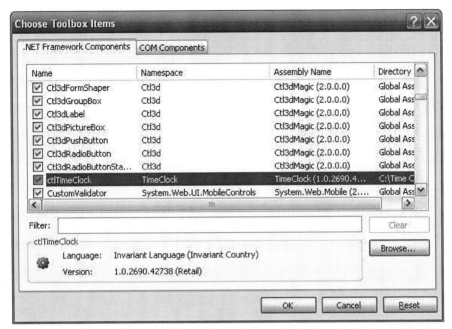

Figure 11.6 displays the Choose Toobox Items dialog with the TimeClock Control selected.

```
Else
btnClock.Text = "Turn On"
ctlTimeClock.ClockEnabled = False
End If
```

Based on the state of *ctlTimeClock.ClockEnabled*, the if then statement toggles the *ClockEnabled* property on and off as well as changing the text property of *btnClock* to reflect the change. When you run the program, you might notice that the clock is not displayed and the button has no text. This is because the timer is disabled. When you click on the button the first time the clock will be displayed and it will remain visible regardless of the timer state.

So now we know how to encapsulate our graphic user controls by creating a rather simple clock. Let's look at a slightly more complicated user control that might be part of a larger computer program to study gambling. MacLin, Dixon, Robinson, and Daugherty (2006) wrote a graphically elaborate program using multiple timers to control a slot machine. The program contained 3 reels and at least 3 timer controls to make the reels appear as though they are moving. For this next section on user controls we will create a control containing one reel and show how multiple controls can be used to program a slot machine with as many reels as one might care to have.

Figure 11.7 dispays the ctlTimeClock Control in the Toolbox window.

Slot Reel User Control

We will now create a control that contains a slot machine reel that appears to spin. You will need to open a new Windows Control Library and name it *Reel* and rename the user control *ctlReel.vb*. Next add a PictureBox, a Timer, and a Panel from the toolbox to be used as a container to hold the PictureBox. Name them *picReel*, *tmrReel*, and *pnlReel* respectively. Set the timer property to enabled = true and add the reel1.bmp (found at http://www.behavioralcomp.com/ BasicSlot/reel1.bmp) as a Project resource file using the *picReel* image property as seen in figure 11.8. Change the *picReel* SizeMode property to StretchImage and its Size property to 89, 719 so reel1.bmp will fit exactly. Making the image a re-source file will ensure it to be packaged with the user control. Drag *picReel* over *pnlReel* to place it in the panel container. Adjust the size of *pnlReel* and *picReel* so they are the same width. *PicReel* will be much longer which is what we want so we can create the moving effect.

Most of the code will be located in the timer subroutine so double click on *tmrReel* to enter edit mode. Add the following code and then run the program:

```
picReel.Top = picReel.Top + 40
If picReel.Top > 1 Then picReel.Top = -504
```

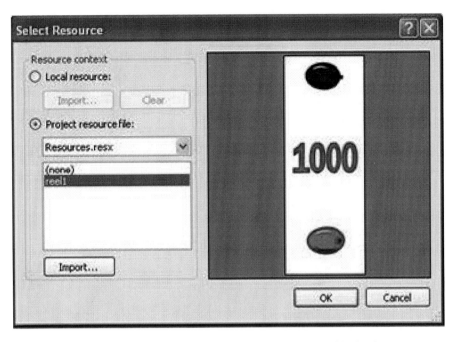

Figure 11.8 displays the addition of reel1.bmp to the Resource files for the project.

Creating Properties

The program works by gradually advancing the reel bitmap each time *tmrReel* fires. When the reel gets to the top (*picReel.Top > 1*) it is moved to the bottom again (*picReel.Top = -504*). Now that we know that the program works, what properties will we want to control when it is added to a new project? We will want to be able to stop and start the reels by creating a property to enable or disable *tmrReel*. We might also want to control the speed of the reel by changing the Interval property of *tmrReel*. We might also want to control where the reel stops by changing the Top property of *picReel*. So let's create these. We need to declare three new variables and then the associated properties using the following code.

```
Public Class ctlReel
Private  ReelOnOff As Boolean
Private  ReelSpeed As Integer
Private  ReelPosition As Integer
Property ReelMove() As Boolean
Get
Return  ReelOnOff
End Get
Set(ByVal value As Boolean)
```

```
ReelOnOff = value
tmrReel.Enabled = ReelOnOff
End Set
End Property
Property Reel_Speed() As Integer
Get
Return ReelSpeed
End Get
Set(ByVal value As Integer)
ReelSpeed = value
tmrReel.Interval = ReelSpeed
End Set
End Property
Property ReelPos() As Integer
Get
Return  ReelPosition
End Get
Set(ByVal value As Integer)
ReelPosition = value
End Set
End Property
```

Run the program and scroll the properties box to the bottom. Try changing the *ReelMove* property and the *Reel_Speed* property. If you change the ReelPos property only the variable *ReelPosition* will change. Since it is not yet hooked up to anything you won't notice anything. We come back to this later. Change the size of the control to be slightly larger than the reels as displayed in Figure 11.9. Go ahead and build the user control using the Build option in main menu. Save the project then open a new Windows Application project called Slots. Rename *Form1* to *frmSlots* and change the text property to "Slot".

Adding the User Control

Right click the toolbox to Choose Items... Click on the *.NET Framework Components* tab on the Choose Toolbox Items dialog box. Select browse and find the ctlReel.dll user control you previously created. Click OK and it should appear in the Toolbox. Double click on *ctlReel* to add it to your form. Repeat this two more times until you have three reels named *ctlReel1*, *ctlReel2*, and *ctlReel3*. Change the *Reel_Speed* property on all three to 50. You can see how easy it will be to design a variety of slot machine programs now that we have this user control.

Let's add some functionality to the program by adding buttons to stop the reels by changing the properties we defined when making the user control. Add three buttons to the *frmSlot* and name them *btnReel1*, *btnReel2*, and *btnReel3*. Change their text property to "Stop". Double click on *btnReel1* and add the following code:

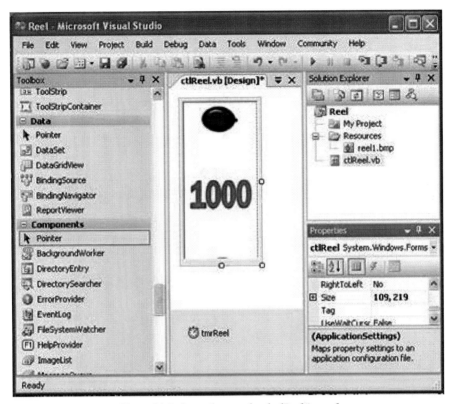

Figure 11.9 shows the completed ctlReel control.

```
CtlReel1.ReelMove = False
```

Add the equivalent code to the other two buttons (remember to change *btnReel1* to *btnReel2* etc.). Finally add a label control to the form positioned above the reels.

Rename the label to *lblSlot* and change the text property to "Your task is to stop the reels on the same symbol to win." Run the program and see if you can match up the reels! There are a couple of slight problems. First, we have to restart the program to reset the reels. This can be addressed by adding a button to reset the reels. Rename the button to *btnReset*, change the text property to "Reset", and add the following code:

```
CtlReel1.ReelMove = True
CtlReel2.ReelMove = True
CtlReel3.ReelMove = True
```

The other problem we mentioned is that the reels just stop where ever they are when you stop the timer. It would be nice if they advanced to discrete positions where they might align better. However this is something that can be done at a later time. For now we have created a user control that spins a reel. We added three of the reel controls to our project to form the basis of a slot machine and added some stop buttons to demonstrate how we can pass properties from the from level to the user controls. The completed slot machine can be seen in Figure 11.10.

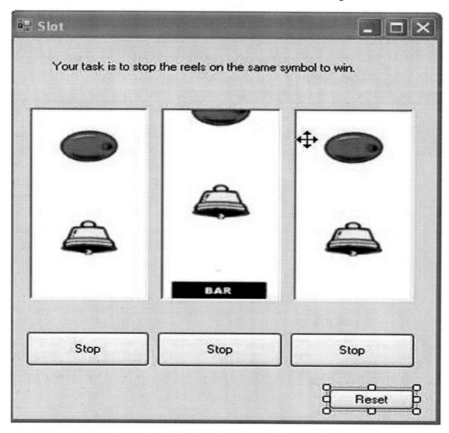

Figure 11.10 displays the completed slot machine.

References

MacLin, O. H., Dixon, M. R., Robinson, A., & Daugherty, D. (2006). Writing a simple slot machine simulation program. In P. M. Ghezzi, C. A. Lyons, M. R. Dixon, & G. R. Wilson (Eds.), *Gambling: Behavior theory, research, and application* (pp. 127-154). Reno, NV: Context Press.

Chapter 12:
Object Oriented Programming

Overview

When we began this book we told you that Visual Basic was an object oriented language in that the language is based on the placement of objects on the screen that perform actions when they are clicked on or triggered by keystrokes or timers. This is only partially true. From a programmers perspective object oriented programming (OOP) is much more than that. The objects that we now refer to are virtual objects akin to an object class. The object class embodies the attributes of object members. We might at this point make a comparison to the behavioral terminology of a stimulus class or a behavioral class. The stimulus class is not really a stimulus, but a collection of properties that comprise the particular stimuli that fall into that class. We might think of motor vehicles as an object class, within this object class of motor vehicles we might find objects such as cars, trucks, motorcycles, and mopeds. These objects share common features such as motors, wheels, steering mechanisms, paint color, number of passengers, and speed capabilities, etc. Each individual object in the vehicle class might have different features setting them apart from one another. For example if a vehicle had 2 wheels and one passenger it is likely a moped. However, if the vehicle had 2 wheels and 2 passengers it would likely be a motorcycle.

At this point you probably thought that these objects themselves could also be object classes. There are many different types of cars and trucks. While car is an object in the vehicle class, a red Chevy 2-door is an object in a class called car. In the example we will program later, we will create an object class called cards as in a deck of cards. There are many types of card decks such as those used for poker, pinochle, or reading tarot. There are also decks of baseball cards, Pokémon cards, and such. However our example for later on will cover a deck of playing cards.

When programmers talk OOP they use words like class, object, method, inheritance, encapsulation, and polymorphism. These terms alone are a good reason to put the chapter on OOP at the end of the book. While it may have been better to learn and practice OOP earlier on, we felt it was best left towards the end at a point where you the reader is more comfortable with Visual Basic programming – we also thought it was a good idea to not have to teach you all of these words. Historically Visual Basic was not considered a real programming language because it was not truly object oriented. Some programmers even considered the early versions of Visual Basic a "toy" language because it lacked the ability to do OOP. As later versions of Visual Basic came out such at VB.Net, programmers had limited object oriented ability. Now with VB 2005, programmers can enjoy the full OOP experience.

We will begin our demonstrating of OOP using a VB Console Application to see the results of our class. Start a new project and select Console Application from the New Project dialog box. Name the project Cars as seen in Figure 12.1. When you click on the OK button you will see that VB opened a Module called Module1.vb this default name will work just fine for this demonstration.

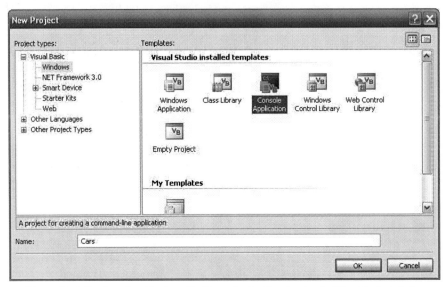

Figure 12.1 displays the selection of a Console Application in the New Project dialog.

Next we need to add a class to our project. To do this, right click on Cars in the Solution Explorer. Select Add... Class from the drop down menus and the Add New Item dialog box will appear. Select class from the available options and name the class Cars as seen in Figure 12.2. Click on the Add button.

You should now have the following tabs in your project as seen in Figure 12.3.

If you click on the Object Browser tab you can see the new class we created (along with an entire list of objects VB automatically supports). If you look through this list you might realize that we have been using object classes all along.

Now let's think about what attributes or properties we want our cars to have. Well for example, we could have the Make of the car (Chevy, Ford, Dodge, Nissan, Saturn, etc.). We could have the Size of the car (Economy, Midsize, and Luxury). We can have the color of the car (Red, Green, White, Etc.) and we could have the number of doors it has (2-door, 4-door). There is an abundance of properties we could list once we put our mind to it. The properties you ultimately use for the classes you program will depend on what you need the classes to do.

We'll start our example using Make of car. Enter the following code in the Cars.vb class:

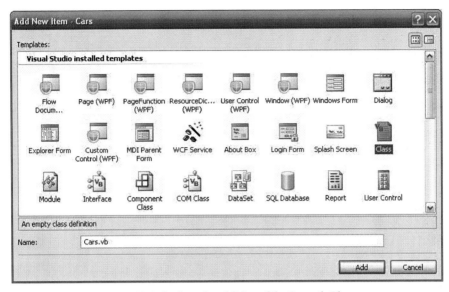

Figure 12.2 displays the addition of the Cars.vb Class.

*Figure 12.3 displays the available tabs in the Object Browser for the
Cars Console Application.*

```
Public Class Cars
Public Make As String
End Class
```

Next open the Module1.vb editor and add the following code and run the program.
Your results should look like Figure 12.5.

```
Sub Main()
Dim myCar As Cars
myCar = New Cars
myCar.Make = "Honda"
Console.WriteLine("I drive a " & myCar.Make)
Console.ReadLine()
End Sub
```

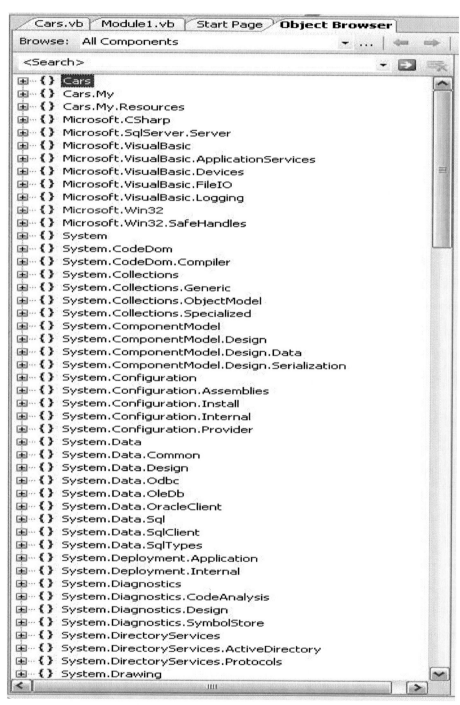

Figure 12.4 displays supported objects in the created class.

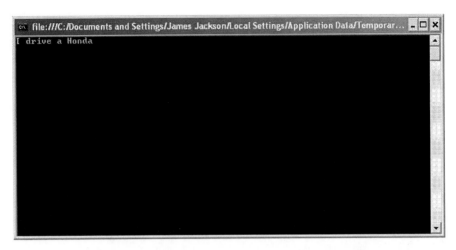

Figure 12.5 displays the running Cars console application.

In our code we have to first create the cars object by declaring the variable *myCar* and then in the second line of code we create a new instance of Cars and assign it to the variable we created *myCar*. Next, we set the make of *myCar* to a Honda. We need to show that we actually changed the make of the car so we use the console to concatenate the string "I drive a " with the make of the car and print it out in the console using the *Console.Writeline* command. Notice that the last line of code is the *Console.Readline* statement. This tricks the console to wait for us to enter something. But in actuality we just want the console to stay open until we get a chance to read the output. Keep in mind we are using the console here to display the output. We could have easily used a form and displayed the output in the form caption by changing the form's text property.

That wasn't terribly eventful either way. In fact, it was rather boring and that is the beauty of OOP. If used correctly, it makes programming easier – and yes, somewhat uneventful.

Now let's add a second line of code to what we already have to define a property for the number of doors.

```
Public Class Cars
Public Make As String
Public NumberOfDoors As Integer
End Class
```

The default value for NumberOfDoors is 0. This is OK because we will change that value later in the module by adding *myCar.NumberOfDoors* = 4. Add this line and the additional *Console.Writeline( )* code. Then run the program.

```
Sub Main()
Dim myCar As Cars
myCar = New Cars
myCar.Make = "Honda"
myCar.NumberOfDoors = 4
Console.WriteLine("I drive a " & myCar.Make)
Console.WriteLine("It has " & myCar.NumberOfDoors & "
    doors")
Console.ReadLine()
End Sub
```

Pretty much like we expected. And this is a good thing. We can play around with what we have so far and see the default value for the number of doors if we remark out that line of code and run the program. Try it.

We can also create more instances of cars. We can create *yourCar* using the same Cars.vb class. Try adding a second dim for a car called *yourCar* and setting its make property to "Ford." Then try creating the new instance. Add a line of code to Write "You drive a..." in the console. Your code should look something like this:

```
Sub Main()
Dim myCar As Cars
Dim yourCar As Cars
myCar = New Cars
yourCar = New Cars
myCar.Make = "Honda"
yourCar.Make = "Ford"
myCar.NumberOfDoors = 4
Console.WriteLine("I drive a " & myCar.Make)
Console.WriteLine("It has " & myCar.NumberOfDoors & "
    doors")
Console.WriteLine("You drive a " & yourCar.Make)
Console.ReadLine()
End Sub
```

Up until now we have either been using the default values or we set the property values during run time. We can initialize property values at start up by using a constructor. Constructors are a subroutine called *New*. We can add the following subroutine to the Cars.vb class to initialize the make, number of doors, and volume so that every new instance of the class will have these values. We can change them later, these will just be the starting point.

```
Sub New()
Make = "chevy"
```

```
NumberOfDoors = 2
End Sub
```

With these values now initialized, every car will start off as a 2-door Chevy. We can try this by remarking out the lines of code in the Module1.vb setting the make and the number of doors. Once you comment out those 2 lines of code, run the program to see if the default values are used. It works, everyone is driving a 2-door Chevy! Now remove the comments from the lines of code and run the program to see if this code will write over the initialized values. It does and we are back to the 4-door Honda.

Sometimes programmers don't want to allow the user to change the properties. Rather than using a Public variable, a Private variable will make it so only the class can change the property. Most cars have sound systems. Let's create a volume property so we can tell how loud the sound system is playing at any given time. In the Cars.vb class add the following line of code to declare a private variable. Notice that we didn't use capitals for the first letter of the variable, this helps us remember that the property is private.

```
Private setVolume As Integer
```

Next write the following subroutines in the Cars.vb class. Remember the previous subroutines were written to the Module because the module was allowed to change the public variables. Now that setVolume is private, we need the subroutine to reside in the Cars.vb class. Of course we will need a way for the module to pass information (called 'set') and a way to receive information (called 'get') to and from the class.

```
ReadOnly Property Volume()
Get
Return setVolume
End Get
End Property
Sub increase_volume(ByVal volumeBy As Integer)
setVolume += volumeBy
End Sub
```

In order for these subroutines to do their job (and this is very important to understand now), we need to pass some information from the module. Using the following line of code located in the module:

```
myCar.increase_volume(10)
```

Technically what happens is when this line of code is reached in the program, it passes the value 10 in this case to the subroutine *increase_volume* (which is located in the class). The *increase_volume* subroutine is designed to receive the value 10 in this case and place the value in the variable volumeby which we declared in the first line of the subroutine. It then increases the private variable *setVolume* by the amount we passed along to the subroutine in the *volumeBy* variable. Notice that we used a different notation for incrementing the variable (+=). This is easier than writing *setVolume* = *setVolume* + *volumeBy*. Both work, one is easier to write – and by the way, if you want to decrease a variable you can use this notation (-=).

All we have done up to this point is to increase the value of *setVolume* associate with *myCar* (If we increased the value of *setVolume* for *yourCar* separate values would be stored). However, we have done nothing to the volume property. We change the volume property when we call on that value, for example, using this code:

```
Console.WriteLine("My volume is " & myCar.Volume)
```

Add the these lines of code to the module if you have not done so already.

```
Sub Main()
Dim myCar As Cars
Dim yourCar As Cars
myCar = New Cars
yourCar = New Cars
myCar.Make = "Honda"
yourCar.Make = "Ford"
myCar.NumberOfDoors = 4
myCar.increase_volume(10)
Console.WriteLine("I drive a " & myCar.Make)
Console.WriteLine("It has " & myCar.NumberOfDoors & "
    doors")
Console.WriteLine("My volume is " & myCar.Volume)
Console.WriteLine("You drive a " & yourCar.Make)
Console.ReadLine()
End Sub
```

As we mentioned before, it is very important that you get this sorted out right now because passing information back and forth to the class is a primary way of communicating with any class and most class variables are private where only the class is allowed to change the values. Now let's step through the program to see what it is doing by pressing the F8 key to start the program and continue to press F8 for each step (as you would in debugging). Notice that the program starts at the *Sub Main ()* in Module1.vb. Next it jumps to the *Sub New()* in the Cars.vb class to initialize the properties. (Remember the subroutine that initialized the properties is called the constructor and it requires the subroutine to be called *New*). As we step through the lines we can put our cursor over the variables and it will tell us the values, this is helpful to see what is occurring. Once the properties are initialized, control is given back to the module when the new instances of cars is created (*myCar* and *yourCar*). Notice for each instance of car, the program goes back to the constructor to initialize that specific instance of cars.

We can tell that these values have been initialized by moving the cursor to the 3 lines of code setting property values (e.g., *myCar.Make* = *"Honda"*) when you step into this code the values will be reset, however if you move your cursor over *myCar.Make*, or *yourCar.Make*, before you overwrite these properties, you will see that they are set at the values set by the constructor.

Continue pressing F8 to step through to the line of code *myCar.increase_volume(10)*. This should pass the value 10 to the Cars.vb class, return control to Cars.vb and run the subroutine. Press F8 and see that it does just that. Press F8 once more so that the code beginning with *setVolume* is highlighted and check the value of *volumeBy* to see that it is indeed 10 as seen in Figure 12.6.

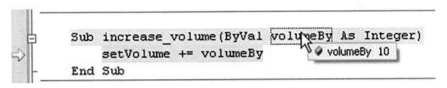

```
Sub increase_volume(ByVal volumeBy As Integer)
    setVolume += volumeBy          volumeBy 10
End Sub
```

Figure 12.6 displays the value of volumeBy *as you step through the program.*

Press F8 again and we can see the setVolume was incremented by 5 to now equal 15 as seen in Figure 12.7.

```
Sub increase_volume(ByVal volumeBy As Integer)
    setVolume += volumeBy
End Sub          setVolume 15
```

Figure 12.7 displays the value of setVolume *as you step through the program.*

Continue the step through pressing F8. Notice that each of the *Console.Writlines* are written to the console until you reach the one dealing with the volume for myCar. At this point, the program needs to 'get' the value by placing control back to the class to 'get' the new volume value by going to the readOnly Property Volume subroutine. The subroutine returns the value stored in the variable setVolume back to the Module as the value of the Volume property as well as returns control back to Module1.vb. The remaining lines are written to the Console. The last line instructs the Console to wait until it has something to read in – at this point we are done so terminate the program.

You can play around with this code by adding another line to increase the volume up an additional 5 units to verify that the subroutine is adding the values. Try adding more cars and modifying their properties.

Inheritance

What happens when we want to create a separate class of cars say SUVs that have all the properties in the Cars.vb class, but have additional properties such as number of seats, number of DVD players, and drink holders? We will need to use what is referred to as inheritance. We can create a class called SUVs that are everything a car is but with a little more. By doing this we are spared the time and hassled of replicating the coding we did for Cars.vb.

Add a new class by right clicking on Cars in the solution explored. Select add, class, name the new class SUVs, and click on the add button.

Add the following code to the new SUVs.vb class so that it inherits the properties of the Cars.vb class and then add a new property for the number of DVD players in the SUV. The subroutine should look like the following:

```
Public Class SUVs
Inherits Cars
Public DVDPlayers As Integer
End Class
```

Next we want to start fresh with the code in Module1.vb so delete the existing code and add the following:

```
Module Module1
Sub Main()
Dim mySUV As SUVs
mySUV = New SUVs
mySUV.DVDPlayers = 3
Console.WriteLine("my SUV is a " & mySUV.Make)
Console.WriteLine("My SUV has " & mySUV.DVDPlayers & " DVD
   players.")
Console.ReadLine()
End Sub
End Module
```

Since *SUVs* inherits from *Cars*, when you run the program and create a new instance of *SUVs* the *Cars* constructor is called on to initialize the properties. Control is then returned to the module and the value 3 is written to the *DVDPlayers* property. The proper information is then written to the console. What happens if we want to have a constructor for the *SUVs* class that might overlap with the *Cars* constructor. This is not a problem and can be illustrated if we create the following constructor for *SUVs*:

```
Sub New()
Make = "Ford"
End Sub
```

What happens now when you run the program is that immediately after the Cars.vb constructor is run, control is directed to the constructor in the SUVs.vb class. Any redundant properties (in this case Make) will be overwritten. Once you create the constructor in SUVs try stepping into the program and watch how it changes control from one class to another and then back to the module.

Now you have enough basic OOP experience to try a more advanced program. Keep in mind that there is much more to know about OOP than what we can cover in this chapter, however you will have a good start on the topic and you can build up from there.

Cards Class

One of the benefits of creating a class is that it can be used each time you write programs with objects defined in the class. One type of class that might be used often is with programming card games. Most card games are common in that they use a deck of cards. The cards may be different, they might be different designs, some cards have jokers and some don't, some card games have different back designs as well.

In this example we will create a very simple card game that uses an object class we found in the Microsoft forums (www.forums.microsoft.com). This class is nice because it taps into cards.dll. This is the same cards.dll that is used in the solitaire game distributed with Windows removing the need for us to have to create and export a set of graphics with the card programs we write. Cards.dll has images for 52 card faces and 13 card backs – thus there are a total of 65 images we can use for our card programs.

To begin with create a new Windows Application and change the name of *Form1* to *frmCards* by right clicking on it in the Solution Explorer and choosing the rename option. Right click on the Cards project and add a new Class, name the new class Cards. Once open, enter the following code based on the Microsoft Forum to complete the class:

```
Public Class cards
Declare Auto Function LoadLibraryEx Lib "kernel32.dll"
    (ByVal fname As String, ByVal dummy As Integer, ByVal
    flags As Integer) As IntPtr Declare Auto Function
    FreeLibrary Lib "kernel32.dll" (ByVal hRc As IntPtr) As
    IntPtr
Private mFront(51) As Bitmap
Private mBacks(12) As Bitmap
Public ReadOnly Property Card(ByVal x) As Bitmap
Get
Card = mFront(x)
End Get
End Property
Public ReadOnly Property Back(ByVal x) As Bitmap
```

```
Get
Back = mBacks(x)
End Get
End Property
Public Sub New()
'- Load bitmaps from c:\windows\system32\cards.dll
Dim     hMod    As     IntPtr    =    LoadLibraryEx
    (Environment.SystemDirectory & "\cards.dll", 0, 2)
If  hMod.Equals(CType(0,  IntPtr))  Then  Throw  New
    System.Exception("Cards.dll not found")
Dim i
For i = 0 To 51
mFront(i) = Bitmap.FromResource(hMod, "#" & CStr(i + 1))
Next
For i = 0 To 11
mBacks(i) = Bitmap.FromResource(hMod, "#" & CStr(i + 53))
Next
FreeLibrary(hMod)
End Sub
End Class
```

As you can see this is fairly simple code in that there are very few lines of code in this class that allows us to use card images from the Windows library for our program. The first two lines of code are required to access cards.dll. The next two lines declare private variables to be used for the front and back card properties. Notice that we have declared these variables as arrays to hold bitmaps. The first array *mFront(51)* holds the 52 face cards (remember the arrays start at 0) and the array *mBack(12)* holds the 13 back designs found in many of the Windows based card games.

The next two subroutines are used to get values of the fronts and backs when called on by the program – note that the fronts and backs are defined as bitmaps so we can use them accordingly. And finally we have the constructor which initialized the property values. In doing so it calls directly on the cards.dll.

That is all we need the class to do for now. Presumably later on if you choose to develop the Cards.vb class it will have more properties and more functions.

Next, return to *frmCards* by double clicking on it in the Solution Explorer. Change the Text property to "Poker Anyone?" Add a button naming it *btnDeal* and change the Text property to "Deal." Next add 5 picture boxes naming them *picOne*, *picTwo* and so forth and set their Size property to StretchImage so that the form looks like the Figure 12.8.

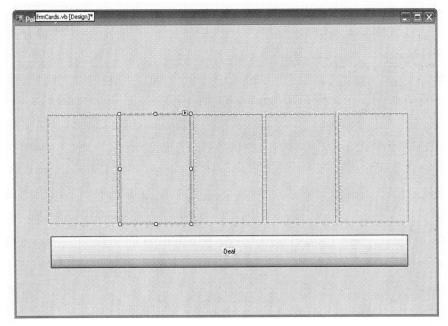

Figure 12.8 displays the initial configuration of frmCards.

Enter edit mode for frmCards.vb and add the following code to declare a variable to keep track of counting the cards (*vCount*) and to create a new instance of cards.

```
Public vcount As Integer
Dim myCards As New cards
```

Next create a sub routine to call on the Cards.vb class and load a bitmap of a card in the picture boxes:

```
Sub deal_cards()
picOne.Image = myCards.Card(vcount)
picTwo.Image = myCards.Card(vcount + 1)
picThree.Image = myCards.Card(vcount + 2)
picFour.Image = myCards.Card(vcount + 3)
picFive.Image = myCards.Card(vcount + 4)
vcount = vcount + 4
End Sub
```

And finally add the code *deal_cards* to the *btnDeal_Click()* sub routine in order to activate the *deal_cards* subroutine. Run the program and click on the deal button several times. Notice in the Figure12.9 that the cards are displaying in sequence as would a brand new unshuffled deck would. Since we did not place an upper limit on the value of vCount, once all the cards have been displayed, you will get an error.

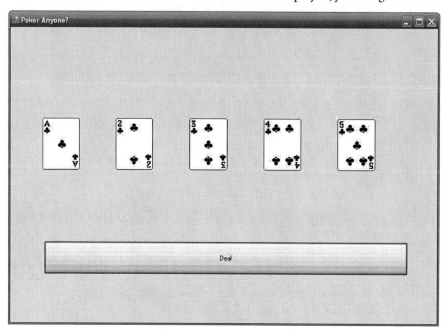

Figure 12.9 displays the initial deal of the cards in unshuffled sequence.

Suppose we want to display the backs. To do this we can create a new subroutine modified from the *deal_cards* subroutine. Create a new subroutine called *deal_backs*, next copy and paste the code from *deal_cards* into the new subroutine. Change each line of code from *myCards.Card(vCount)* to *myCards.Back(vCount)* to look like this:

```
Sub deal_backs()
picOne.Image = myCards.Back(vcount)
picTwo.Image = myCards.Back(vcount + 1)
picThree.Image = myCards.Back(vcount + 2)
picFour.Image = myCards.Back(vcount + 3)
picFive.Image = myCards.Back(vcount + 4)
vcount = vcount + 4
End Sub
```

Change the code under *btnDeal* to *deal_backs* and run the program to see the backs of the cards as shown in Figure12.10.

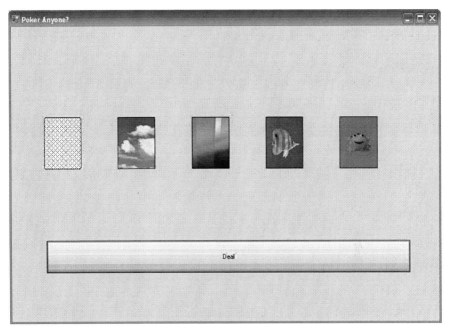

Figure 12.10 displays the dealing of 5 different types of card backs.

Now let's give this class a bit more functionality by having it shuffle the cards for us. Return to the Cards.vb class either by clicking on it in the Object Browser at the top of the screen or by double clicking on it in the Solutions Explorer and add the following function to Cards.vb class:

```
Public Sub shuffle_deck()
Randomize()
Dim i, r As Integer
Dim x As Bitmap
For i = 0 To 51
x = mFront(i)
r = Int(Rnd() * 52)
mFront(i) = mFront(r)
mFront(r) = x
Next
End Sub
```

This subroutine is very similar to the randomization subroutine we describe elsewhere in the book so we won't go over it here in detail. However, there is an important difference between this and the previous randomization function. Previously we used x to hold the content of the array which was an integer. Here the content of the array is a bitmap so we had to declare x as a bitmap to be able to randomize (shuffle) the deck here.

Now we need to add some code to frmCards.vb to be able to run the program and see that the deck has been shuffled. In the form load subroutine add the following code that calls on the shuffle subroutine in the Cards.vb class and then run the program.

```
Private Sub Form1_Load(ByVal sender As System.Object,
    ByVal e As System.EventArgs) Handles MyBase.Load
myCards.shuffle_deck()
End Sub
```

With poker we are dealt a hand and then we usually have a chance to hold the cards we want and discard the others to hopefully improve our hand. Let's add 5 buttons below each picture box changing their text to "Hold" and calling them btnHold1, btnHold2, etc.

To make this work we will need a variable to flag the state of the game. Let's declare a variable called *vFlag* as a Boolean variable. Return to the code level of *frmCards* and beneath the code we added to declare the *myCards* variable type the following:

```
Dim vFlag as Boolean
```

If *vFlag* is 0 then the program will shuffle and deal new cards as we have been doing. However, if *vFlag* is 1, then it will not shuffle and will just deal the next card in the sequence to any picture box without a hold button pressed. We also need a way to determine of the hold button has been pressed or not. We can accomplish this by changing the enabled state of each button to false when clicked and then deal cards only to those which the hold button is still enabled. Add the code for each button to disable it when clicked. For example:

```
Private Sub btnHold1_Click(ByVal sender As System.Object,
    ByVal e As System.EventArgs) Handles btnHold1.Click
btnHold1.Enabled = False
End Sub
```

Now let's make a subroutine to replace the discards. This will evaluate each Hold button to determine if it is enabled or not.

```
Sub replace_cards()
If btnHold1.Enabled = True Then
vCount += 1
picOne.Image = myCards.Card(vCount)
End If
```

```
If btnHold2.Enabled = True Then
vCount += 1
picTwo.Image = myCards.Card(vCount)
End If
If btnHold3.Enabled = True Then
vCount += 1
picThree.Image = myCards.Card(vCount)
End If
If btnHold4.Enabled = True Then
vCount += 1
picFour.Image = myCards.Card(vCount)
End If
If btnHold5.Enabled = True Then
vCount += 1
picFive.Image = myCards.Card(vCount)
End If
End Sub
```

We still need to make a subroutine to tell the program what deal state it is in. Change the code in the *btnDeal_Click()* subroutine to the code below which simply alternates the value of *vFlag* and then either deals or replaces the cards.

```
Private Sub btnDeal_Click(ByVal sender As System.Object,
    ByVal e As System.EventArgs) Handles btnDeal.Click
If vFlag = 0 Then
deal_cards()
vFlag = 1
Else
replace_cards()
vFlag = 0
End If
End Sub
```

Run the program and test our progress thus far. You may notice that we need to add a subroutine to enable the hold Buttons with each new deal. We will then call on the subroutine once we deal the cards. We will create a new subroutine called *clear_hold* which should contain the code listed below.

```
Sub clear_hold()
btnHold1.Enabled = True
btnHold2.Enabled = True
btnHold3.Enabled = True
btnHold4.Enabled = True
```

```
btnHold5.Enabled = True
End Sub
```

Now move your cursor back to the *btnDeal_Click()* routine and add the following code beneath the line *vFlag = 1*.

```
clear_hold
```

The main purpose of this program was to illustrate how a class could be used along with OOP to program a card game. The game is not optimized and could stand a few improvements. For example, we make the backs of the cards appear on the discards for a few seconds before they are replaced. To do this we would need to add a timer, set its interval to 1000 and then modify a few lines of code. First remove the line of code that is located in the *btnDeal_Click()* routine that calls on the subroutine *replace_cards* and relocate it to the Timer1_Tick() subroutine for our new timer. Add a second line of code to *Timer1* that disables the timer. The *Timer1_Tick()* subroutine should look like the following:

```
Private Sub Timer1_Tick(ByVal sender As System.Object,
    ByVal e As System.EventArgs) Handles Timer1.Tick
replace_cards()
Timer1.Enabled = False
End Sub
```

We now need to make some adjustments to the subroutine that shows the card backs so that the number that is passed to Cards.vb class represents one of the 12 back styles. The subroutine to show the backs should look like this:

```
Sub deal_backs()
If btnHold1.Enabled = True Then
picOne.Image = myCards.Back(6)
End If
If btnHold2.Enabled = True Then
picTwo.Image = myCards.Back(6)
End If
If btnHold3.Enabled = True Then
picThree.Image = myCards.Back(6)
End If
If btnHold4.Enabled = True Then
picFour.Image = myCards.Back(6)
End If
If btnHold5.Enabled = True Then
picFive.Image = myCards.Back(6)
```

```
End If
End Sub
```

We also need to adjust the *btnDeal_Click()* subroutine a bit. The code for this subroutine should now look like this:

```
Private Sub btnDeal_Click(ByVal sender As System.Object,
    ByVal e As System.EventArgs) Handles btnDeal.Click
If vFlag = 0 Then
deal_cards()
clear_hold()
vFlag = 1
Else
deal_backs()
Timer1.Enabled = True
vFlag = 0
End If
End Sub
```

Some features you might add on your own could be sound. Perhaps make the hold buttons more realistic. Additional graphics could also be included to make the game seem more realistic. At this point we could even attempt to use some of the programming skills you have developed thus far to develop some methods for creating a scoring system based on the hands dealt. With the skills you are beginning to refine the possibilities are endless.

Index

This index provides a quick reference to many frequently used features of Visual Basic 2005. Indexed pages are not exhaustive but rather indicate the initial presentation of the feature as well as highlight selective examples of application.

About the Authors

Dr. Otto H MacLin is a faculty member in the Psychology Department at the University of Northern Iowa. Otto has been writing computer programs for over 25 years, the last 10 have included Visual Basic versions 3.0-6.0 and .NET, Visual C++, JAVA, and XML. Otto's programs have been incorporated into a variety of areas of research including gambling, stimulus equivalence, eyewitness lineup administration, examination of the cross-race effect, and face recognition.

Dr. Mark R. Dixon is Professor and Coordinator of the Behavior Analysis and Therapy Program in the Rehabilitation Institute at Southern Illinois University. Mark has been writing computer programs for the past 20 years, the last 15 exclusively in Visual Basic versions, 2.0-6.0, .NET, and VB2005. Mark's programs have been incorporated into a variety of research including gambling, verbal behavior, choice and self-control, and relational frame theory. Mark also serves as a private consultant for organizational and experimental software development.

James W. Jackson, M.S., is currently working on the completion of his Ph.D. in Rehabilitation from Southern Illinois University. He holds a bachelors degree in Physiology and Psychology and a Masters degree in Behavior Analysis and Therapy from Southern Illinois University at Carbondale. He has consulted on various projects for the development of computer applications for both Pocket PC and Desktop computers for the collection of real time data for behavioral service providers and for human operant research. Jim has authored journal articles and conference presentations in the areas of the study of gambling behavior and in the development of mobile computing solutions for behavioral data collection.